In The Arms of Merlin

by

Margaret Bevan Lee

In the Arms of Merlin

To my Dad

Copyright © Margaret Bevan Lee 2014
All rights reserved

ISBN 9 781497 470408

Cover picture by Caprice Graphics

CHAPTER 1 – GOING INTO SERVICE

It had been snowing on and off all day. Annie had walked miles from her home – if you could call it home. She was so happy to leave No. 2 Ellwood Lane, but on the other hand, she was scared about going into service, but it was better than being at home with her father around. Little did she know what was in front of her.

    She was very wet and very cold when she arrived at the big house. She rang the bell, waited for a few minutes, then a girl about her own age opened the door. She must have known who Annie was, because she just took her bundle from her and told her to follow her. They went through a kitchen, down a passage, then up a flight of stairs that was never ending. At last they arrived in a small room which had two small beds, a table, two chairs and four narrow shelves on one wall, a small window in the other wall, a doorway but no door.

    Mrs Owens, Annie's mother, had been very glad that her daughter had been accepted at the big house, so that she could get away from her father's rages and beatings. There were four other children younger than Annie, one brother and three girls. Annie was very mixed up about her parents' life together. What with all the rows and beatings her mother had had, Annie thought she would have been long gone. There was never any food in the cupboard, nor coal in the old shed out the back. There were times when Annie or her mother would have had to go to the woods to collect some wood. Sometimes the wood was so wet it took ages to light the fire. If it was very cold the little ones had to go to bed to get warm.

    Mary, the other scullery maid, although a little plumper than she should have been, was a pretty girl with rosy cheeks, freckles and a mop of red hair. She and Annie had never met before but they soon became firm friends. After the introductions to each other, Mary said, "That's your bed, Annie."

After a few minutes of shyness Annie started to undress. "Hey," Mary said, "what are you doing? We don't go to bed yet; we have to go down to the cellar to get the coal for tomorrow morning."

Annie dressed quickly so as to catch Mary up; she was flying down the back stairs. They arrived in the kitchen at the same time. There was a boy there, a little older than the girls. Mary introduced him to Annie who took to him straight away and he to her. They spent about an hour getting the coal up to the kitchen. They weren't allowed to take it any higher than that. They had a few laughs and chatted about their families, then the boy, whose name was Jack said he was going to bed because the morning would come all too soon. They all said goodnight and made their way to the top of the house. Mary and Annie had a quick wash, undressed and got into bed and went to sleep in a while, Annie wondering what the future would be like in this large old house.

The first thing Annie heard as she opened her eyes was a loud banging on the wall outside their room. It was Jack calling them to get up. Annie thanked him very much, got out of bed and got dressed but Mary didn't move. Annie tried to shake her but she wouldn't have any of it so she waited a while, then in burst a very large woman. She came flying through the doorway nearly knocking Annie over. She got hold of Mary by the hair and dragged her out of bed. Poor Mary, she was screaming, so was the large woman. Ten minutes later they were running downstairs to start their day's work. It seemed that Mary was like that every morning so Annie took it on herself to get Mary out of bed herself so as to keep Cook happy. Mary wasn't very pleased but got used to it in the months ahead.

In the Arms of Merlin

The family didn't exist as far as Annie was concerned because she was down in the kitchen all of the time getting on with her work and her life, which was very hard and heavy. Jack would help her sometimes if he could, but he was pushed from pillar to post with all sorts of jobs but he never moaned because life in the big house wasn't too bad really.

Annie did not see her mother and family for six months; she was getting to the stage that it didn't upset her when she thought of them at home. Cook, whose name was Mrs Brodie was in charge of the junior staff, Mary, Annie and Jack, who was older than the girls. He used to clean the boots and shoes of the household and carry the buckets from the bedrooms then bury everything, poor boy. There was many a day that he wouldn't be able to eat anything.

He was much happier working in the stables as he was crazy about horses. He was the youngest son of a smallholding two miles out of town. His father couldn't afford to keep him at home, so he had to go out to service like most young children had to do. There wasn't much Annie knew about Mary. She had been brought up in an orphanage. She had no one to cry over, so she was quite happy with her lot, as thank goodness, there was no one really nasty to them. As long as they did their work properly and didn't cheek anyone, because then they would have a clout off Mrs Brodie and Jack would have one from James, the Butler.

Four o'clock in the morning would come all too soon for Annie. They went downstairs to start their usual jobs, then about seven they had a spell. They would have a bowl of oats, a piece of bread and a mug of cocoa; it would go down like nectar. After they had eaten, it was Annie's job to wash their dishes. Annie got on with it then started back on her routine jobs. It must have been midday, when Mrs Brodie called Annie into the main kitchen and in her broad Irish accent said "now be off with you my dear, get yourself

In the Arms of Merlin

changed and go to your home for the afternoon but see that you are back by six o'clock."

Annie couldn't believe her ears, "go on with you" Cook said again. She didn't have to say another word as Annie was off. She ran up to their room. Stripped off her working clothes, put on her Sunday best – they weren't much better than the clothes that she worked in but they were kept for best.

As Annie walked down the road she remembered how it was when she walked to the big house six months ago. Summer was here now, the hedgerows were full of wild flowers and she could smell the hay. It was so different to the day that she had walked the opposite way. It was so cold, there was a thickness of snow and a keen wind and she was so frightened not knowing what was in front of her and here she was happy as she had ever been, in her job and on her way home to see her family.

As the miles went by she was really getting excited about seeing them all again. She even missed her father, even though he used to beat her, she must have had a soft spot for him because he was quite nice when he was sober, but that wasn't often.

Annie's joy wasn't meant to last. As she turned the last bend, when her house came into sight, her heart stood still, her home was in ruins. It must have gone on fire and now it was just a shell. Where was her family? The first house was intact but the third house was also burned to the ground.

Annie just stood there not knowing what to do. After a little while she realised that she could ask Mrs Wilson who lived in number 1. She walked down to the house and as she approached the door the old lady opened it and took Annie into her arms and they both wept. After the initial shock of seeing Annie through the curtains, Mrs Wilson took Annie into the house, led her to an armchair and kneeled down by her side. Annie was in a trance and couldn't speak. She couldn't think what could have happened but it must have been pretty awful. Mrs Wilson was so upset she held Annie's hands and tried to tell her what had happened but Annie couldn't take any of it in. After a while she stopped sobbing. Mrs Wilson went to make a pot of tea. Annie said, "do you mean that all my family are dead?" Mrs Wilson nodded and they both started sobbing again.

A little while later Annie pulled herself together as she was giving Mrs Wilson a hard time, she realised that the poor woman had been through hell because of the fire and the tragedy that had happened next door.

She had been very fond of Annie's mother and the children, so now she listened to what Mrs Wilson had to say. It seemed that Annie's mother had gone to look for fire wood. When she came back the house was well alight.

Her father had come home from the Alehouse very drunk, so her mother had put the children in the bedroom out of his way. He must have gone to the fire with a piece of paper to light his pipe and he must have dropped the paper on the rag mat that her mother had made and not noticed it and fell asleep on the sofa in a drunken stupor.

By the time her mother had arrived she tried to get in through the front door, failed, so she went around the back. She must have got in that way and was never seen alive again. Everyone was upset because they all loved Mrs Owens and the children but there was no sympathy for the father.

After they searched the debris, they realised that number 3 was empty, one of the children was sick and they had taken him down to his granny to get a remedy. The father was at work so they were all very lucky. Now a relative was putting them up until they could find another little cottage for themselves.

It was much later that they realised that Annie had to be told about the tragedy. They sent word to the big house but nobody mentioned anything to her. In all fairness to the cook, she didn't know about it either.

The time had come to talk about the funerals. Annie didn't have a clue what to do, she was just a young girl who knew nothing much about death and what had to be done, but Mrs Wilson came to her rescue. She walked into town to the Parish Relief and asked them if they could help.

The funerals were held a few days later. They were buried in Pauper's graves. Annie didn't know any different, as Mrs Wilson didn't tell her. After the funerals were over, Annie was allowed to stay with Mrs Wilson for a few days. Mrs Wilson was very kind to Annie and on her last day at the cottage she told her to now treat this house as your home and I will try to help you like your mother would have done. Annie was overcome but she also knew that Mrs Wilson meant every word that she had said and her parting words were "Call me Auntie May from now on" and that is how it went. Pity that she didn't have more time to spend with Auntie May but Annie had to work every day. There were no days off in service in those days.

It was six months later that Annie had another day off and went to see Auntie May. They had a lovely time together and went to see her family's graves and put wild flowers on them. Annie was very happy and contented as she walked back to the big house and back to work again.

As the days went by Annie got stuck into her work. There were extra duties to do as visitors were on their way to the big house.

Spring was also on its way. The days were getting longer; the buds were turning to leaves and flowers. One evening as they all sat around the fire, having a chat and a laugh, all the work had been done and the staff had eaten, when in came Mrs Withers, the housekeeper. She pointed at Annie and said "come along with me." Annie hesitated but Mrs Withers caught hold of Annie's arm and took her out of the kitchen and up to James, the butler in her dining room. She sat her down on a chair and told her that her job was going to change in the next few hours. "Your Mistress needs a maid and you are the one."

Annie was flabbergasted. She didn't want to be a maid. She would rather stay down in the kitchen and the cellars rather than meet the people upstairs. She felt so scared, that Mrs Withers told her, "Stop crouching like that, girl. You don't have to be frightened, the Mistress is a very nice and gentle lady, she won't harm you at all, so pull yourself together and get these clothes on. Then you must come with me to meet the Mistress."

A week had gone by before she started to like her new job. Mrs Withers was quite right; the Mistress was a real lady. She was so gentle and kind to Annie, but Annie couldn't get used to the job yet, but she thought that in a few weeks everything would come to place.

As the weeks went by, Annie was gradually getting over the loss of her family and getting used to her new job.

She hadn't been to see Auntie May as she didn't have any time off but they kept in touch through Jack, he had to pass the house to go home so Annie would send verbal messages because Auntie May couldn't read or write either.

When the master came home he wouldn't talk directly to Annie, just look at her, she was really scared of him, she dare not lift her eyes to him. Lady Barbara knew of the situation so she kept Annie away from him as much as she could.

While they sat around the fire at night they used to chat and laugh. And one night they decided to learn to read and write. It was a marvellous feeling when they got everything together; they took it in turns to read aloud to everyone. Their elders were very impressed, the only thing was, it didn't help with Auntie May's messages.

In the Arms of Merlin

It was Annie's sixteenth birthday, everything was going great, she was so happy doing little things for her Mistress and she seemed happier than usual.

The first shock was pounced on Annie. Jack's father had died and his mother couldn't manage on her own so he had to go home and not only that, he had to go to another town to work to keep them going. Mary and Annie were heartbroken but they couldn't do anything about it. Jack came back for a few days after his father was buried, then left the big house the following week.

After another few days the second blow fell. News had arrived that the Master was coming home at the beginning of the week and bringing his cronies and floozies home with him. The poor Mistress was beside herself with worry.

Annie could see the fear in her eyes as she looked at her reflection while Annie was brushing her hair. Monday arrived, so did the Master with all his motley crew. Annie, as a young country girl, had never seen anything like it before; she was too scared to walk up the main staircase, so she used to scuttle up the one from the kitchen like a rabbit.

One evening she had made her way to the main bedroom to help her Mistress bathe, as she did every day. Lady Barbara was lying on the bed with her nightgown all torn, her face all bruised and blood coming from her mouth. Annie was beside herself. She did no more, ran down the stairs to the kitchen to get a bowl of water, some lint and ointment. She also called Mrs Withers to help her. When they got back upstairs, her Mistress was still lying on the bed with her eyes wide open but she didn't say a word. Mrs Withers looked at Annie as if to say "keep quiet", and she did. Perhaps that is where she went wrong.

The Master wasn't seen for a few days after the incident. Then Annie had another shock to upset her again. It seemed that they were short of a maid in the dining room, so

In the Arms of Merlin

Annie had to serve the food as well as looking after her Mistress.

Annie was very upset with the situation, she didn't think that Lady Barbara was happy about it either. It must have been the Master's orders. Damn him, thought Annie.

It was a big problem for her, so she confided in Mrs Brodie. All she told her was to get on with her work or "you will be finding yourself walking down the drive", so Annie thought that she had better leave well alone and carried on with her work.

Things just went on as usual; she got used to her new job but spent far less time with Lady Barbara, but she was lucky that he didn't take her from her altogether.

When Annie was serving meals, she was afraid to look at her Mistress, but when Annie wasn't looking she could feel her eyes on her. Annie thought it was all down to the Master.

There must have been twenty guests for every meal. It was hard work but she didn't complain.

Mary moaned the whole time.

One day Annie couldn't help it and said, "It's already for you; you are lucky to be down here, it's hell up there with all those men leering at you and catching hold of you as you pass. It is getting me down and there is no one to complain to." She was getting herself into such a state and she didn't know what to do about it.

A thought came to her. Perhaps her Mistress could help her out but she didn't think it was such a good idea after thinking more about it.

Two days later, she had had enough. One of the men had put his hand right up her dress. It took all of Annie's willpower to stop herself from hitting him. They all could see the look on Annie's face and thought it was really funny. All except the Mistress.

The following afternoon, Annie thought that she would take a risk and go up to Lady Barbara's bedroom to see if she

In the Arms of Merlin

could do anything to help her. Off she went up the back stairs. She thought that she had nothing to lose as she tapped the bedroom door.

She couldn't hear anything, so she opened the door as she always did when she worked for her Mistress before, when all of a sudden she could hear gasps and moaning. She could see what was happening. Annie couldn't believe her eyes.

She now opened the door really wide and could see what was going on. The Master was holding Lady Barbara down on the bed.

To stop her crying out he had his hand over her mouth. One of his cronies was on top of her doing something terrible to her. The two men had been taken by surprise, so the Master had let his grip go for a second or two. Lady Barbara gave such a scream that the man on top of her hit her across the head and blood was trickling down her forehead.

Annie saw red. She flew from the door and jumped on top of this monster, she managed to get him to the floor. She bit him and he had full blast of every nail Annie had. They might have been worn down with hard work but he had every bit of nail that she could muster.

They were struggling on the floor, the man was screaming and Annie had her hands wound in his hair and she was giving him hell.

By now the Master had realised what was happening, so he let go of his wife and made his way over to Annie. Annie was oblivious of that as she was giving the man on the floor all the way to go. All she knew was that Lady Barbara was absolutely howling and it was making Annie angrier.

Annie didn't think that she could hurt this man any more but her thoughts about the matter were interrupted by a change of position of her body. She felt herself being wrenched away from the man. Annie had been turned on her back and she could see her Master's eyes as he looked down at her. They were red. Annie had never seen anything like it in all her life. She thought now for it. He is going to beat me within an inch of my life but Annie was wrong. She didn't have a clue what she was in for. A beating would have been heaven to what she was going to have.

Annie was now trapped under the Master's body. He was a tall slim man, but was as strong as an ox. Poor Annie didn't have a chance; he had pinned her down with one hand and with the other hand he was tearing at her clothes.

Annie's clothes weren't flimsy like the ladies' clothes, so he had his work cut out to rip them off but eventually he succeeded. Annie's mind was in turmoil, she struggled with all her might but her battle was lost.

He had his wicked way with her three times. Annie was screaming and asking God to take her, because she thought she was dying. After he had finished with her he got up and kicked her until she lost consciousness and as he walked away he said, "Now scram, you little vixen." He didn't take a bit of notice of his wife but went over to his friend and took him out of the room.

In the Arms of Merlin

CHAPTER 2 - THE WORKHOUSE

It was ages before Annie came round, she opened her eyes and everything was in darkness, she couldn't make out where she was. She sat up with great difficulty and realised that she was in the room where the logs were stored over the winter. Someone must have carried her down and dumped her on the floor.

She tried to sit up but had searing pains where young girls of Annie's background only knew about when they got married. Annie was ignorant about the facts of life and really didn't know what had happened to her or what the consequences could be. The only thought she had in her mind was that she wanted Mrs Brodie or someone to help her, to hold her in their arms and take the hurt away. She had never had such pain in her life.

She knew where the shed was and started to crawl over to the door. It took her ages and she managed to reach up for the handle and open the door. She fell flat on her face. Then she crawled for hours, so she thought, and had nearly reached the kitchen when one of the scullery maids came from bed to start her work in the kitchen.

In about ten minutes Mrs Brodie and James had been sent for because Jane, who had found Annie didn't know what to do. Annie was in a sorry state, her clothes were all ripped, she was covered with blood and her face was all swollen.

As the senior members of the household entered the kitchen, they saw the situation and cleared the room. They were flabbergasted and weren't sure what to do. They also didn't know who had done these terrible things to Annie.

Mrs Brodie took control and had James help her to carry Annie to the sofa. She covered Annie's nakedness as best she could and got some water and lint to clean up some of her wounds. The bottom half of her body was black and blue. Mrs Brodie could do nothing about those. She called one of the maids to go to Annie's room to get a dress or anything for her to wear.

By the time Annie came round properly she saw Mrs Brodie and clung to her sobbing. Mrs Brodie kept asking, "Whoever did this to you child?" and all Annie was say was "Master." James looked at Mrs Brodie and she looked at him. They just didn't understand.

They knew that he was wild and reckless and had a very nasty streak in him, but they couldn't believe that he could do such a thing to Annie, who really was only a child.

James went down to the cellar and got some brandy from his Master's special liquor store. He poured a glass for Annie and one for Mrs Brodie and one for himself. James kneeled on the floor by the sofa, rose Annie up gently by the shoulders and tried to get her to sip some brandy. Annie was choking on it and was crying out in pain. James could feel her whole body quivering in pain and fright. His heart went out to the young girl and he said, "by God, someone has got to pay for this."

Annie was quite calm by now but was full of hatred for her Master. She told James and Mrs Brodie everything from the very beginning. They were absolutely stunned and they both knew that they could do nothing about it to help her.

Before another hour had gone by, the Master barged into the kitchen and told Mrs Brodie that Annie was to leave at once because she was a bad lot and he didn't want the other young girls to work with someone like her. Mrs Brodie made a protesting gesture to the Master. He knew what she was going to say so he stopped her in her tracks and commented about her position in the Big House. Mrs Brodie had to shut her mouth or she would have been dismissed.

She was so angry that she couldn't talk, she just glared and really worried that her Irish temper would have got the better of her, but she held her tongue with great difficulty. By now the Master had stormed out as he had come in. What was Mrs Brodie to do now?

Annie was completely out of control; she was sobbing from her boots. It was like a knife stabbing into her heart to heart that poor girl and now to do what the Master had told her to do. James and Mrs Brodie whispered together to see what they could do for Annie They came up with the only thing that they could think of. They both agreed. They nodded to each other, got hold of her as gently as they could and took her up to her room to get her belongings together. Mrs Brodie rolled them into Annie's shawl and because it was a very cold day, Mrs Brodie gave her hers.

Annie still didn't realise that she was going to be thrown out until Mrs Brodie said, "Come now, my darling, it won't be so bad. It will be better than here. You will never be able to work here after what has happened and I don't think that you would want to work here."

Annie kept crying and sobbing and saying, "Where will I go? I don't know anybody."

James interrupted her and said, "Don't worry now; you make your way to town, then ask someone where the workhouse is and they will look after you."

It was beginning to rain and James didn't have the heart to let the child walk on her own to the town, it was about ten miles, so he saddled up a horse, jumped on and drew Annie up behind him. Mrs Brodie was overcome to think that James was doing this for Annie.

James' comment was, "If I was more of a man I would have taken a whip to the swine, but I am too old to go to gaol."

Mrs Brodie agreed with him and also thanked him. There was no fear that the Master would find out, as he had gone back to bed and wouldn't surface for hours, so James felt quite safe.

They rode for hours and hours so Annie thought, she was hurting so badly. Every step the horse took, Annie's body shuddered with pain and James could feel it as she held on tightly to him. At last they arrived at the workhouse.

James got off the horse and helped Annie down. He gave her the shawl with her belongings in and rang the bell on the big door. He then proceeded to go back down the hiss leaving Annie to her own devices. It was the first time that Annie had been to the town, she had only been out of the Big House twice the whole time that she had been working there, they worked very hard and their lives were quite sheltered really.

An old man with funny eyes answered the door. He stared at her and she stared at him until he shouted at her and demanded, "What do you want?"

She told him that she wanted a place to say, as she had been thrown out of the place where she had been in service.

He said, "Come in" and told her to go into the room on the left side of the courtyard, and so she did.

Annie was standing in the Porter's Lodge while the old boy went to look for the Master of the Workhouse. He came in about half an hour, looked Annie up and down and asked her what sort of trouble she was in to have to come to the workhouse. Annie told him the truth because she didn't know what else to tell him. This man is going to throw me out now Annie thought, but no, Annie was pleasantly taken aback when he took her arm and escorted her upstairs into a small room with someone lying in the second bed.

Annie wasn't bothered about the other person in the other bed, she was just glad to be able to put her head down and rest her aching body. Seven o'clock and Annie was awakened by a gentle shake, she opened her eyes and there was Sarah standing in front of her. It was Sarah in the bed when she arrived in the early hours. After the shock of seeing

In the Arms of Merlin

her here, they started talking; Sarah told Annie all about how she had landed here in the workhouse.

At eight o'clock Master and Matron sent for Annie to come to the office to have a chat about herself and what had happened at the Big House. Annie sat down and poured her heart out to them. She was just repeating a similar story to Sarah, but Annie was far worse.

After a bit of consultation, Matron got up and told Annie that she could stay, but would have to work for her keep and there would be a few pence over for her to put away. She accepted their offer straight away with deep gratitude. Another stage in her life was just beginning.

Annie was put to work in the wash house because Sarah had to finish there, as she was having a baby in two weeks, so now Annie knew why Sarah left so abruptly and that is why Annie was taken in without much fuss.

There were about fifty women sitting at a very large table in this very large room. It was so cold when Annie sat down, that she drew her shawl tighter around her body as she was still shaking after her terrible ordeal of yesterday. On one side of her Sarah sat and on the other side a woman about the same age as Annie's mother. She looked old and very tired, she wore a wedding ring on her finger and her clothes were very shabby. She looked as if she had had a rough time too.

They all ate their food in silence. There were not allowed to talk at meal times.

After they had finished eating, they all got up, took their plates and cutlery to the corner of the room, where there was a large sink pan with very hot water and soda. As Annie was told later on, they washed their own utensils, shook the surplus water from them and took them back to their rooms, visited the closet and made their way back to the wash house to work until eight o'clock when it was supper time again. Did the same to their utensils, then went to their rooms for the night to sleep until five o'clock when it was time to start work again.

Morning came all too soon. Part of their work was to wash the linen of the Infirmary. It came every morning in two very large 'gambos' and most of it was most foul. The girls used to talk if none of the staff were around. One girl was telling us about an arm she had found in a sheet. Annie was horrified. Another girl blurted out "I found a dead bay" and that, for Annie, was the last straw. She just folded over and was in a heap on the floor.

Everyone gathered around her, someone came from somewhere, cleared everyone back to their jobs – it was the Matron. She helped Annie to her feet and asked her what had happened. Annie was in tears. Matron gave a smile, told her not to listen to anything that Ray had to say. She kept that story for all the new ones. "Try and forget it my dear" and immediately went over to Ray to rebuke her for upsetting Annie. Nobody said a word, but after she had gone they all had a laugh at Annie's expense.

Life was not too bad at the workhouse, she had a clean bed (a bit hard) but bearable. Two good meals a day, enough work to make her go to sleep as soon as her head hit the pillow, so one did not have time to think of things to make one cry. Annie was thankful things were as they were.

It was a few days later, after their meal, Sarah and Annie went straight to their room as Sarah didn't feel well, her back was nearly breaking. She thought she had worked too hard that day even though she was on a light job. She had to iron all the pillowcases from the Infirmary and they were made of heavy material so as to last longer so what a light job that was.

Annie got undressed and put her night gown on. She sat on a chair and rubbed Sarah's back as hard as she could. After a while it wore off a bit so the two girls went to bed to sleep. An hour or so had gone by so Annie thought. She

In the Arms of Merlin

could hear Sarah groaning. My God, Annie wondered, What's wrong now? She got out of her bed and asked Sarah what the matter was; Sarah garbled out something about the baby coming.

Annie fetched her shawl and ran upstairs to the Master and Matron's room. She hammed on the door several times but could not hear any movement from within. She was so desperate by now she even kicked it, but to no avail. Her thoughts were turned back to Sarah, so she ran back to their room.

By this time Sarah was out of control and Annie didn't know how to get on top of the situation. She did no more but just ran to the woman who sat next to them at mealtimes. Annie didn't even know her name as the woman always kept herself to herself. Annie blurted out what the problem was. She just got out of bed, put on her shawl and they ran over to Sarah, who just lay there quietly but was shaking either with fear or the cold, a bit of both they thought.

Bessie, as they later learned was the woman's name, got some matches from somewhere and lit the candle and that helped things a little. By the time Bessie had thrown back the bedclothes and pulled Sarah's nightgown up, Sarah gave another howl of pain. Bessie was telling Sarah in a gentle but firm voice to push down. Annie by now, was holding the candle and her eyes were nearly popping out of her head.

There must have been about ten more screams, nine more pushes then one more howl and a huge last push and the baby was on the bed. It was quiet for a few seconds. Bessie told Annie to run down to the kitchen to get sharp knife, then to go to her room to get some wool from the cupboard by her bed. "Don't walk", she said, "run!"

Annie did as she was told and was back in minutes. By the time Annie had arrived back the baby was crying.

Bessie had had to give it a few smacks on its bottom and blew on its face. After the cord was cut Bessie tied both ends tightly and handed the baby to Sarah who took the baby into her arms and sobbed gently while Bessie got on with getting the afterbirth away. It took much longer than she thought but did come away eventually.

After about an hour they had cleaned everything up. They sat on the bed, laughed and talked and gazed at the baby. It was three o'clock before they got back to their beds.

After a short sleep, Annie got up, got dressed, then went over to see Sarah and the baby. They were both asleep so Annie left them and went over to Matron's room to tell her about the happenings of the night before. Matron was very nice when Annie told her and made an excuse about not hearing Annie knocking the night before.

All was well, so Annie didn't worry about it. Instead of eating her breakfast Annie took it to Sarah. When she first got to their room, Sarah was feeding her baby for the first time. It was a wonderful sight for Annie as she felt part of the little family that was in front of her. Sarah ate her breakfast as they talked about naming the baby.

Sarah thought it would be nice for Bessie to name the boy, so that's what happened. They called him Lewis.

"What a great name," Annie remarked, and Bessie smiled weakly and said it was her husband's name, and later on told the girls that he had been killed in the war.

They got closer to each other as the days went by and she told Annie and Sarah about her life and what had happened to her for her to be in the workhouse.

It seemed that Lewis and Bessie had met in the annual fair, that servants used to go to to look for a better job, with more money at the end of the year, so they could save more to buy their own piece of land and start a living for themselves.

As soon as they met each other they fell in love and they knew that they were meant to be together. The waited for their contract to end. Lewis and Bess (as he used to call her) pooled their money and rented a very small holding with a small house, which was marvellous to them.

After all the papers were signed they started to clean it up and white limed the walls to freshen them. Bess' sister had given them a bed and a couple of chairs, also a couple of home-made quilts which her mother had given her. Lewis' sister gave them a table and a dresser that her husband had made when they had first got married, which was a good few years ago. As Lewis' brother in law had got on in his job as a carpenter, they could afford to give them a helping hand. Their mother had died many years ago when Lewis was quite small and his sister had helped to bring him up.

Bess and Lewis were in seventh heaven in their little love nest.

Things started to go wrong two months after they got married. Bess found out that she was pregnant. She was not too worried about it until Lewis came in from the field when she told him. He was beside himself as he knew how much money he had spent on seeds and other things that had to be bought to start things going. As Bess said, "there is nothing we can do but get on with it" but Lewis was not convinced. They both had a very restless night that night and for Lewis, many more to come.

When Bess was six months into her pregnancy, it rained for six weeks and everything was flooded. A few weeks later the water had all drained away. Lewis saw what it had done to his crops and land. It was just a quagmire and would take weeks to dry out and they could not afford this loss. What with this and the baby on the way it would be impossible to manage.

Bess saw Lewis talking to Policeman James on day and couldn't understand why he was doing so, so she did not mention anything to him straight away but when they got to bed they lay together. He had his arms around her and was gently kissing her eyes, her nose and then her lips. He said, "I do love you, my darling, and that is why I have to leave you."

Bess freed herself from his arms and was crying. "What are you talking about?" she asked and he then told her what he had in mind for their future. What Bess heard him saying she did not like one bit, but as they talked about it together it seemed more sensible as the night went on. Eventually they must have gone to sleep but Lewis had gone to the town before she had woken up.

In the light of day the thought of Lewis being away from her terrified her, but it was the only thing they could do to get out of the mess they were in.

Two weeks later Lewis was dressed up in his Sunday clothes, on his way into the Recruiting Office to join the Army. He was told it was a good life and they would look after their families too, so Lewis said, "Where can we go wrong?" So that is how it went.

Everything was going well, Lewis sent money home to Bess and by the time she was full term with the baby she had no debts at all. Lewis was on his way home on his first furlough.

He had caught a train to Carmarthen, the next town and had walked home to find Bess in the middle of her labour. After four and a half hours their little girl was born. They were both delighted and to think how he was able to be home for the actual birth was a blessing in itself.

Lewis had joined the Infantry as a regular soldier; it was quite a good life after he got used to it. He also had a few good pals, which made a difference to army life. After his two week furlough he went back to barracks and carried on as best he could.

One evening a few months later, one of the officers came in to tell the boys that they were going to be transported to a port and shipped over to Africa and that was all they got to know.

In the Arms of Merlin

All the men had a chance to write to their wives and relatives, so Lewis sat at the table and wrote a long loving letter to Bess and told her about them being shipped abroad somewhere.

That was the last time she heard from him. He was reported killed in action and a thank you from the War Office and a frugal pension.

Three months had gone by and Bess was still grieving over Lewis. She used to sit for hours crying with little Lizzie in her arms. She was not eating much and was not drinking much either, so her milk was getting less and less.

Lewis' sister had died not long after Lewis. Bess did not have anyone else to turn to, so things just went on and on until the baby was taken ill. Bess too her to the doctor and was diagnosed as consumption. Within days the baby was dead. Bess had the baby buried and it took every penny she had left. She had no money for food or anything; she just lay on the bed waiting to die.

Fortunately for her, her brother-in-law had a bit of a guilt complex and called to see how she was getting on. He had such a shock to see Bess that he broke down in tears, thinking what help he could have been to her but it looked as if it was too late as far as Bess was concerned.

After thinking things over for a few minutes, he realised that the only thing he could do to help was to take her to the sick area in the workhouse and that is what he did.

Davey, Bess' brother-in-law, who had not bothered about anyone since his wife had died, had certainly saved Bess' life.

Two days had passed before Bess woke up. She had no idea where she was. She knew it could not be Heaven, because it was too shabby. The next person that came along she asked. She had quite a shock when she got an answer from this woman but poor Bess was so weak that she did not care where she was as long as she could go back to sleep.

As the days went by Bess got stronger and started to walk about the ward. There were a few people ill and a few very ill. Seeing those very ill people she came to terms with what had happened in her life. There were twenty patients, including herself. One or other was dying about three times a week, then a few more would arrive all times of the day and night.

One morning as she was eating her porridge, the matron arrived at her bedside with a well-dressed man, he asked her how she was feeling. Bess told him that she was much better. He was a doctor from one of the town practices who did voluntary calls and treated the down and outs like poor Bess and her kind. Dr Clayton gave Bess a thorough examination and said the consumption had cleared up and if she looked after herself it would not come again.

Bess was so pleased but as the couple was moving away she realised the predicament she was in. Where could she go? What could she do? While all these things were going through her mind Matron came to see her. "Now then Bess," she said, "have you thought anything about your future?" Bess started to cry and matron caught hold of her arm and told her not to fret as they would sort something out for her. Little did Bess know that Matron had a soft spot for her, knowing about her circumstances, which were similar to her own, but that is another story.

Later on that morning, Bess was taken to a small room at the top of the stairs with two narrow beds in it, one cupboard and two chairs and that was it. She wondered what was going to happen next. Master came into the room, he was not as sympathetic as Matron but nice enough. First of all he asked if she had any relatives.

"No," she told him.

He then asked if she had a place to go. She shook her head. "Right," he said, "would you like to live and work here? You will have a clean bed, two good meals a day, clean clothes every week and a few shillings in your hand at the end of the week. We need an extra worker so it might as well be you if you want it. Think about it and come to the office as soon as you have made your mind up."

Bess had no other alternative but to take the offer. She was lucky that it had been made to her. It must have been at least ten minutes by the time she got to the office and told them both that she was going to accept. Matron gave her a smile, as she turned her head away so as not to show too much to her husband that she cared what happened to this young girl who had been in real trouble. Bess was lucky of that kind streak in Matron.

All that happened twelve years ago. Bess had no favours given to her or any preferential treatment. She just did her work and got on with her lot.

Annie had been at the workhouse for six weeks, working very hard and doing what she was told and not feeling too good. She could not make out why she felt so unwell.

Sarah and Lewis were also getting on fine. Sarah was back in the wash house in her old job. She was as strong as an ox. One of the women who used to work in the ironing room had pneumonia, was getting over it but still not fit enough to go back to the heavy work, so she was looking after Lewis. Sarah fed the baby until he was six weeks old. Now he's on the bottle with cow's milk. Everything has worked out for Sarah, she seems happy enough in her own way. She has blocked all the past out and is just looking at the future. I hope that one day Sarah will meet a nice boy and settle down but there does not seem to be any hope of that happening here at the workhouse.

Annie went to bed straight after work; she did not even have a wash. She felt so unwell. Sarah was so worried about her that she took the liberty to tell the matron. After Sarah had left, Matron had a word with her husband. They had both come to the conclusion at what was ailing Annie.

Dr Clayton arrived about an hour later. He had a few words with matron and they made their way up to Annie's room. Annie was shocked to see Matron and the doctor and wondered what was the matter. After Dr Clayton had asked Annie a few questions, he examined her and gave his diagnoses. Poor Annie was shocked, she could not believe what the doctor was telling her. Here she was in the same position as Sarah. What was she going to do? Crying came easier as the time went on.

She was very quiet in work but as soon as she got to her room she gave vent to her feelings. She did not take it like Sarah had. Annie was full of rage, inside of her she was seething and could have, and would have, killed the Squire without batting an eyelid.

As the weeks went by Annie got a little better. She seemed to have cooled down a bit after she felt the baby stirring inside her. The months went by quickly then Annie had to go to the ironing room because it was not so hard. By the time Annie was full term she was looking forward to having her baby and put all the bad thoughts aside.

It was the turn of the century, in the second month, the 22nd day at midday that Annie's son was born. He was a beautiful child. He had no hair at all, so she knew he would be a fair headed boy like her mother and her brother and sisters. Memories came flooding back to her, she held the baby close to her, marvelled at the blueness of his eyes and shuddered when she remembered how he had been conceived, then the tears came again.

Everyone was kind to Annie and they all loved the baby. When he was six weeks old Annie had to go back to work again. Sarah and her were working together and another woman, who was getting over an illness, was looking after the two babies. Annie and Sarah often talked about what they would do if they could get out from the workhouse. They both had different thoughts about the subject.

Matron called Annie and Sarah into her office one day and asked the girls if they had considered having the babies christened. The girls were very pleased to think that Matron thought so much of them. They talked about it for a few minutes and said "yes." Matron was very happy. One of the inmates had died and he was to be buried from the workhouse, so Matron thought she would catch the vicar at the burial. Not many Vicars would christen illegitimate children but she knew this one would.

After the burial the two babies were baptised. Sarah's son was named Lewis Hall and Annie's son was named William Owen. They held the two boys in their arms and were very proud and very thankful to Matron and to the vicar.

One day Matron asked Annie if she had any relatives and Annie said "no, only Mrs Williamson who had been so good to her when she had lost her family." She asked where she lived and Annie told her. She then asked if Annie would like to take the baby to show her. Annie was not too sure about this as she did not want to tell Auntie May anything about what had happened.

In bed that night, Annie lay with the baby in her arms and let a few ideas go through her head. She called quietly to Sarah and Sarah woke up with a start as she thought that there was something wrong, but Annie reassured her and told her what she was going to do, but she made her promise that she would not tell a soul and she promised.

Next day Annie went up to Matron's office and told her that she would like to go to see her Auntie May, so arrangements were made for the following Sunday. Master was going to town in the morning and would drop Annie off, then she could make her way to Auntie May's under her own steam. This suited Annie. They came to the church in the middle of the town. Annie got off the trap and Master handed

William to her in his basket. Annie took him and thanked him and started to walk towards Auntie May's. It was a lovely spring day, the sun was shining and the birds were singing and Annie thought this was how it should be. "Master and Matron have been more than good to us. William," she said. "This is the only way out." The die was cast.

All of a sudden it clouded over and it started to rain. "Drat!" said Annie to herself. She did not expect it to rain and it spoilt things a bit but never mind, William we'll be alright. She covered William's little face and walked quickly up the drive around to the front of the house. There was nobody in sight. She got to the front door without anyone seeing her. She kissed William tenderly and quickly turned away with tears in her eyes and said "goodbye" to William.

She got past the front of the big house and was making her way towards the drive when two boys chased her and caught her and threw her to the ground. Her knees were bleeding, so were her hands, but they didn't care. They dragged her back to the big house.

Annie was aghast because this was not what she intended to happen. She knew that she was going to be in deep trouble as all her plans had gone terribly wrong.

Mrs Brodie was finishing off the sauce to go with the salmon for lunch when she heard a terrible noise from outside. She tried to look out through the side window but she only heard screaming and shouting. It was getting closer and all of a sudden the kitchen door burst open and three people rolled in onto the floor. She had the shock of her life to see those horrible thugs that the Master had employed to look after the woods and grounds after Willie had left. Struggling between them and covered in blood was Annie. "You poor love," Mrs Brodie said "what is going on here? Get off, you brutes!"

But they did not leave her go until the Master arrived and then all hell was let loose.

In the Arms of Merlin

Mrs Brodie still did not know what was going on until they dragged her down the cellar and locked the door and went away. Annie's sobbing could be heard all over the house but none of us could do anything about it. Around four o'clock one of the boys came in for a drink. Mrs Brodie did not ask him anything because she knew he would not have told her in any case. He then blurted all the story out. Mrs Brodie was not a bit shocked to hear what he was saying. James and her had gathered what had happened the night poor Annie was thrown out, but she did not reckon on Annie bringing the child here to the big house. Mrs Brodie did not know what poor Annie had in mind and that it had all gone so terribly wrong.

After things had died down a bit Mrs Brodie went to the top of the main stairs to see if the Master or any of the others were around. Everything was quiet so she went to get the key of the cellar door and made her way down to the cellar. Annie was just sitting on a chair holding her head in her hands and sobbing. Mrs Brodie made her way over to her and put her arms around her and said, "Come on now, love, it's not as bad as you think. What did the Master tell you?"

Annie just kept on sobbing and said that he was going to get the constable. Mrs Brodie held her breath and said to Annie, "I have to go, love, I think I can hear voices." Off she went and by the time she arrived in the kitchen and locked the door and put the key back, the Master was there with a constable from the village. They took Annie away and Mrs Brodie did not see her again until she went to the Shire Hall in Carmarthen for her trial.

CHAPTER 3 - THE GAOL

Annie was sent to trial for abandoning her child and endangering his life.

There was no-one to help Annie as no-one would come forward to speak on her behalf, as they were all afraid of the Squire.

The took Annie in a covered wagon to the gaol. It was a short ride and was over before Annie had time to get her thoughts together. She got off the wagon and there were a few older women waiting outside the prison gates. They pelted things at her and jeered at her. Poor Annie, by the time she was taken right inside she was nearly collapsing but the wardens would not let that happen as it would mean more work for them. This was not the workhouse, this was a prison with hard taskmasters and hardened criminals.

She was taken to a room, made to strip and put on prison clothes. The clothes that she had taken off were very old and shabby but they were silk compared to what she was wearing now. Dressed in her official garb she was taken up an iron staircase, along a wooden corridor, up another iron staircase, along a short landing then into her cell. There were two very narrow beds, a small table, a small window with bars, a slop bucket and nothing else. On her way out the wardress said, "My name is Miss Smith and you see that you keep your nose clean or you will have me to reckon with. I will send one of the other inmates to get you when it is time to have your last meal for the day." Then she slammed and locked the cell door.

Everything had happened so quickly that Annie's head was swimming. She could not get her thoughts together to even think what had happened to her.

It was six o'clock and the door opened and a young girl came and said "come on, I've got to take you down to the food hall, where you are to sit next to me", so off they went down to have food.

There were dozens of people making their way to the tables. Annie had no idea how many of them there were and she did not much care either. The girl who had fetched her said, "Come on, or we will lose our seats." At last we sat down, then as soon as they did a voice boomed over all the noise and told them to make their way to the table to pick their food up.

On arriving at the very large table, Annie could see that the inmates were serving the food. We were given a tin plate, a fork and a spoon. We moved down a little, then a very large woman sloshed a piece of meat. Annie was not sure what it was but it looked as if it had been killed about six months ago. They moved on a little way again and were given a large mug of cocoa.

Annie did not raise her eyes from the plate; she just walked behind the other girl. Half an hour later they had finished their food and had taken their plates and cutlery back to another large table on the other side of the hall.

As the young girl walked she jabbered to Annie, but Annie had no idea what she was saying. At last they arrived at the door of their cell, walked in and sat on their respective beds and just looked at each other.

It seems that Martha, as she was called, had only arrived a few days before. She was from a village not far from Carmarthen. She had been badly treated by her father, could not take any more so she had stuck a knife into his side. He did not die but was very ill for a long time. Martha was not a bit sorry about stabbing him. The only thing she was sorry about was that she had not killed him.

She worried about her mother because her father was about to go home, as he had been at his sister's because there was no room at his own home. It was only one up and one down and there were six children so poor mam will have to look out from now on and it's all through me.

She broke down and sobbed. With that a figure stopped in the doorway and said, "Stop that snivelling and get into your beds." She turned around and locked the door behind her.

Annie looked at Martha, Martha looked at Annie and they both started crying together.

It was still dark when the cell door was unlocked and the gaoler shouted for them to get up. Annie thought they had early calls in the workhouse but this was really early. They got dressed in double quick time and by the time they had finished the woman was back. "Come on slow coaches," she said, and we joined the line of women slowly walking along the landing.

They made their way down the stairs, along another passage, then into a big room. We were about thirty females, some very young girls, some Annie's age and some very old women. God help, they looked as if they had had a terrible life but Martha said it was life in prison. Annie shivered, wondering how she would look when she came out in three years.

Today was 'pull your socks up day' or else. The Governor read the riot act to them. The men prisoners had already had their talk and had gone to their jobs. Annie had no idea what was in store for her as no-one had said a word to her. After the Governor had finished talking, the women all went in their different way except Martha and Annie. Miss Smith came up to us, told Martha to go down to the washhouse and took Annie into the kitchen, right down to the bottom, where it was darkest.

Annie's job was to clean the pots and pans that had been used for the cooking. They were all black and ingrained with stale food. She tried her best to get them clean but was fighting a losing battle.

In the Arms of Merlin

One of the men cooks came along and said, "Get a move on you, or the staff's pots and pans will be here before you finish these. You've got to clean them until they are shining or there will be hell to pay."

After doing her best with the inmates' washing up, Annie carried on with the gaolers' pots and pans. As she rubbed and scrubbed the pans, the cook was watching her like a hawk. He said, "If you don't do them properly you have to do them all over again because I get it in the neck. We don't want that, do we?" So Annie scrubbed until they gleamed. Poor Annie's hands and nails were in a terrible state and this was her first day of her three years.

What had she done? Annie thought. Why, oh why had she done it? She thought that she was doing the best thing. The Mistress would have taken pity on the baby and would have had one of the kitchen staff to bring it up until Annie had enough money to have the baby back. Her plans had gone hopelessly wrong.

She did not know that the Mistress was very ill, more or less dying. She had asked if the baby could be brought up in the Big House. She knew whose baby it was, so she thought, as she could not have any children of her own, perhaps she could have a little hand in bringing him up. She had thought a lot of Annie but when she told her husband he went berserk and the Mistress had to be taken to her room and has been there ever since.

It had been quite good in the workhouse. Why had Annie not been satisfied with her lot? She worked hard in the washhouse. Sarah and her had little laughs to themselves sometimes. They had a few shillings put aside for them every week and not too bad food, much better than what she was having now. It was all Annie's fault and she could do nothing about it but grin and bear it and hope that the time would go quickly.

In the Arms of Merlin

It was the middle of June, the weather was really hot. The head gaoler came down to the kitchen to see Annie. He told her he was taking her up to the washhouse as they were one short. Annie was quite pleased to hear his news, the best she had had since she had arrived there. It was the first time Annie had been up in the washhouse and didn't know any of the women there. They could be a nasty lot if they took a dislike to you so Annie thought, keep your mouth shut and you should be fine, but it didn't work like that. There were the bullies there, all in their middle forties, real hard nuts. Whether life in gaol had made them like that, or they were like this before they came here? Annie tried to carry on with her work as best she could because it wasn't like the workhouse wash-pool, it was more archaic than that and much harder and heavier.

Annie, nor Martha, knew all the women by their names, so that made it much harder to try to be friendly. One morning Annie was up to her elbows in boiling soda water when the woman in the next tub started talking to her. Annie was quite surprised but was very pleased and started talking back. She said her name was Esther and she was from the town, had never been in trouble before but was serving life – for stealing.

It seems that she was walking down to the town one day, she was feeling quite happy this particular day. She could not remember even why she was so happy as things were not that good. There on the pavement was a lady's purse. Esther stooped to pick it up, looked around to see if anyone was looking for it, but there was no-one in the street.

It was a black dressy little bag, like a wealthy woman would wear. It had black jet beads all over it, like women wore when they were in mourning, Esther opened it. There was a handkerchief, smelling salts, a key and another purse with twenty golden sovereigns.

In the Arms of Merlin

Esther's knees went like jelly, she felt quite faint and got really flustered. She did not know what to do, so she put it in her pocket, turned around to go back home to ask her mum and dad's advice. As she was in the process of turning around, there was a hand on her shoulder and she was led away to the round-house. She didn't know what had hit her from the minute she picked that purse up, she didn't stand a chance.

The owner of the purse was screaming at her. The constable was bullying her, then the woman's husband came in, then that was it for poor Esther. She did not have a leg to stand on. She was taken straight away to the gaol and was there until Monday morning.

At nine o'clock she was taken down to the Magistrate's Court, had a farcical trial, sentenced to spend the rest of her life in gaol and her parents didn't even know that she was in any sort of trouble. Esther had picked the wrong person's purse up. She was the wife of one of the most powerful men in the shire.

It took three days for Esther's mother and father to get to see her. John Evans was a shoemaker in one of the lanes in the town centre and was not too bad off really. He used to do quite a lot of work for the gentry, as a good shoemaker was hard to find outside the cities.

One of the Magistrates happened to be one of John's customers and was very upset when John told him about Esther, as he had known Esther since she was a child and knew she would not do anything like that.

It was Mr Oliver who had got special permission for Mr and Mrs Evans to see their daughter, as visitors were not allowed for three months.

As John and Mary walked through the main gate of the gaol; Mary gave a shiver and held back a flood of tears, not wanting to show Esther that there was no way anyone could be of any help to the poor girl. They were taken to a small room with three chairs and a table. There was Esther looking as white as a sheet, with tears cascading down her cheeks and running towards her mother. The gaoler came between them and said "sorry, there must be no bodily contact."

After a few minutes Esther settled down as she realised the time was getting on and her parents were only allowed a short time to talk. After the first question of how she was, her father threw question after question at her. She told him the truth and he believed her.

He said; "Look now, Esther fach, try not to be too upset. I know it's easy enough for me to say but give me some time and I will do my best to get you from here." Esther cooled down a bit and knew her father meant every word he had said.

That was five years ago. John Evans spent every spare minute had had, obviously he had to do his work, to make money to try and get Esther released and exonerated.

Mary Evans had died six months since of a broken heart and that made John more determined to get Esther out of that hell hole. One morning as John opened the shop, his friend, Mr Oliver walked in. "I think I may have got some good news for you, John," he said, and they huddled in the corner and talked for an hour or so.

John Evans was in tears when Mr Oliver finally said, "I have to go now, John, not a word to anyone."

As the days went by and very slowly I may say, Esther and Annie got really close. Martha wasn't put aside because of Esther, she was still Annie's friend, but there was something different between the other two. It might have been because they were both innocent of the crimes that they were sent to gaol for. Annie did leave baby William on the doorstep so she did do a more criminal act than Esther but that is by the by.

It seems that the Honourable Oliver Stevenson was in a spot of bother himself now, by what John Evans had been

In the Arms of Merlin

told by Will Oliver. The husband and wife had gone to their London house for a few months, as the Right Honourable was a wheeler and dealer with money, especially other people's.

He had got to be a bit more clever than he should have been. He had got mixed up with the big boys, because London was the place where it all happened.

At one of his bawdy parties, his wife, who was a social climber, invited a German Baron and his wife, thinking that it would take them up a few more rungs of the social ladder by asking them. As soon as Oliver met the Baron he knew his wife had made a mistake but it was too late. He was in his clutches from the minute they met.

Weeks went by and Oliver had not seen or heard a word from the Baron but the Baron was waiting in the background for Oliver to make one wrong move. It was something to do with foreign currency and if it had worked out as it should have, Oliver would have been a very wealthy man but the Baron was keeping a close watch on him and his cronies. There would have been a lot of businessmen going bankrupt through Oliver's deals but it did not worry Oliver as long as he made more money.

It wasn't because businessmen throughout Europe would have lost everything but the Baron had taken an extreme dislike to Oliver and his frivolous wife, so the time had come to put a spoke in his wheel. Oliver did not have a chance. He drove down to Wales in his coach and six of his best horses to get from London and to his bank in Wales, to get his money out before his creditors found out what he was doing.

The watertight deal, crooked as it was, had fallen through because the Baron had intervened. Any other time the Baron would not have taken part in such a deal but for the Right Honourable Oliver Stevenson, he could not and would not.

In the Arms of Merlin

In a matter of two weeks, Oliver and his wife were deported to America by Steerage and that could not have been so pleasant for a couple like them who had been born with silver spoons in their mouths.

It was a week later that John Evans heard from Mr Oliver. It seemed that he had been to see the Chief Magistrate to discuss Esther's case. They now realised that they could change the sentence as she had really been wrongly imprisoned. It took a few more days to get the case through the legal system. John was over the moon, the only pity was that Mary was not here to see John going to get Esther from the gaol.

Esther had no idea what had been going on, as Mr Oliver had told John not to say anything in case things went wrong.

We were all in the wash house on the Monday morning when the warden came in, spoke to Esther and took her out with him. We were all puzzled and could not understand what was going on. An hour must have gone by, then in walked Esther. She was sobbing like a baby, we thought that something had happened to her father. We all crowded around her bombarding her with questions, then Miss Smith walked in. We all scattered, leaving Esther just standing there, still crying, when Miss Smith told us all we needed to know. Esther had been released, exonerated from her crime and her criminal record taken from the files, so she was a free woman.

Esther put her arms around the women she had befriended. She left Annie to the last, they had their arms around each other and were clinging to each other, until Miss smith caught hold of Annie and dragged her from Esther and gave her a push into the corner, told Esther to get moving and told Annie to get on with her work. Work! That was the last thing she had on her mind but there was nothing else she could do.

Annie went back to her washing and so did the others, they dare not talk any more or Miss Smith would be down on them again and they didn't want any aggravation from her.

It must have been seven o'clock by the time they got down to the food hall. They picked up their food, moaned a little, then went to their usual seats. Their meal consisted of potatoes, turnips and onions which had been boiled in a very large cauldron with more water than should have been. It was so tasteless, the cooks didn't even put salt in it. They really did not want the inmates to enjoy anything in that place.

After the meal was over, they did the usual thing and took their utensils to be washed, dried and put away, then all hell broke out. The three women who had been subdued for the last three weeks just could not contain themselves any more. They just went berserk. Whistles blowing, women shouting, screaming, banging things. It seemed that they have a good few of these mini riots. Lil, May and Rose had been quiet for a few weeks as Miss Smith had been watching them very closely, because she knew that they were ready to explode any day.

While Esther was there they had a plaything but since she had been released they had to find someone else to torment. It was a verbal thing with Esther; they had not harmed her at all. It was just the fact that Esther was a nice girl, well-mannered and quiet, she was perfect for those thugs to pick on. Who was going to be their next victim?

All the other inmates were old lags and had been there many years, so it all fell on Annie. She was next in the firing line. She did not realise what was happening, until a few days had gone by. Miss Smith seemed to be off the scene, no-one knew where she was; not a word was said about her. Things were going quite smoothly without her, so they thought that they could get away without replacing Miss Smith. That was the mistake they made.

As soon as Annie got into the wash house, the first job was to get one of the men to help her to carry the boiling water to the very big zinc pans. Jim, who had helped this morning, seemed to be in a good mood so Annie made the most of it. She chatted to him and he was quite civil to her. It was a nice change; things did not seem so bad on a day like this, Annie thought.

With the zinc full to the top she started to drop soda into the water. Before she had time to turn around, two of the women were on top of her, taunting her about Esther and calling Annie terrible names. Annie was struggling to get free from the, when suddenly they let her go as one of the gaolers had come in and they ran to another part of the room. Annie thanked God that she had been reprieved this time but she knew that sooner or later they would have her.

The following morning she started to carry the water again with Jim when here they come. The three of them held her, punched her, kicked her and the next thing she knew Lil had her hand and was dragging her over to the boiling water. Annie was screaming. The other women were too afraid to do anything to help her, or they would be the next ones in trouble.

Annie's fingers had gone in the water once. She had struggled so they had to pull her hand back out. Lil found extra strength from somewhere and Annie's whole hand was on the way into the boiling water. There was a terrible yell and the three women were sprawled over the floor. Annie couldn't make out what had happened until she saw Jim. He was giving Lil a good kicking, she stayed down. Rosie ran away and he punched May in the mouth. There was blood everywhere as she fell to the floor. She spat a few teeth out.

By this time two gaolers had arrived. They had heard the commotion, realised who it was and let Jim do his handiwork on them before they moved in. After Lil and May had been put in solitary confinement, Annie was taken to the

In the Arms of Merlin

woman who looked after anyone who had been got at. The skin was hanging off Annie's fingers and she was still shaking with fright and pain.

The head gaoler was called to assess Annie from work and suggested that she be put on the ironing, as that room was nearer to the gaolers' room so they could keep an eye on things.

It was time to go down for food by the time Annie had settled down to her new job. It was not the same without Esther but she would be safer here than in the wash house. At the table all eyes were on Annie, some sympathetic and others mad that the two women had been locked up. It was a relief for Annie to know that she did not have to look over her shoulder every two minutes.

As the days went by Annie's hand got better. It was examined by a local doctor who came in about once a month. He said, "She can be without the bandages to let it dry up but keep her on the ironing as I don't want her to get her hand wet for a while."

Annie thanked him and he gave her a smile, as it was a change to speak to someone tidy in this terrible place. Dr Morris was not very happy coming to this place but every penny helped, as his father was not very well and whatever money he made, he helped his mother with a little hand out now and then.

After two weeks had passed, Annie's hand had completely healed. So back to the wash house she went. Lil and May were also out of the lock up, but things were quiet.

It was on a Tuesday morning that Annie was called to the Governor's room. Annie was scared and puzzled as she could not make out what he wanted with her. She stood in front of him. He asked her full name. She told him, then he asked, "Can you read?"

She nodded and said, "Yes."

In the Arms of Merlin

The Governor was surprised with her answer, which had solved the problem of why she had been sent a letter. Annie was given the letter and removed from the room. She put the letter deep down in her pocket, thought about it for a while, then forgot about it until she got back to her cell.

Martha and Annie were both very tired. They both laid on their beds, chatting about the day's happenings. All of a sudden, Annie jumped off the bed and dug deep into her pocket and pulled out the letter. They were both excited as Annie tore the letter open and had the shock of her life. It was from Mrs Brodie. Her writing was not very good and it was quite hard to read but eventually Annie knew what Mrs Brodie wanted to tell her.

It seemed that after Annie had left the Big House, the Mistress had gone into a decline and had just faded away until the Lord had taken her out of her misery. Mrs Withers, the housekeeper and her new maid had looked after her the whole time, as the Squire had not been home since Annie had been imprisoned.

As she read the letter out to Martha, she started to cry, as the Mistress was very good to her and she was so sorry that she had had such a bad time with monster who was her husband. Lady Barbara was buried in a family tomb in the grounds of her parents' home about twenty miles away. They had insisted, as they knew that their son-in-law did not care two hoots where she lay.

It was coming up to Christmas. Annie shivered to think that she would be in this terrible place over the festive season. Not that it was marvellous at home. They did not have much as children but they used to go to Church on Christmas morning and they would have something different for dinner, even if it were only a pheasant that Annie's father had poached from the Squire on the few occasions that he was sober. Goodness knows what happened here on Christmas Day. They would have to wait and see.

In the Arms of Merlin

It was Christmas Eve morning. Annie got up at the usual time, did all her little jobs before she came down to the food hall. Everyone was in a nice mood, even Miss smith. She was quite pleasant but still strict. They had finished eating their breakfast and were making their way to wash their plates and cutlery, when Lil came from nowhere and pounced on Annie, puncher her, scratched and gouged her eyes. The last thing Annie felt was a searing pain in her head. Annie did not struggle anymore because she must have fainted.

She came to, feeling something cold on her head and she realised that someone was putting a cold compress on her head. She could not make out why. She could feel water pouring down her face, then all of a sudden everything went red. Annie started to panic and really struggled until Miss Smith came to her side and told her what happened.

Half an hour later Annie was on a bed in the sick ward. Once again her head was heavily bandaged and it seemed to be on fire. Lil had really got to her this time. After all the punching and kicking she had taken a home-made knife from her pocket and cut a big chunk of her hair and scalp. Annie did not know it but her skull was in sight.

They had to call the doctor from the town but he could not do much about it. He told the attendants to keep the wound as clean as they could but in a place like that there was not much that anyone could do. Annie just lay on the bed holding her head. It was really painful but she just had to grin and bear it. The only consolation she had was that she did not have to work in the wash house or see those women again for a while, so Annie made the most of it.

Christmas morning arrived. It was no different to any other morning. There were a lot of very ill people there and two died before midday. Annie just 'cwtched' into the pillow as deep as she could. Even though it was rough hessian, she felt safe while her head was covered up.

It must have been two o'clock by the time the attendants started to bring the food in. Today they had like a broth and it did not taste too bad, unless it was because Annie had not eaten since breakfast the day before. She dipped the bread into the broth because it was so hard and her face was hurting so much she could not even chew, so she sucked the broth through the hard bread. They had the same thing for supper but Annie did not mind, as long as she had peace to nurse her wounds.

She woke at down, got up with great difficulty and walked to a room where there was a large zinc pan. Annie just wiped her face as best as she could, washed her hands, went to the water closet then back to her bed. She looked around the room and all she could see was misery, so she just bent back on her bed and wallowed in her own miserable thoughts.

Her mind started wandering. She thought, *I know I feel ill, I'm aching all over, my head hurts but I am alive and I am going to stay alive with the help of God, so Annie,* she told herself, *make the most of it.* She had not lain on her bed like this since she had been home in Ellwood Lane.

She started thinking about her mother, her brother and her little sister and she started to cry softly. She was sure that her mother wasn't happy that Annie was in this predicament but Annie's fate was planned as soon as she left home and went to the Big House to work. Why couldn't things have been different for her?

What had Annie done to deserve all that happened? She hadn't been nasty to anyone or hurt anyone. To lose her family was enough for any young girl to bear on her own. Annie gave a deep sigh and turned on her side and went to sleep.

Two days had gone by when there was a bit of a commotion in the passage. Annie could not make out what was going on. It seemed that a Minister had just called to see if anyone had wanted to talk to him, or to receive Holy Communion. There were only two of us fit to do anything. The Reverend took us down to the end of the room and talked to us as if we were human beings. It was a lovely feeling.

As the days went by, Annie got stronger. She could see that the attendants had more work than they could cope with so Annie offered to help out. They were very pleased and gave her a few jobs to do, which she did. At the end of the week the Doctor came, went around to the very ill patients first, then he went to Annie's bed. He took the bandage off and was surprised that the wound had started healing so quickly, but as he remarked, Annie was a young strong girl.

As he was talking to her he wondered what a nice young girl was doing in this 'hell hole'. He then asked her why she was there and she told him all her tragic story. He was quite impressed with her story. Annie said goodbye to him and he left the attendant to re-bandage her wound. As he was leaving he turned around and said, "Please put a clean bandage on that wound. Thank you."

The attendant who was seeing to Annie was shocked with the doctor's concern for her. He had not been going to gaol for long and was very thorough, seeing to the inmates, so different to the last doctor. He used to come in once every two weeks, just walked past the beds glancing at them, then go over to the governor's quarters where they used to drink themselves silly.

Mrs Elliot, who was the attendant looking after Annie, sat by her bed for a minute and they had a chat. The other women attendants appreciated Annie's help because it took some pressure from them. As the days went by, Annie got discharged from the sick room. It had been like heaven there, even though people were so ill around her. Annie did her best to help them but now she was back to reality.

She was taken back to her cell, she put the few things she had in her shawl on the shelf, went to lay on the bed, then heard the key was in the lock. A little grinding squeaky noise and the door was locked. It was hours later that Annie went to sleep and as soon as she did someone was hitting the door with a tin can, terrible noise.

Annie got up, dressed, had a little wash then made her way down to the food hall. As she sat down after getting her food, she realised who was sitting next to her. It was the woman who had helped her the first time she had gone to the sick ward. She had been admitted because Lil had slashed her face. She was another quiet person so it seemed. They started talking very quietly, as you were supposed to just eat, so they whispered to each other and Annie got to hear about everything that had gone on while she had been in the sick ward.

It seemed that Lil was still under lock and key, day and night and would be for another week, so Annie could breathe easy for another few days. Jane, the woman who had her face slashed was the same as Esther, very quiet and tried to ignore Lil, that is where they went wrong as it annoyed Lil to be ignored and that is why she used to go berserk. It was too late for them to find out now but it would help them in the future when Lil came back the wash house, God forbid.

After a week of good grafting Lil came back. She looked at Annie as if she could have killed her. Annie thought that Lil was more subdued than she was before she went to the lock-up. By what the others were whispering, it was really tough down there. The only thing Annie consoled herself with was that she would not have to go there.

It was four o'clock and Annie was beginning to flag when the door opened and Miss smith came in and made her way over to Annie and called her to one side. She said, "After you finish here, make your way to the Governor's room, as he wants to see you." Annie was terrified, Miss Smith could see this but did not tell Annie anything, so Annie had to suffer until she got to his room.

A quick knock on the door and a voice shouted, "Enter."

Annie was shaking all over. The Governor was a tall, large man with steel grey hair and a large moustache. He really looked frightening. He enquired about her health and asked if she was feeling stronger after starting back to work. He seemed pleased as she nodded and he said, "Having talked to the attendants in the sick ward, I have come to the decision to let you work there for the rest of your sentence. Everyone I have spoken to has told me you are a good worker and that you were sympathetic to the ill patients. This new doctor we now have insists that people in the sick ward be treated more humanely and seeing to them will now be your job. I have given you this chance to get away from that woman, and nursing these people may put you in good stead when you get out from here."

After a terrible night Annie got up, did her usual ablutions and made her way down to the food hall. As she walked into the hall the first person she saw was Lil. She started on her straightaway. Annie tried not to take any notice of her, but that made Lil worse. Nobody knew what made Lil tick, it really was getting Annie down. She didn't know how long she could take this. Miss Smith came from nowhere, got hold of Lil and frog marched her out of the hall. She was put under lock and key once again, so peace reigned in the hall for a while.

As soon as breakfast was over and Annie had put her plate and cutlery away, a gaoler came from nowhere and spoke to her gently, but firmly and then proceeded to take her to the sick ward. She took her to the woman in charge, who looked a 'tough one', but when Annie was a patient she was quite good to her, but how was she going to be now? Annie didn't know, only time would tell.

She took Annie to one side and told her; "You do your job and listen to what you are told. Be as nice as you can to the patients and you won't go far wrong." She then told Annie what she wanted doing through the morning and that is how Annie started to be a nurse.

This new doctor was certainly making many changes in this place. There were two of us and the woman in charge. The woman who worked opposite to Annie was about the same age as her mother. As a matter of fact she reminded her of her mother, not in looks, but in her ways and it was quite pleasant working with her.

It was very heavy work, especially on the male side. There was one man with an amputation and an ulcer on his other leg looked as if it had gone to the bone. The smell was terrible, poor man, he must have been in agony. It would have been kind for the good Lord to take him out of his misery, but it doesn't work like that.

After Annie had fed a few of the old ladies with some broth, the other woman, whose name was Mary, fed some of the men that needed feeding and they talked as they did so. Annie found out that she was from Bristol and came down to Wales into service. Her father had a smallholding and to supplement their income, he used to break in horses for the gentry. A Welshman, who had connections in Bristol, used to bring horses to him as he was very good at his job.

Mary was getting old enough now to go into service, so her father asked the Welshman if he knew of a place for Mary. He was delighted when he told him that he would take her to his own home, as his wife was looking for help with the children and Mary would be perfect. Everyone was over the moon, even Mary, because Mr Bevan had been coming back and forth to their home for years.

Mary was a bit nervous and upset when she left with Mr Bevan. She had to ride astride a horse to get to Wales, it was a good job that she was used to it or she would have been in a mess by the time they got to Wales. They left at 6 o'clock in the morning and rode for three hours. They stopped at an inn. The Master went in for a meal but Mary sat in the stable, eating some bread that her mother had put in a cloth for her. She asked the stable boy for some water, so there she was, sitting in the straw, eating her mother's bread and drinking water, which tasted like nectar.

The young lad was very talkative and spoke very highly about Mary's new Master. It seemed that he always called on the way up to Bristol and on the way back. It didn't take Mary long to eat her bread because she ate sparingly, as she didn't know how long the journey would take and she didn't want to go hungry. They rode for another three hours then came upon another inn. Arrangements were made for Mary to sleep in the stable. She found a good place in the corner, away from the horses. She put a little more hay on the ground and just lay down looking up at the roof of the stable. She could feel her eyes closing but held back, because she realised how hungry she was. She sat and fumbled in the cloth bag to get her bread out. The only thing was, there was nobody there to ask for water. She just had to grin and bear it. The bread was very dry going down but she managed it. She felt much better after eating and had put the last piece of bread back in the cloth when a young girl came into the stable with a jug of milk. Mary couldn't believe her eyes, the girl said it was from her Master, with a message that they would be on the road by six o'clock.

After Mary had downed the milk she felt all warm and contented. She just lay back in the hay thinking about what lay ahead of her. She woke up at the crack of dawn; lay for a few minutes until a young lad came in. He started seeing to the horses, then he realised she was lying in the hay. She got up, shook the hay from her clothes and her hair, then went to a trough of water and had a quick wash. She went back into the stable and there was another jug of milk waiting for her. Her bread all eaten and her milk all drunk, Mary was ready to finish the journey to her new job and new home.

In the Arms of Merlin

The village clock struck six times and by the time it had finished striking the master was in the stable. A few words and off they went. They arrived home early evening. It was a very big farm with a huge house. They must have been very rich to live in a place like this. When he called with her father she thought he was just an ordinary farmer, not a rich landowner.

It was very good working for Mr and Mrs Bevan. They had five children, two teenagers, one seventeen years old and one nineteen years old. They were really good looking, very blonde hair with blue eyes. Next came a ten year old, then a seven year old and the baby who was nine months, a gorgeous little girl and her name was Maggie.

Mary didn't have much to do with the bigger children, just the three little ones, Edward and Ernest were always naughty but not nasty naughty. They were always up to something. Nevertheless, Mary was very happy in her new job.

A year had gone by before Mary was able to go home to see her family. There were times that she felt so homesick, that after all her work was done, she would just go to her little room, get into bed under the clothes and just cry for hours. All the staff knew that Mary had been crying because her eyes were all puffed up. Mary didn't show anyone how she felt, she was too ashamed for them to know, because everyone treated her so well. She thought about it for hours in her room, thinking to herself, What if I wasn't happy here? I would have something to cry about.

After her first trip home, things got better for Mary. She lost all the homesickness that she used to have. She was so pleased, because everyone was so good to her.

Little Maggie was four years old when things went wrong. Mary used to take the children to the woods for walks most days and everything was fine but things went wrong this day. The two boys ran on ahead, which they nearly always did. Mary tried to catch them up and was running with little Maggie. She caught up with them, had a little laugh and then they played hide and seek. They were having a great time until it was Mary's time to hide her eyes.

She could hear the children giggling, counted to a hundred and said, "Ready or not, I am coming." She went to the right, she went to the left, she looked up and down. Found the two boys but couldn't find little Maggie. Mary looked everywhere. The boys were now crying and Mary was crying. She didn't really know what to do.

The only thing she could do now was to go back to the house and break the bad news to the family. Mary was out of her mind when she was telling her story. The mother was in deep shock and the father was furious. He rounded up all his workers to look for little Maggie. They were out until sunset and as they made their weary way back to the farm they all had the same story to tell. No sign of little Maggie.

There was no sleep for anyone that night, Mary at her wits end. What was going to happen to her if they couldn't find her? It seemed that a few children had vanished in the last couple of years. Mary couldn't even let the idea enter her head but it was starting to burn into her brain.

On the third day, the constable called Mary into one of the big rooms. It was a big shock when the constable made his thoughts known to her. She just screamed and screamed and didn't stop until the doctor, who had been called to Mrs Bevan, had to give Mary a draught to knock her out.

It was the next morning when Mary was taken to the gaol. She was tried for selling the child to some person or persons unknown for gain.

It seems that gypsies used to abduct children and sell them to wealthy people in other parts of the country. It was a very popular and profitable scheme.

There were some gentlewomen who wanted children but as childbirth was such a hazardous pastime, they would pay anything for a child rather than have one of their own with the risk of dying.

As it happened, someone was very happy with a beautiful little blonde girl called Maggie. There was no peace for Mary, her mind was in turmoil for years.

Mary had been in gaol for fifteen years. She was just about coming to terms with things. There were rumours that the Penal System was going to be changed, so Mary was living in hope of a new trial.

At first Mary had been in the kitchen, then she had been sent to the wash house but clashed with Lil's personality. After a few beatings off Lil, she was sent to work with the sick inmates and has been there ever since and enjoying it.

This new doctor, he certainly was causing a commotion amongst the big wigs of the gaol. There were no floggings, which happened all of the time, but things were changing for the best, some folk said.

It was a new thing for the patients to be washed. It was never heard of with the last doctor but it was part of this doctor's treatment to get a patient back to health again.

It used to take Mary and Annie hours to wash a few people, half of them struggling because they didn't want to be washed, the other half because they were too cold.

It was really freezing in that big room. There was a fire at the bottom of the room but it was miles away from where the men were. It was not so bad right near the fire, so we put the very ill ones up there.

Mary and Annie got on very well together. They chatted about their lives before they came to gaol. As the weeks went by, Annie could see more of her mother in Mary, whether it was wishful thinking on Annie's part she didn't know. She even had the same mannerisms as her at times. It was quite upsetting for Annie.

She went to bed one night after a terrible day. One of her favourites, an old lady, who had been in the gaol for thirty three years, had been poorly all the week and the day before she died, they sent for the doctor. He shook his head and walked back to the senior nurse's room. He talked to her for a few minutes. She went to the medicine cupboard, took out a bottle and poured some dark stuff into a mug then called for Mary. Elizabeth took it without any fuss. Mary put her head back on the pillow, the old lady smiled, went to sleep and didn't wake up. She passed away the following morning. She had gone out of her misery, poor old thing. Every time the nurse went into the cupboard, Annie knew what was going to happen.

Annie had been laying on the bed for a short while, thinking about her mother, her brother and sisters, when all of a sudden her mother was standing by her bed. Annie had such a shock. She sat up straightaway and said, "Mam, what is the matter? What do you want here?" Annie was talking as if she was home and everything was back to normal.

Her mother smiled at Mary and said, "There is nothing wrong, my dear, I just want to see you and have a chat with you." She asked if she was happy in her new work and Annie said; "Yes, but I am not happy here Mam." She said: "I know, but you have to make the most of your time here, so you can follow up with the nursing when you get out of here."

Annie was taken aback at what her mother had said. She had not thought of anything like that at all. She had not even thought as to where she was going to live after this nightmare was over. By what Annie reckoned, she had about another year to do again, but that was so far away she didn't let it enter her mind.

Mam had started her thinking. Annie's mouth dropped open when her mother said, "You don't often think of your son."

Annie just couldn't say anything to her mother. She just cried. After she had pulled herself together, Annie looked up.

In the Arms of Merlin

Her mother was gone. It had all been so real but Annie realised she must have been dreaming, it gave Annie food for thought. She hadn't thought about her baby for a long time. She seemed to block him out of her mind but from that minute on she thought of nothing else.

Every time she had a minute to spare, she would get a bucket of hot water, add some soda in it and scrub as much floor as she could. After a few weeks the whole floor was clean all of the time.

Doctor Morris was very impressed with Annie's work and her whole attitude to looking after the patients. More inmates came out of the Infirmary than used to. Also fewer people were dying.

By the time another six months had gone by, Annie was a very capable nurse. The senior nurse gave her quite responsible jobs and Annie was thrilled to think that she was able to do them.

One morning there was a scuffle in the dining hall between Lil and one of the women that Lil had slashed a few months earlier. There was a terrible fight and for a change Lil got the worst of things. Two gaolers and two inmates carried Lil into the ward, put her on the bed and assessed her injuries. The head nurse hesitated for a second, then changed her mind and said, "Get someone to call the doctor or this woman will die." Everyone thought that the thought had entered the woman's head to leave her to die but something must have changed her mind.

What sort of a patient Lil would be, goodness knows. Only time would tell.

Annie nearly fainted when she saw who she was. Her face drained of colour, the other woman could see the effect Lil had on this girl, but it was too late now, the die was cast.

Head Nurse Hughes said; "Come on now, girl, help me to get some clothes off this woman or it will have been a waste of time sending for the doctor."

In the Arms of Merlin

After Annie had got over the first shock of Lil being there, they managed to take clothes off her. As they got near to the wound, they both gasped as they saw Lil's side. There was a very deep slit and it was just pumping the blood out. Lil's face was getting whiter as the minutes were going on.

When the doctor arrived he went into action straight away. First job he did was to send Annie away because he could see the colour of her face and thought, A woman on the floor is going to be no good to me. He told Annie to get Mary. Annie was really glad, perhaps she would have been different if it had not been Lil.

After her dismissal, Annie scampered everywhere, trying to do everyone's job. She didn't do too badly. By the time they had got Lil's wound stitched and cleaned her up, she started to come around, then started up with her antics. They could do nothing with her, so they had to manacle her to the bed. What an afternoon they had with her.

Annie was glad to go back to her cell for the night. She didn't even go for food. She was physically and mentally exhausted. She lay awake for hours worrying about the time she was going to spend looking after this terrible woman, but do it she had to.

She got up at the usual time feeling very hungry, but when the food was in front of her she couldn't eat it. She made her way to the sick ward. There were screams, abusive language, cursing, you name. it. The only consolation Annie had was that Lil was tied down to the bed. The other two saw to Lil for the first few days. She got quieter as they were sedating her but they didn't want to do too much of that as she could go into pneumonia and that certainly would have killed her and they didn't want that after taking so much trouble to save her life. They all hoped that Lil realised that they had made that effort. Not that she would, because she wasn't that intelligent.

In the Arms of Merlin

The first encounter Annie had with Lil, was giving her a wash, with the help of Mary. It was a mammoth job. Annie nor Mary had ever seen such strength and temper. As the days went by, Lil seemed to calm down and they cut her sedation to see how she would be. She didn't seem to get any worse and had stopped spitting her food out every time Annie came to feed her. Things were looking up.

One morning Annie went to Lil. First she seemed to be quite subdued, so Annie thought she would try to converse with her by asking how she was feeling and if she was still in pain. Annie got the shock of her life, she answered her quite gruffly in her usual tone of voice, but she did answer her, so things were getting better.

Doctor Morris was very pleased with Lil's progress and he was really surprised at her attitude. Perhaps Lil's life had been worth saving after all.

As the days went by Lil got better. She wasn't good every day, but when she had a 'pull' she wasn't as bad as she had been, so that was some consolation. Before Lil's recuperation was over, she used to follow Annie and Mary and help them with little jobs on the ward. Everyone was so surprised, even the Governor made his way to see the miracle of the sick ward.

The day finally arrived for Lil to be discharged. She was very quiet all morning and we all thought, Here she goes, she is going to go berserk again, but things didn't happen like that.

Nurse Hughes, the head nurse, came to see her before she went and gave instructions to the two gaolers who had come to take her back to her cell. She was to be put on light duties until she had healed up inside. Doctor Morris told her several times that there was to be no fighting, or any sort of messing about, as she could start bleeding again and perhaps they wouldn't be so lucky the second time.

In the Arms of Merlin

It did sink in with her, because as she was leaving the ward, she put her arms around Mary then Annie and was really crying. It a sight that nobody had ever seen. Lil must have seen the light or something. From then on Lil was an exemplary and reformed character, who tried to get the other old lags to be the same as she still was 'top dog' in the gaol.

In about 60 days (if all went well), Annie would be on the other side of the big wall. A shiver went down her spine as she thought about the outside world. She didn't have a clue what she was going to do, where she was going to live or how she was going to live. It got too much for Annie, so she shut it out of her mind completely.

As she was helping Mary to get old Joe up to the chair, they started talking about Annie getting out. Annie didn't want to know and tried to change the subject but Mary was adamant. She wanted Annie to sort things out, sooner, rather than later and she suggested that she had a word with Doctor Morris. Annie wouldn't hear of it but Mary was worried for Annie. She was still only a young girl with no experience of life in the outside world. Mary wished that she could take care of her when she got out but poor Mary was surely doomed to die in this terrible place.

It was a few days later that Mary had a chance to have a word with Doctor Morris. He was a very approachable man and very down to earth, not a bit snobbish. He wasn't a bit like the last doctor, he could hardly touch the inmates. He had no compassion for anyone that was in that place. He used to say that it was their own fault that they were there in the first place and that was that.

After the usual good morning and a bit of 'chit chat', Mary came straight to the point and asked Doctor Morris if he could help Annie get a job in the Infirmary when she was released in a week's time. He was taken by surprise that Mary had approached him about Annie, because he had actually been thinking about asking Annie himself about her taking a job in the Infirmary, but held back because of his position, but things were different now.

He was delighted that Mary had asked him because he liked the girl and she knew how to work hard and was good at her work. As he left the gaol, he called Mary to one side and told her that he would enquire at the Infirmary when he went there this afternoon, to see if they would take Annie. The big wigs at the Infirmary might not be as benevolent as Doctor Morris because Annie was coming from gaol, so he told Mary not to say a word in case it didn't work out. That was how things went.

It was the morning before Annie was due to be released, when the doctor called Mary to one side and told her the bad news that they didn't want to know about Annie, as she had committed a crime and had been to gaol, so that was that.

CHAPTER 4 - THE INFIRMARY

It was six o'clock the following morning. Annie was standing in front of the Governor in her own clothes and a few things wrapped up in an old piece of cloth. A lump of bread was wrapped in another piece of rag.

The Governor was looking sternly at Annie and told her: "I hope you realise what you did and that you are truly repentant and will never do anything like that again. Perhaps the next time you won't be so lucky and you will spend the rest of your life here and you don't want that do you?" Annie shuddered and looked the Governor straight in the eye and said in no uncertain manner, "Indeed, sir, you will never see me again."

'Farewells' had already been said. Even Lil had given Annie a hug and thanked her for helping to save her life.

Mary and Annie had talked nearly all night and the last thing Annie said was that she would come to visit Mary whenever she could. They hugged each other several times and sobbed in each other's arms, until the time came for Annie to go to the Governor's Office.

Annie had now left their cell and was making her way to the office. All was behind her now. She was escorted by a gaoler down the stairs, along a corridor and down to the main gate. She turned around, gave a long look and wet out through the open door, back into civilisation.

"God help me," she said, as she started walking down the little hill that she remembered going up in the wagon. Things looked much different than they did on that terrible day, three long years ago.

After a short walk down the hill, Annie came to a square. It was alive with people jostling here and there. Annie's eyes were popping out. She had never seen anything like it. She hadn't really been to the town, only when she was

In the Arms of Merlin

brought by the constable and the scenery was the last thing she had on her mind but she was here now.

A few rags for clothes, a large piece of bread that they give every prisoner when they leave and half a sovereign, which she had earned in the workhouse before she arrived in gaol. It was put aside for her, so thank goodness for small mercies.

There was a long road going up in front of her. One going down to the left, towards the river and one going to the right. She thought for a minute, looked left, then right and looked straight up the road and decided to take the right turning and off she went.

She walked a few yards, there were several small lanes. She was so positive now, she took the one on the right again and started walking up the little lane. There were tiny houses on the left.

She walked straight to the top and came out at a wider road with shops on both sides of the road. There were long wagons, gambos and one or two governesses' carts going back and forth.

She walked right up the narrow street, until she came to the Church. It was a very old and beautiful looking Church. Annie knew that she had taken the right road, wherever it would lead her. She made her way to the Church door, held the latch and pressed it down, it opened immediately.

Annie breathed a sigh of relieve and walked down the aisle. As she nearly got to the front pews a man's figure came from the vestry and made his way over to her.

"Can I help you?" he asked.

"I just want to sit in one of your pews and give a prayer in solitude," Annie replied, "as I haven't been able to do that for three years."

The vicar looked closer at Annie and realised that he knew the girl. He was the vicar who had christened her son William, in the workhouse a few years ago.

In the Arms of Merlin

He told Annie that he remembered her. Annie was so taken aback that she kept stuttering and couldn't make any conversation with him. He realised her dilemma and led her to one of the pews, sat her down and told her to take as long as she liked and he would come back later.

There must have been an hour gone by when he came back. Annie had said her prayer of thanks and had composed herself a little. The vicar came and sat by Annie and started talking to her. He asked her if she had anywhere to say. Annie shook her head, then he asked her if she had eaten. Again Annie shook her head. "Right" he said, "we will go over to the Vicarage, it is only over the road and we will chat about things while you eat."

When they arrived at the vicarage they were met by a large woman who looked really bad tempered and by the sound of her voice, she was. She found out from the vicar in two minutes who this young girl he had brought over to his home was.

After a lot of whispering in the pantry, the woman brought some things out and started cooking Annie and the vicar some food. Annie was very embarrassed, because she knew the woman didn't like her. She was called by the vicar to come and sit at the table. When Annie saw the food on the plate, she didn't worry about any embarrassment. It was plain food but Annie had not eaten like this even when she was at home. She thought she had gone to heaven but obviously she knew she hadn't. After the meal was over, she thanked the housekeeper very much for it and also thanked the vicar.

He got up, looked at Annie and said; "Now we must look for somewhere for you to live." He turned to Mrs Pugh, the housekeeper and asked her, "What about your sister, doesn't she take in lodgers?" She nodded but wasn't very enthusiastic about the question and tried to edge away from the vicar.

The vicar said; "speak up woman. Is it because she has been to gaol?" Mrs Pugh went red and confessed that it may well be. The vicar retorted back to her, "have you no compassion woman, don't you have anything beating in that body of yours?"

Mrs Pugh lowered her head in shame.

Annie interrupted and said, "Don't worry, Mrs Pugh. I suppose I would be the same if it was me, because everyone thinks the worse, don't they?"

Mrs Pugh made her excuses and left the room.

In the meantime she must have gone to her sister's to ask her about Annie, came back later and told the vicar that Annie could stay with her sister until she found somewhere else to live. The vicar was pleased, so was Annie.

After a lot of questions and answers, Annie told the vicar that she had the knowledge to be able to work in the Infirmary but didn't know if they would accept her because she had been in gaol. She wasn't aware that the doctor had tried for a job for her there, neither was the vicar, so he said he would go up to the Infirmary first thing in the morning.

Annie was a very young, lonely girl on her way down to Mrs Pugh's sister's lodging house.

Mrs Evans, Annie's new landlady for a while anyway, was a very nice lady, very jolly and smiling all the time and what's more she was a marvellous cook. Her food was plain but it had a great taste, because that was what she hadn't had for three years.

Annie was shown to her room. There was another bed in it but it was empty. Annie was made to understand that if someone wanted it, it had to be given. That didn't bother Annie at all. As there was no-one in it now, she was glad for her to get herself together.

She was called a 6.30 am, that was a lie-in for Annie. It was great, there was a bowl on the washstand and a big jug of cold water. She had never seen this before and enjoyed it.

In the Arms of Merlin

After she had dressed, she made her way downstairs and was met at the bottom by Mrs Evans. She said, "Come along now, girl, you are late, I need to finish so that I can go on to my work." Annie didn't know what that was all about but would know later no doubt.

Annie was allowed to come and go as she pleased, as the front door was always open, as Mr Evans was at home all day. He was out of work. He had had an accident in the tin works a few years ago and had never worked since.

Annie walked back to where she started from the day she was released from gaol. It was a very busy little town. There were little shops everywhere and there was one very big shop. It had clothes in the window, scarves, shawls and beautiful boots and shoes for the ladies. They looked so soft and delicate, so obviously they were for the gentry. Annie had never seen anything like them in her life.

She walked further down into the town, turned left and landed down by the river. There were hundreds of people here, mostly men and some looked very rough. Annie thought it was time to make her way back to the square. She was quite uneasy there, so she thought she had better make her way back in case. She must have walked for about an hour up this road, down that one, looking in shop windows and looking at the people as they were passing her.

She realised that she felt a bit hungry and found a bread shop, went in and bought a small loaf, paid for it and scuttled out. Annie was delighted. That was the first time she had ever bought anything in a shop in all her life. She felt good. Perhaps things are going to get better, Annie thought.

As she walked out of the little shop, she put the bread under her shawl for no-one to see it. She hadn't asked Mrs Evans about eating in her room. She closed the door, sat on the bed and ate half the loaf. She thought that she would keep the rest for this afternoon.

Annie felt a little better now. She checked that there were no crumbs anywhere as she did not want to upset Mrs Evans. After the cleaning operation was over, Annie lay back on the bed and looked up at the ceiling and started thinking about the future. She had to look for a job because her money would be gone in a few weeks and she would be thrown out and be destitute and back in the workhouse again and she didn't want that.

After a long think, she must have dropped off to sleep. It was a marvellous feeling just to lie there and no-one to bother her. It was three o'clock when she woke. She jumped out of bed, had a quick wash, tidy her hair. While she was doing this she looked at herself in the little mirror and was quite pleased at what she saw. Since coming out of gaol she had piled her hair in a knot on the top of her head and after a while little tendrils crept down onto her face and added softness to it. She had very good skin considering that she didn't pay much attention to it. She was on the lean side, more than likely that was also due to being in gaol, because the food sometimes was simply awful.

All that was behind her now, so she must get on with the rest of her life.

On arriving downstairs, Annie went into the kitchen to see if Mrs Evans wanted any help; she got the shock of her life when she found out that it was Mr Evans doing the cooking and whatever it was it smelled delicious.

Annie was a bit shy when it came to men. She hadn't had much to do with them, only that time when she helped in the sick ward in gaol. It must have been 7 o'clock when Mrs Evans came home. She was very tired and moaned a little, which was unusual for her, as she was a very jolly person.

It seemed that a few of the workers were ill and with nobody to replace them, they had to get on with it. After a chat with her about her job, Annie realised that Mrs Evans worked in the Infirmary and had been there for years. It was a great opportunity for Annie to ask Mrs Evans if she could help her to get a job as Annie couldn't go on indefinitely without working. Mrs Evans let the idea go through her head for a while and spoke her thoughts and said that there was no harm in asking. "You understand, my girl, that perhaps when they find out that you have been to gaol, they won't have you."

"It's all right, I'll take my chance," Annie said. "I have got nothing to lose, only to gain."

The following day Mrs Evans went to work and as soon as she saw her superior she asked her about Annie taking a job there. The woman was delighted knowing that Mrs Evans was recommending this girl. She knew that it would be alright, because good girls were hard to come by.

Mrs Evans was very pleased with herself, she had taken a liking to Annie as soon as she had seen her. She didn't know why, but she had. She wondered when she was going to tell her about the gaol sentence? I had better tell her before I go home, she decided.

They had been so busy that Mrs Evans had forgotten about it until late afternoon. They had not even eaten that day. They always tried to find time to eat a few scraps from the kitchen, but not today.

Miss Jones, the head of the cleaners, cooks and odd job men told Mrs Evans, "I think you can ask your girl to start tomorrow if you will. We can't go on like this."

Mrs Evans decided now was the time to break the news. She told Miss Jones all about Annie's life so far.

After a thoughtful pause Miss Jones said, "Who do these so called gentry think they are to do such a terrible thing to a young girl like that?"

Mrs Evans was quite taken aback and stuttered a few words but Miss Jones was still thinking about what poor Annie had gone through on her own. It must have been awful for the poor girl. Now when she comes to work in the morning not a word is to be said about the matter. "Tell her she is not to tell a soul."

It was four thirty when Annie came downstairs. Mrs Evans was already there and had made some cocoa. It was lovely and hot. She had been quite cold getting up this morning, it was a very damp bedroom, but Annie didn't want to complain as Mrs Evans had let her stay with her after all.

After they had drunk their cocoa, they put on their coats and hats and made their way to the Infirmary. It took them about 15 minutes to get there. They couldn't go very fast because it was still dark and there were no lights at all. They had to be careful where they walked. Once they turned the corner past the Church, the Infirmary came to sight. It was a big old place with big windows and a big door at the entrance.

Once they got inside, they made their way down the stairs to the basement, then over to the kitchen. There were a few women scuttling about. Mrs Evans and Annie then went to the outhouse and fetched a load of kindling, paper and some coal. Mrs Evans explained to Annie that the first thing to do was to rake all the ashes out from the stoves, then re-light them. That meant twelve of them. It was the first time Annie had ever lit a fire in her life but as Mrs Evans said, "There is always a first time." Annie raked all the ashes and Mrs Evans laid the fires then lit them, trying to show Annie how it was done.

While Mrs Evans was laying the fires Annie was going up and down the stairs carrying buckets of coal. It was no mean feat. Annie must have carried twenty buckets up to the second floor. Her back was breaking and this was only the first two hours of the day. Twelve lit fires and twelve clean stoves.

They made their way down to the closet where all the cleaning material was kept. Their next job was to scrub all the floors of the wards. Mrs Evans took Annie into the front ward where the women were. She said she would make a start on the men's ward. As there were only two women in the ward that Annie was in, it would be done quicker.

After Annie had finished her ward, she went over to Mrs Evans to help her. She had never seen anything like this in all her life. It was filthy; there was vomit on the floor someone had had his bowels open in the corner by the stove. There was food everywhere. Annie couldn't believe it but Mrs Evans said it was all due to no staff coming in for a few days.

It took them at least an hour to clean that ward, then they went onto the next and the next. It was never-ending. It was now time for dinner. One of the nurses came up from the kitchen with a sort of *wagon*, on it was a very large cauldron of broth, tin basins and spoons. She asked us if we had finished our work and Mrs Evans said, "Yes, off you go," and off they went.

They scrubbed one more ward, then went back to the closet to take their buckets and cloths back. They had one little spell, then off again to carry more buckets of coal upstairs. After they had taken the coal to every ward, they had to go out to one of the outhouses for blocks of wood to supplement the coal.

Another hour must have gone by before they finished with the wood. Mrs Evans whispered to Annie, "Come on, girl, you and I deserve a break and a little sustenance but don't show anyone."

I won't, don't worry! Annie thought.

They went outside to the outhouse via the kitchen. Mrs Evans picked up a piece of bread and a lump of cheese. She hid them under her apron and off they went to the outhouse.

It was a very large place, very cold and damp. You could see water running down the walls and it wasn't even raining. Where it was coming from she didn't know and really didn't care. She was just interested in crouching down on haunches and eating a little something and that is what they did.

Annie thought that she had to ask Mrs Evans if it was like this every day but she thought better of it in case she thought that she was ungrateful or something and she didn't want that because she had been very good to her.

While they were eating, Mrs Evans with her mouth full of bread said, "Annie, I hope that today hasn't scared you too much, because it isn't always like this."

"Thank God," Annie said with a chuckle, then they both started laughing.

It was so nice to be with someone with some humour in them. After they had finished their snack, they went back upstairs, took the food *wagon* with them and collected all the basins and spoons from all the wards and took them to a small kitchen on the same floor as the wards.

There were two big zinc baths there, on two narrow benches. There were large tin trays on a very large table and loads of shelves, where they put the basins and every other container for food.

Mrs Evans said, "Come on, girl, we have to go down to the kitchen to get the hot water and soda."

Oh! Annie thought, I am back in the workhouse and gaol again, and a little shiver went down her spine. But as she thought some more, she knew she didn't work as hard in either of the two places as she had worked this day, but she was free - that's what matters, and she made her way down to the basement, to the kitchen to get the water to wash the things up.

It was from a distance that she saw Doctor Morris but he didn't see her, because she ran like a scared rabbit. She didn't know why but she actually blushed when even she thought of him.

In the Arms of Merlin

After hours of different jobs, Annie and Mrs Evans made their way home. They were absolutely whacked, it was no wonder that Mr Evans did all the work in the house.

After a quick wash, Annie came downstairs to a lovely meal. It was a rabbit stew. It was the best meal Annie had ever tasted in all her life. Mrs Evans had certainly taught Mr Evans to cook, what a gem he was. They ate their meal in silence as they were too tired to talk.

Mr Evans asked Annie, "how did the job go, do you think you will like it?" Annie didn't commit herself. She didn't know how Mrs Evans managed to keep going because she was years older than Annie.

After Annie finished her dinner, she offered to help with the dishes, but neither of them would have any of it. "No," they said, "off to bed you go. The morning will come all too soon."

Annie didn't have to be told twice and was in bed like a shot. She lay there for a few minutes thinking of the day behind her and started wondering about the one in front of her and drifted off. She must have woken up after a few seconds, realised that she had not said her prayers, so she started them, but didn't remember finishing them.

The morning came all too soon. She awoke with a start. She thought that she had overslept but she was alright, because it was now Mr Evans was giving her a knock, so everything was fine.

After she had finished her usual ablutions she went downstairs, sat at the table and ate her breakfast. Very think oats and a chunk of bread. Mrs Evans told Annie to take some bread with her to work in case there was someone around and they would not be able to pinch something.

They walked up to the Infirmary in double quick time. They were a bit behind time today. They arrived early though, went through the front hall, down the corridor and down the stairs to the basement and to chaos.

Annie couldn't make out what was wrong, but after a few minutes they realised that the cook had not turned up. What a row. Mrs Evans took control straight away to the others' amazement. In no time she had cook's big apron on and told Annie, "You stay here with me, girl" and there we stayed all day. We were very busy but it was a much easier day.

Annie thought that Mrs Evans was more than pleased with her. She felt quite happy with the way that she had coped. It really made her feel good.

As they walked home that evening, Annie commented that it would be nice if they could do that job all the time. "There is no chance," Mrs Evans said. "We more than likely will be scrubbing and carting coal about the place again."

Things went on like this, as if Annie had worked in the Infirmary all her life. It wasn't too bad now that she had got into a routine. Annie thought that she could put up with the job, but was a little worried about her lodgings. She was quite happy there but didn't think that she could afford to stay much longer. She was earning a few shillings a week, most of it going to Mrs Evans for her keep. Annie reckoned that she would have to find somewhere else to live and very soon.

When she finished work, it was too dark to go out. She was very tired but she would have to go soon.

It was the very next morning that she was having a chat with one of the patients as she was lighting the fire. He asked her where she lived, she told him that at the moment she was with Mrs Evans but explained her situation to him, as he seemed to be a decent sort of man.

He said, "I own some property in the town, perhaps you would be interested. They are not too special mind, but they are not terrible either." Annie said she would let him know after she had thought things over.

David Jones had been watching Annie from the first day that she started at the Infirmary. She was so young and

In the Arms of Merlin

had such sadness in her eyes, he reckoned that she had been through some sort of trauma in her young life, but he didn't mention his thoughts to her or anyone, it was just that he felt sorry for her.

David had been to Pembroke on business a week earlier and had started his way home on horseback, which is what he always did. When he had got half way, he stopped overnight at an Inn. He had a meal and some ale, then he made his way to bed earlier than usual. He made his way down to the stables and must have disturbed someone and got a bump on the head and two fractured ribs for his trouble.

He was lying unconscious on the stable floor when the young stable lad arrived. There was hue and cry, they got him up, took him into the Inn and put him to lay down. The sent for the doctor and constable.

They both came at the same time but the doctor took over first because he kept going in and out of consciousness and the doctor didn't like it one bit. After he had been examined, the doctor bound his chest and put cold compresses on his head.

The constable had a few words with him then, but he couldn't tell him anything really because he hadn't seen his attacker.

After thinking things over, the doctor decided to take David up to Carmarthen to the Infirmary because of his concussion.

The Innkeeper and the stable lad helped to load him into the doctor's carriage and off they went.

It took about two hours and David didn't know where he was for about two days. He had been in now for nearly a week and was hoping to be discharged in the next few days. His head was still fuzzy but the pain was gone. His sides were still sore and hurt when he coughed, laughed or made a sudden move.

They had told him that the pain would stay with him for a week or two, so that meant that David wouldn't be able to work for a while. It was a good job that he had a good manager in charge of everything. John, the Manager, had been brought up with David and his sister. They were children together.

Their father had been a manager to David's father and had got killed in an explosion down the pit. Something had gone wrong and David's father felt responsible and took the children under his wing. He gave them both an education. John passed as an engineer. Letitia went to a finishing school in Bath and now she was a fine figure of a girl with beautiful red hair, bright green eyes and those eyes were for David Jones only – and she also was an accomplished pianist.

Annie saw this young girl when she visited David Jones and wondered who she was. Mrs Evans put her right on that score and Annie didn't think much about it again.

When they got home that night they had eaten and were having a chat, when Annie approached Mrs Evans and told her about David Jones' offer. She was quite surprised, as was Mr Evans, but Annie explained to them it was nothing to do with them, it was just that she needed to spend less on her accommodation, as there was hardly anything left after she had paid Mrs Evans. "You see," she said, "I want to save enough to get my son out of the orphanage and be able to look after him like I am supposed to do."

Mr and Mrs Evans were amazed, because Annie had never ever mentioned the child before, but Annie didn't talk to anyone about him, or what she had in her mind.

After the initial shock of Annie's intentions, they threw question after question at her but Annie couldn't say why David Jones had offered her a cottage out of the blue. They both knew the man, not personally of course, but had nothing but admiration for him. They knew that he wouldn't harm Annie in any way.

In the Arms of Merlin

Mrs Evans told Annie that she would speak to David Jones in the morning. "Discreetly of course," she added.

While Mrs Evans was scrubbing under David Jones' bed, she had a quiet word with him, not showing anyone. He was quite pleased that Annie was at least considering it. He told Mrs Evans to bring Annie to the house about a week after he had gone home, whenever that would be. Mrs Evans nodded her head and carried on with her scrubbing and passed the news on to Annie when they were sneaking a bit of stew in the woodshed.

Annie was delighted and so was Mrs Evans. She told Annie that she would help her with a few bits and bobs from the house. Annie thanked her very much. A warm feeling came over her thinking about the future, which wasn't going to be too bad after all.

Annie slept restlessly that night and was worn out when Mr Evans knocked her door. She would have given anything to go back to sleep, but out she had to get.

They got through the morning pretty good but the afternoon was another kettle of fish.

As Annie was making her way to the basement, there was a crowd of people in the front hall where patients were brought in to be treated if they were hurt.

There was a terrible hullabaloo going on. Annie couldn't see who they were, but she had an idea that they were gypsies. It seemed that a young gypsy boy had been knifed. There was blood everywhere. Even a few of the gypsies had it on them. In the middle of the was John Philips, David Jones' manager. He was also covered in blood.

Annie hoped that John wasn't involved in any way. It was John Brown's fair that day and the railings of the Church were used to tether the horses that were up for sale. About half of them belonged to the gypsies, the rest were from local farms and a few land owners.

In the Arms of Merlin

It was a very big day in the town, there was a lot of toing and froing. Lots of provisions were bought and lots of ale was drunk and this is how that knifing had come about.

Annie could hear someone coming up the stairs from the basement, so she thought that she had better move or she would get into trouble, she didn't want that, so off she went up the stairs to the front ward. The first person she saw was David Jones and he was dressed ready to go out. Annie blushed as he approached her. He stopped and spoke to her in a low voice and told her not to forget to come and see him in a few days' time to discuss the little cottage. Annie was so flustered that she just nodded her head said "thank you", and walked quickly away from him. She thought that her face was going to burst, she was so ashamed, that she couldn't have behaved better. She couldn't understand why she blushed so much when she saw him, or when she thought of him.

After she had finished seeing to the fires she made her way down to the basement again and had a quick look to the front of the infirmary, but the commotion had died down a bit.

Arriving in the basement, Annie found Mrs Evans and queried her, but she didn't know any more than Annie. It must have been two hours later that the young gypsy lad was taken upstairs to one of the front wards. There must have been about five gypsies left and they all traipsed up the stairs to be with the young boy.

Annie was wondering how long it would be before they would be sent out from the ward. The sister was a stickler and nobody would get one over her. Sure enough, down they came. Four of them – she must have let one of the stay – he must have been his father.

One of the maids and Annie were collecting the last of the dishes and were on their way downstairs with them. As they got to the corner they nearly knocked John Phillips over. He had his arm all bandaged up and held up high in a sling.

In the Arms of Merlin

He also looked as white as a sheet. He must have been injured too. He nodded as they made way for him and made his way to the bed of the young boy. The girls couldn't stay too long to listen but did catch a few words and learned a little about what had happened. If John Phillips had not intervened the boy would certainly have been killed.

It was the first time the boy had come to town on Fair Day, because things could get pretty rough. The boy whose name was Liam, had got on the horse and ridden him up the street twice for the two men who were interested. The boy got off the horse and tethered him up again, to one of the railings of the Church. The dealers who were from London started to mess the boy about because they couldn't see anyone with him, so they took advantage of him.

One of the men wanted to take the horse for himself and when Liam said "no", there was a scuffle and they had the boy on the ground. John who was parading a horse himself, was passing at the precise moment that Liam was getting up and was strongly protesting about their behaviour. There was a flash in the sunlight and this cockney struck him with his knife. John jumped at him straightaway, let go of the horse and just piled into the man with the knife and down they both went.

The man was taken aback when John helped Liam. He thought that because he was a gypsy he would get away with anything, but he was wrong.

By the time Liam's father had arrived, the blaggard was lying on his face, with his arms held firmly behind his back until the constable came, then they were both taken away.

Someone got a flat cart and put Liam on it and pushed it up to the Infirmary and advised John to follow him. John hesitated because he had to get someone to look after the horse. He looked around and saw someone he knew and asked him if he would take the horse back to the farm. The man agreed to do what he asked.

In the Arms of Merlin

By now John wasn't feeling too good, he felt faint and sweaty and all of a sudden everything went black and down he went to the ground, so they both ended up riding on the cart. After a few minutes John came around and felt a little ashamed, but the doctor assured him that anyone who had lost so much blood would certainly do the same thing.

No-one at the farm knew anything about what had happened, until the man brought the horse back. The master couldn't go back to town, so Letitia, his sister took the trap and went to see what was going on. As she arrived at the front hall, John was coming down the stairs from the ward as he had been to see the boy, his father had thanked him very much for saving his son's life and more than likely he was right.

Liam lay in bed for four days, he had an infection and was burning up with fever. On the third day, the surgeon had a look at his wound and was shocked to see how bad it was. So the next thing the boy was being opened up again for the surgeon to clean all the puss out of the wound. He re-stitched the wound, cleaned the outside with some sort of alcohol and sent him back to his bed saying, "That's all I can do. Let's hope this will do the trick."

John on the other hand, got better quickly. He was about his work in a few days and nearly forgot to go back to the Infirmary to have the stitches taken out.

When he went back the second time, he met Annie on the stairs carrying two big buckets of coal. He caught up with her and took one of the buckets from her. She protested but he wouldn't have any of it and actually took it right up to the stove.

One of the nurses was looking very disapprovingly at Annie, but she couldn't do anything about it. She was so embarrassed, she didn't even say thank you. John didn't mind about that, instead he followed her to the little room off the ward and asked her when she was going to come to the office

In the Arms of Merlin

to see about the cottage. Annie was surprised that he knew anything about it. She pulled herself together and told him that she would be around in the next few days and John looked quite pleased with her reply.

When Annie got down to the basement, she had big stories to tell Mr Evans and Mrs Evans had bigger stories to tell Mr Evans when they got home.

It was three days later that Mrs Evans covered for Annie, just for her to slip out to the office. "Now, Annie, don't let me down, that 'eyes like a hawk' nurse will certainly miss you if you are away too long. Just do your business and make your way back for both our sakes."

Annie promised on her honour and off she went shaking all over.

She ran up the last lane and landed on the step of the office out of breath. She waited for a few seconds, knocked the door, waited again, then gently opened the door. It was quite a large room, just one small window, a very large desk and chair and in the corner of the room there was a smaller desk and chair and sitting at the desk was a middle-aged lady with a large bun and thick spectacles.

"Yes?" she said, "can I help you?"

Annie started stuttering and stammering but was saved by John Phillips who had come in from a room at the back of the office. Annie didn't know him really but was glad he was there, because that woman really frightened her, reminded her of the women in the gaol.

"Mr Phillips, I am Annie Owens and I have come about the cottage."

"Yes, I know," he said. "Come over here and sit down and I can tell you all about it."

Annie was very relieved. Mr Phillips put a chair out for her. That was the first time that had ever happened to her and it felt quite good. As she sat down, Annie explained that she didn't have much time to spare because she had to go back to work. He nodded his head and said, "Well, let's get on with it."

He explained that Mr Jones had told him all about the renting of the cottage, so he told her where it was, how much a week it would be and he gave her a key and wished her good luck and said if there was anything that he could do, just ask for me.

Annie thanked him very much and asked him to thank Mr Jones as well and as he shook hands with her she said, "I shall bring the rent money here every Monday, if that will be all right?"

He nodded and escorted her to the door.

Annie was back in the basement with her apron on and ready for anything in fifteen minutes. When she found Mrs Evans, she told her all about it.

Mrs Evans was very pleased for Annie; she was a lovely girl and had had a hard time through no fault of her own. She had been living with them for a few months and they had really got to know her and had grown very fond of her. What worried her was the interest that David Jones had in her. It would all come out one day, as long as Annie would not get hurt again.

They arrived home about eight o'clock and sat down to a perfect meal. Mr Evans had excelled himself once again. It was as if he knew that they had something to celebrate. He had roasted two sheep's heads with roast potatoes, onions and turnips, in the same tin. It was absolutely delicious.

After they had cleared up after the meal, they started talking about the cottage. Mrs Evans said, "It is too late now to go and see it, so perhaps," she told her husband, "you could make the dinner tomorrow night, take everything off the fire and leave it on the hob and meet us at the cottage?"

"Good idea," he said and that was how they got round to see the cottage together.

In the Arms of Merlin

Annie had a very fitful sleep that night and as soon as she woke the first thing that came into her head was the cottage. She got up straight away, went downstairs, ate breakfast, went to work. How Annie got through that day she never knew.

At last the time had come to go to see the cottage. Annie was beside herself. The three of them made their way to see the place, which would be another start in Annie's life. That is all she seemed to be doing, was going down new roads in her life. She hoped that this one was going to be a good one.

CHAPTER 5 – A NEW HOME

Mrs Evans opened the door, then stood aside for Annie to be the first to see her new home. Annie was amazed, it had even been white washed, but whoever had done the job, had put a bit of *nott coch in with the white. Annie thought that the colour of the wall, a deep pink, was absolutely beautiful. It made Annie feel warm all over. She wondered where he had the idea.

There was a small fireplace. Annie wondered where she would get enough wood to keep it going. The room was not very big, but big enough for her. There was a little lean-to going off the main room. She went into the tiny scullery and could see a small window and no back door.

Annie was glad that there was no back door, she would feel more secure. She realised that deep down she was a little nervous. This was the first time that she had lived on her own. "Please God, don't let me start thinking about it."

Mrs Evans said; "come on Annie, let's go and see the bedroom," so up the rickety little stairs they went. The stairs were so narrow that Mr Evans was filling them. They had a chuckle about it when they got to the top of the stairs. They went straight into the bedroom. It had a very low ceiling. Mr Evans had to bend his head slightly. They had another chuckle and Mr Evans passed a remark about gentlemen friends, that Annie would have to look for short ones. Mrs Evans gave him a nudge, Annie blushed to the roots of her hair. She even felt her body go red. Mrs Evans changed the subject then took Mr Evans to one side and gave him a mouthful. He apologised to Annie but Annie had got over the thought of any man coming up to her bedroom.

They went downstairs and talked about what furniture they could find. "Leave it to me," Mrs Evans said, "we'll set you up, don't you worry."

They took one more look around, went outside and locked the door and started their way back home. It was a four-minute walk to Mr and Mrs Evans' home, so Annie wouldn't be too far away if she needed them or they needed her. They ate their dinners with gusto, first of all they were starving and the walk must have given them an appetite.

It was as Annie was scrubbing the men's ward that she saw Doctor Morris. It was the second time that Annie had seen him since she had left gaol. But this time he saw her. He stopped what he was doing and made his way over to Annie and he said, "Annie is it you?" Annie felt quite embarrassed as Mrs Hughes, the head nurse was looking daggers at Annie. To think that a maid should look at a doctor, leave alone talk to one.

Doctor Morris turned around to Mrs Hughes and asked her would she wait a minute while he had a word with Annie. The woman was dumbfounded and walked away.

Doctor Morris told Annie, "come here into this little room and we can talk without any interference." Annie was black red in the face. She held her head down and waited for him to start talking to her.

He asked her how long she had been working at the Infirmary, where she was living and wanted to know why she hadn't asked him to find her a job in the first place?

Annie shook her head and said she didn't think that he would be able to help her in any case. "You have been here all this time and I haven't seen you. You should be looking after the patients, not scrubbing the floors. Tomorrow morning, I will have a word with one of the governors for you to come and work on the wards. You are being wasted scrubbing floors my dear," he said, "I shall see you in the morning."

Annie's heart was pounding when she arrived at the basement to give the news to Mrs Evans. She was as shocked as Annie was, told Annie not to put her mind on anything that the doctor had said, because nurses were young ladies who were daughters of gentry, who were doing their work, some of them voluntarily and Annie didn't have a hope to be a nurse.

Annie went quite flat, because she thought that she would be able to do the job and also liked looking after ill people. Annie went to bed that night a very disappointed girl. She was sorry that she had seen the doctor that morning, in case she couldn't have a nurse's job.

As soon as they finished work, Mrs Evans and Annie made their way to the cottage. They didn't have to do any cleaning because the place was spotless. They were now deciding what to put where and what they needed. Annie was at sixes and sevens. She had only a shilling left, but Mrs Evans reassured her that everything would be alright.

There was a second-hand shop at the bottom of the lane, so after work the following night Mr and Mrs Evans and Annie called in to see what they had.

They bought a double bed, a chiffonier, which was dirt-cheap but damaged. Mr Evans said, "don't worry about that, I can repair it." Two armchairs, a large tub, a fender and an ash pan and the man threw a kettle in for nothing. There was a table for the kitchen and a smaller one for the scullery.

Annie was very pleased and thanked the couple several times, but Mr and Mrs Evans were only too glad to help her because she had made a difference to their lives. She had risen them up from the rut that they were both getting into.

Mr Evans paid for the furniture with two gold sovereigns. Annie tried to protest but they both just tut-tutted her away. They told the shopkeeper that they would pick up the stuff the next evening. So off they went, to have their meal, another perfect one, as Annie told him.

After all the chores were done, they all went to bed.

In the Arms of Merlin

Annie was so excited, her mind was in a whirl, so sleep was far away. She must have dropped off about four o'clock and the next thing, Mr Evans was knocking the door.

The day just dragged on and on. Annie thought it would never end, but eventually it did. They made their way to the shop and there was Mr Evans, with a handcart, waiting for them. He was as excited as the women were. The only thing was that they would be losing Annie, but she was quite close and he didn't think that she would keep away from them.

He told Annie to go to open the door of the cottage, to receive the furniture, so off she went. They put the bed, the small table upside down on top of it and they managed the kettle.

The door was ajar, so they carried the bed upstairs and set it up, little table in the scullery and kettle on the hob. Back they went, but Annie insisted that she went to help to push the cart this time. They were back in ten minutes with the armchairs, the fender and the ash pan. Dropped them off and made their way once again and all was finished.

The little cottage was furnished, ready for Annie to start her life.

While they were eating dinner, Mr Evans said that tomorrow he would go and look for kindling, because you have got to give the cottage a good airing, goodness knows how long it has been empty. That is how things went.

Annie was not allowed to live there until it was really aired.

There was a man living up the road who used to walk to the country and collect wood. He would saw it up and bring it home in his flat cart, sell it for a few pence. Mr Evans got in touch with him and asked him to see that Annie had plenty of wood all the time and he would see to the cost of it.

Fire was lit every day for three days. By now the cottage was like toast. Mrs Evans had brought some of her quilts from her coffer upstairs and other bedding, and gave them to Annie.

Annie was the luckiest girl in the county. Her luck had changed the day she met the vicar and now that she thought of it, she had not seen him since, but through no fault of her own because it was all work. There were no days off for Annie to visit anyone. As Annie was drifting off to sleep she decided to write a letter to the vicar, not for him to think that she was ungrateful.

It was two days later that Annie met Doctor Morris on the landing, dividing the two wards. He was pleased to see her, as he had been looking out for her since they had had their last chat. He explained to her that he had talked to the Governors and they were quite impressed with what the doctor had told them about Annie.

There were plenty of girls who would work hard, but they could not read and write. Doctor Morris had also told them how good she had been in the sick ward in the gaol. They were very impressed, but the only fly in the ointment was the fact that she was an inmate there.

Doctor Morris had explained to them why she had been sent to gaol but it didn't make much difference to them. He explained all this to Annie and she knew that she would never be able to be a nurse.

Doctor Morris said, "give them time, I am sure that they will come round to my way of thinking," but Annie knew that it was useless.

It took until the following Monday for Annie to move into the cottage.

She had been to the baker on her way home from work, bought a loaf, some flour and yeast for her to make her own bread, she wouldn't be able to afford to keep buying bread, even though it was much easier. Annie hadn't even tried to make bread before but she had to try.

In the Arms of Merlin

She got into the house and there was a lovely fire going, the place looked really nice. Mr Evans must have come to light the fire early. Annie was very glad, but he couldn't keep doing this. Also there was a pan of broth simmering on the hob. Annie did no more. She got a big bowl from her cupboard and a spoon, sat down, ripped some bread off the loaf and ate a very large helping of the broth.

When she met Mrs Evans the following morning. Annie thanked her for the broth and for lighting the fire. "It was Mr Evans who had been there," Mrs Evans said, "don't you worry about that, we shall help you as much as we can, that is, if you don't mind, we think of you as the daughter we didn't have."

Annie felt an inward glow, she had not had anybody to take care of her, or love her, since her mother had died. Annie swallowed hard trying not to break down in front of Mrs Evans but put her arms around her, gave her a big hug and thanked her and said she would do the same to Mr Evans.

"By the way Annie," Mrs Evans said, "how about calling us by our names? We have known each other long enough now."

Annie nodded and went quite shy and said; I can't call you by your Christian names, it seems too disrespectful."

"Well," Mrs Evans said, "you can call me Auntie Sal and you can call Mr Evans Uncle Will." And that was how it went.

It was six months later that Annie had her first time off. She was now to have a half day every two weeks. She was over the moon, because by the time she got home, made food, lit the fire, it was time to go to bed.

They had an arrangement now. Uncle Will came three nights a week to light the fire and leave something or other on the hob. It was a marvellous arrangement for Annie.

It was dark when she went to work and dark when she got home. When they were making their way to work they didn't see a soul. There were a few people out when they were coming back but now Annie would be able to see the town in the day time and look around. She was so pleased with herself.

Straight after all the dinner things had been cleared and all the dishes had been done and put away, cook told Annie, "off you go, and don't be late in the morning." She didn't have to be told twice, she was home in two minutes, opened the front door, went to the scullery, fetched a kettle of water, brought it into the front room and proceeded to clear the ashes. She put them into a flat tin and opened the front door and took them across the lane and tipped them in the corner by the closet. That was where everyone put their ashes.

It took a few minutes and the fire was roaring. Annie put the kettle on before she put the logs on the fire so as to boil the kettle. She brewed a lovely mug of tea in a few minutes. Later she went to the scullery, put some cold water from the tin can into a pan and had a quick wash, tidied herself up, saw to the fire, then went out for the first time.

Usually she walked down the lane but today she thought she would walk up the lane and landed in the main street of the town. There were lots of people there, horses and carts were coming up and down the street. You had to keep your wits about you.

Annie did not move off the pavement, even though it was very narrow. She was making her way up the street. She had never been up there before and landed by the Church. She thought of the vicar but decided to leave a visit to him until the next half day. So instead of going past the church, she turned down left, then left again and landed in a small square.

A few people passed her, as she walked along and all of a sudden she came across a small shop. There were shoes in the window. Annie stopped in her tracks and realised whose shop window she was looking in to. She walked on a few feet, until she came to the door, turned the handle, opened the door and there, squatting down with a boot in his hands was Mr John Evans, Esther's father.

Annie was speechless when the bell on top of the door tinkled. Mr Evans looked up and didn't recognise her for a minute and said, "can I help you?"

Annie had pulled herself together by now and said, "don't you know me?" Mr Evans took a closer look, got up and put his arms around her.

There were tears rolling down his face. "Annie," he said, "where have you been? We knew that you were out from gaol but had no idea where you had got to. Come along," he said as he took her arm and opened the door into their living quarters and shouted, "Esther, come and see who I've got."

There was a scuffling from down the cellar and all of a sudden Esther was on the top stair leading from the cellar. She took one look at Annie and ran towards her and hugged her until Annie couldn't breathe. It was ages before they stood apart and the three of them were crying. They all moved into the kitchen. Mr Evans put the kettle on the fire and said "we'll all have a cup of tea."

Esther was throwing questions at Annie and Annie was trying to answer them. Esther eased off after a while.

Mr Evans had to leave them, as someone had come into the shop, so they just talked and talked. Esther told Annie that she would have been dead if Annie had not been in gaol the same time as her and that she was the one that kept her sane. Annie said it was the same for her and that Esther had done the same for her too. After a very long chat Annie decided that she had better go home, but told Esther to come over later and they could eat together and chat some more.

If Annie had not had a half day, she would never have found Esther, because it was dark when she went to work in the morning and dark when she got home at night. Not that she would be able to go anywhere, as she was too tired by the time she made some food and lit the fire, the night was gone. That was when Uncle Will didn't come over.

Since Annie had heard that there was no chance of her being able to go nursing, the rebuff had triggered something off. She now realised that she couldn't go on living like she was, so it started her thinking. She had saved a few sovereigns, as she didn't have time to spend them. She didn't tell Auntie Sal in work, because they didn't work together that morning so instead of going to her own home she went to Sal's home.

When they both arrived together Will thought that there was something wrong and asked immediately what was the matter? "Nothing" said Annie, "I have got a proposition to put to you." Will couldn't get over what Annie was telling him.

"She has an old head on those young shoulders," he told Sal later after Annie had left to start the ball rolling.

Annie wrote to Mr David Jones, asking to see him when she went to pay the rent. The following Monday, there was a message for her in the office, with Mr John Evans. He told her that David Jones would see her tomorrow and that John would pick Annie up in the trap and take her to Plas yr Arad.

It was a very large mansion on the hill outside town surrounded by hundreds of acres. They certainly were a very wealthy family and had been for generations.

Annie was a bit shocked at the message and explained that she couldn't possibly go with him because she would be at work until eight o'clock. John was shocked at the long hours that they had to do and said, "I will have to get back to you and explain to the boss."

It was two evenings later. .Annie had just come into the cottage, the fire was lit and there was some stew on the old hob. It looked so homely. Annie was quite happy with her little cottage and realised how lucky she had been.

"Now then" she thought," who could be at the door at this time of night?" She went nervously to the door and said, "who's there?"

A voice said, "It's me - John Phillips - with a message from David Jones."

Annie blushed when she heard his voice and garbled a few words while she was trying to unlock the front door. As the door opened, he was there standing in all his glory. By this time Annie was black red. John noticed this and tried to make her more at ease, but poor Annie seemed to get worse.

John said, "Is this a bad time?"

Annie knew she had better pull herself together or he was going to think she was simple," so she said, "No, Mr Phillips, it's all right, please come in." She shocked herself at the way she had taken control of the situation.

"No thank you," he said, "I can't stay too long, as there are things to do. Now then," he said, "Mr Jones has given me full control here, so what did you have in mind?"

Annie thought that she had better start from the beginning and she told him about working late every night, she didn't have any life at all. Also she said that it was very hard work, she didn't mean for herself, but for her Auntie, who had been so good to her. She had thought things through and wondered if Mr Jones would object to her opening a Team Room in the downstairs of the cottage. If it went all right, would she be able to rent the cottage next door at a later date? It would take Auntie Sal from that job as well as myself; she is not as young as she was.

"I was hoping," she said, "that I could keep the rent as it is, until the trade would pick up. It is going to be hard at first, there is not much room here but we will have to manage. I have been down the lane to see about buying the small tables and chairs. The only thing I was worried about was how I was going to bake cakes, as the oven is in the front room where the tables and chairs are, but my Auntie only lives a few minutes down the road and she has suggested that we bake the cakes in her house, as she was going to be involved in the venture."

John was very impressed with her plan. She certainly was a go-getter and he admired her immensely for that. But on reflection, he admired her in any case.

He took himself from his thoughts, told her that he didn't think there would be any problem at all and that that she could get on with the arrangements.

Annie was very pleased and thanked him most sincerely. "Will you please thank Mr Jones?" she added.

John nodded his head in acknowledgement, rose from the chair and started to walk towards the door. "If you are stuck or need anything, please let me know," he said, "and I will do my best for you."

Annie dropped her eyes to the floor and thanked him once again.

He went out through the door and out of sight down the lane. Annie hugged herself and really felt good. She was too excited to eat much tea so she just tidied up, put the fire safe and made her way to Auntie Sal and Uncle Will to give them the good news.

It was quite late when she got there; they were surprised to see her at this time of night. Annie spilled the story out to them and they were delighted. Uncle Will was glad because his wife Sal wouldn't have to work so hard and she would be home on a Sunday. She hadn't had one Sunday off for years.

His first thought was that they could go to Church together once again. The rest would be a bonus.

Will watched the girls talking about the things that they had to do. Nothing could be done tomorrow because they were both working, but Annie had a half day the next day.

Poor Auntie Sal never had a half day but God willing, things were going to get better for the three of them.

They worked hard all the next day, they both wondered how they were going to tell the head cook about their intentions. The opportunity arrived when cook was having a break, an unofficial one of course. She had gone into the wood shed to have a quick smoke. She was a clay pipe smoker and was missing quite often. Everyone knew where she was and sometimes she would have a swig of port if there was no-one about.

Auntie Sal and Annie had hold of her and asked if they could speak with her. She wondered what it was all about and got the shock of her life when they told her. Annie was such a good worked but Mrs Evans was priceless. She had got cook out of trouble many a time. She told them that she was shocked at what they had told her but wouldn't stand in their way because it sounded as if they had a good thing going and gave them her blessing.

Mrs Evans and Annie finished work in the Infirmary on the Sunday night, at eight o'clock hoping that they were doing the right thing.

Well, if they were or were not, the deed had been done.

CHAPTER 6 – THE TEA ROOMS

They both got up very early the next morning, took the one armchair up to Annie's bedroom and they carried the other one down to the second hand shop down the lane. They were changing the one armchair for four dining chairs.

The three of them ferried the furniture back and forth to the cottage until all the swapping and changing had been done.

The three of them went down to the market to buy crockery and cutlery. They had a good bargain with another second hand dealer. Uncle Will put everything on the flat handcart with a couple of quilts under the crockery so that it wouldn't break.

They pushed the cart up to the cottage, washed everything and put them away, then Auntie Sal went back to the market and bought some lengths of good calico, measured the tables and went back home and made lovely tablecloths. They looked great. Auntie was pleased.

They now only needed one larger kettle and one large teapot. The man down the lane thought that he could find a kettle for them. Auntie said, "alright, get it for us and I will get the teapot." She remembered seeing a very large teapot in one of the cupboards in the kitchen in the Infirmary and it was never used. "I think I will go now for it."

Uncle Will was never a forceful man, always quiet and unassuming, but on this subject he was adamant. "You will do no such thing," he told his wife, "do you think that I would survive if you were sent to gaol? Ask Annie what it was like and that should make you think twice about the stupid thing that you suggested."

His wife was as white as a sheet. She didn't think the same way as her husband; she would have just gone into the kitchen, taken the teapot not thinking about the consequences. That idea went right out of the window.

Joe, the second hand man was lucky, he found a teapot as well for them.

Now they were ready to go.

After a lot of talking, the two girls – as Uncle called them – had decided to take it in turns to bake the cakes early in the morning so that they would be fresh and that is what they did.

Auntie was taking the first turn because she was the better cook. After Auntie and Uncle left, Annie made herself a cup of cocoa and took it upstairs. Her armchair was up there, so up she went and sat down on the chair in the candlelight and let the day's events run through her mind.

She had locked the front door, so didn't bother to take the cup downstairs; she undressed and went wearily into her own bed, in her own house and in the morning she would be starting her own business.

She put her hands together and said, "please God, let things work out for us, if it is your will." She went into a deep sleep.

It was five o'clock when Annie looked at her clock. She lay with her eyes closed for a minute then opened them and jumped out of bed and said; "now Annie Owens, let's see what you are made of."

She ran round the cottage like a rabbit. It was half an hour before she was able to slip up to Auntie Sal's, who had started the baking. The smell was gorgeous.

At about eight o'clock they started to carry the cakes to the Teashop. Uncle had made a small sign saying 'Teas and Fresh Cakes'.

They arrived at the Tearoom, went inside, put all the cakes and Victoria sponges in tins and started laying the tables. Everything was ready by nine o'clock.

In the Arms of Merlin

They all waited with bated breath. They didn't see a soul until ten o'clock, then two navvies came in and asked for two mugs of tea and sat down on their lovely clean chairs with filthy clothes. Annie was really disappointed. They wondered how they could make it known that they wanted clean and tidy clientele. They would have to work something out before they would go any further. The two men went after they drank their tea and complimented them on the brew.

Auntie was a little embarrassed. She didn't want their kind in the Tearoom and felt guilty because they were so nice.

They tidied up after the men and then the door opened and in walked Letitia and two friends. Annie took them to a table near to the fire and gave the list of cakes. The girls were giggling and laughing most of the time, but eventually had three pieces of Victoria sponge with cream and jam in the middle.

Annie thanked them for their order and went out to the scullery where Auntie was waiting. Annie gave the order, Auntie cut the sponge, while Annie brewed the tea. She carried it all on a large tray, put everything on the table and retreated to the scullery. They could hear the girls still giggling but they were also eating at the same time. They finished in about twenty minutes and Letitia called for the bill. Annie came in and gave it to her. They were amazed at the cheapness of the tea and told Annie so, and they complimented her on the cake; they said it was delicious. They paid their bill and as they made to leave they said they would come again and they would tell their friends. The scullery staff were over the moon.

They had twelve customers that first day. The second day the trade doubled and they went from strength to strength.

By now Annie had enough money to buy a small teapot, milk jug and sugar basin for each table and after the meeting they had last night, Annie was going to see David Jones to ask about the little cottage next door to extend the Tearooms.

They all realised that Mr Jones would put up the rent, but they had it all worked out and it would be worth it.

They had a really nice clientele frequenting their Tearooms and Annie had to admit that it was all down to Letitia. Word must have gone around and people must have enjoyed the food or they would not have come again but Letitia had sent them in the first place, thank goodness.

While Auntie and Annie were out in the scullery in between serving customers, they were having a chat. Annie was telling her Auntie that she thought that she would like to go to the Emporium in the main street to look for something to wear. Annie wondered if they would let her in the shop, she had never been to a shop like that before.

"Don't be daft" said Auntie, "as long as you have got the money they won't refuse you."

But Annie protested, "I don't look as if I have got a penny to my name."

"Don't be worrying about that," said Auntie. "once you show them a sovereign or two, they will be running around in circles for you."

It would be the first time that Annie would have bought anything in a shop. She found a blouse that wasn't too bad, gave her skirt a good brushing, cleaned her boots, brushed her hair until it was shining and swept it up into a top knot. She couldn't do anything more to improve herself.

She made arrangements with Auntie to go out, because it was quiet at this time of day. She put her coat and hat on, if you could call it a hat. It was a very large beret, made from some velvet that her Auntie had found on the market. "Never mind love," Auntie said, "you look lovely, so off you go, but be back before the crowds come for you to make more money to help to pay for your outfit."

In the Arms of Merlin

So off she went up to the top of the lane. There was a keen wind blowing. She kept her head down because it was catching her eyes. She was going quite quickly and went 'bang' into someone.

"Oh!" she said. "I am so sorry, I should have been looking where I was going." She looked up and there in front of her was David Jones.

"Miss Owens," he said, "I was just coming to visit your Tearooms and to have a chat about the cottage next door."

Annie was dumbfounded, he had to come today of all days. She didn't go anywhere ever and here she was gallivanting to the town and this man was coming to talk business with her.

"You seem to be in a great hurry so I won't detain you any longer. Carry on with your mission and I will make my way to the Tearooms and have a nice tea. Will you be very long?" he asked.

By now Annie was scarlet. "No," she said, "I will be back by the time you finish your tea."

"Right ho," he said, doffed his hat and strode down the lane towards the Tearooms.

Annie went to the Emporium, her little outing had been spoilt really, because she had to rush things now and she was worried what he was going to tell her about next door.

In the meantime, Auntie nearly had a fit when he put his head around the door, looked around and walked to a table, took off his hat, sat down and greeted Auntie in a very respectful manner.

Auntie was all fingers and thumbs when she served him but he took it in his stride.

As Annie pushed open the door of the shop she walked in and she could feel all eyes on her. There was nobody looking at her, it was just her nervousness.

She arrived at the counter eventually; it could have been a mile away from the door in Annie's mind.

In the Arms of Merlin

There was a young lady waiting behind the counter and she asked Annie politely what she could do for her. Annie stuttered that she needed an outfit. Not too expensive and not too bold. The girl was amused at Annie's candour and gave a little snigger as she took her up the wide staircase to the dress department.

She handed her over to the manageress. By then Annie thought that she was going to swoon. She asked the older lady if she could sit down for a minute and the lady took her to one of the gilt chairs. Annie was as white as a sheet. "What a good start," she thought, "I'm only coming to buy an outfit. How am I going to be when I get back to talk to that man. Things are not as simple as one thinks."

All the joy had gone out of the shopping expedition but she found something that she thought she liked. It was quite reasonably priced and the lady said it looked good on her.

Annie was quite shocked when she looked in the mirror. She was not a bad looking girl, with a sylph like body. It couldn't be otherwise with the food she had eaten in gaol and the workhouse. She thanked the lady for helping her.

She had bought a skirt, blouse and a small fitted jacket. It was pale grey with a pale pink stripe running through it and the blouse was the same colour as the stripe.

"Would madam like to go to the millinery department to try on a hat?"

Annie shook her head and made an excuse that she had no more time spare. She had no more money to spare either but she didn't' mention that.

She went downstairs with the assistant to pay. She handed over the sovereigns, received her change and as she walked out of the shop the manager said; "thank you madam, it's been a pleasure and we hope to have your custom again."

"Thank you," Annie said and was out on the road once again.

As she was making her way back to the Tearoom she realised about the parcels and would have been embarrassed if David Jones saw them, so she took to her heels and landed in Auntie's house. Left the parcels there and ran all the way back to the Tearoom.

Between the running, the cold and the shyness, Annie was blooming. She opened the door and he was still there. He looked up when she walked into the room. She smiled at him and passed him to get to the kitchen. She took her coat off and put on her apron, tidied her hair but couldn't do anything about her cheeks and walked out to meet him again.

He got up immediately and pulled out a chair for her to sit on.

Annie felt a shiver going down her spine. She had never had anyone hold a chair for her before. It felt marvellous, compensated her for the thrill of buying the clothes, which he had spoiled for her earlier in the day.

"Now then Miss Owens, let's get down to business." David Jones said. "Do you think Miss Owens, that your Tearoom needs extending?"

"Well, yes I do," Annie said, "we are doing very well and I know that we could do better if we had more space. If you rent us the cottage next door we would have more tables and we could put in a range, so we could do the baking here. It would be much better all round, that is if you would be willing for us to negotiate about the rent."

"We will get to that later," he said. "I have been keeping an eye on you and your business. I hope you don't mind but I have been interested in you since I first saw you at the Infirmary. I don't know what it is but there is something about you that I like. You have got more work in your little finger than some people have got in their whole bodies. And you've got plenty of guts."

Now if that is not a compliment I don't know what is.

In the Arms of Merlin

Annie was quite taken aback with his remarks. She had no idea that he really knew her but she did wonder why he had offered the cottage to her in the beginning. Now she knew.

She offered him another pot of tea and he accepted. She poured him a cup while he was talking and he passed another remark, he said, "you even pour a good cup of tea." By now Annie was speechless.

It didn't bother him that he was making Annie blush. He was a man of the world, could say what he wanted. He also enjoyed Annie's blushing. New and fresh to him, he hadn't seen a young girl blush like this for a long time but now he thought "I must stop, or I'll scare her and I don't want to do that."

"Miss Owens," he said, "there will be a letter in the post tomorrow morning, giving you all the details of everything regarding the cottage. Will that be all right with you?"

Annie said, "Can't you tell me how much you are going to charge us? If the rent is too much, we will have wasted your time."

"Now don't worry," he said, "I might as well have a few shillings from you every week, the cottage next door will be used, kept warm and dry, rather than be empty, so if you want it tell me now and things will get dealt with by the morning. Now do you mind if I finish this great cup of tea?"

"Not at all," said Annie.

Little did he know that she was on cloud nine wherever that was.

He was up on his feet in a few minutes. Annie went to get his hat and coat; he turned around to take them from her and their hands touched, just for a second. He stopped short, hesitated, then carried on with putting them on.

By now Auntie was in the room. He turned around and thanked her for looking after him so well. "It's quite all right," she said, "you must come again."

"I certainly will," he said. He smiled to Annie, then went out through the door and was out of sight in no time.

Annie and Auntie just collapsed on a chair and talked and laughed until another lot of customers came in.

Annie couldn't even serve them so Auntie had to do it.

Annie couldn't believe what was happening to her. Her life was definitely turning around. As she was making up the pots of tea and hot water, she said quietly to herself, "I must give a little prayer of thanks tonight when I get to bed."

At six o'clock they closed the front door and started clearing up. They washed all the crockery and cutlery, changed the tablecloths, cleared up the scullery then Auntie made a lovely cup of tea for them both.

They sat down and talked about all that was said that afternoon. "What a lovely man he is," Auntie said, "and a fair one too, but a very good businessman. Now that the cottage next door is empty, he will make money off it. Not a lot mind, but if it's not lived in it will quickly deteriorate, so we are doing him a favour too."

"Not as much a favour as he is doing for us," Annie said.

After all the events of the afternoon, they suddenly remembered the outfit that Annie had bought. Annie had forgotten all about it and disappointed her Auntie by saying that she had taken them to her house. They both started to laugh and decided to leave the two cups in the pan and wash them up in the morning. Off they went to Auntie's house to tell Will and to see the clothes.

"What a day," said Annie, "I have never had one like this before."

Auntie said, "I think this is going to be one of many if you ask me."

In the Arms of Merlin

In bed that night she was telling Will about the conversation that she heard from the scullery. Will was a little upset because he didn't want Annie to be made a fool of. He said, "if he makes a fool of Annie, I will have something to say to him. That girl has had enough trouble in her young life without him messing her up again."

"Hold your horses now, Will," she said, "let us see how things go. Perhaps the man is genuine enough so let us wait and see."

They waited quite a while and nothing happened, so they carried on with their work in the other cottage.

There was an old boy that lived in one of the yards. He was a mason but didn't have a job, so Uncle had made arrangement with him to come in on Sunday morning very early, so that he would have all the noise finished by the time people went to Church and Chapel. Between the two of them they had made an entrance into next door.

Annie and Auntie had covered everything up with old quilts that had seen better days. After the opening had been made for the door, the two women cleaned up everything. The place looked presentable again for a while.

John Thomas said, "I will be here tomorrow morning at four thirty to fill the sides for the door. Do you want me to hang the door for you?"

Will asked, "Can you, John?"

"Of course I can."

This man was a treasure; he could turn his hands to anything. He used the stones that he had taken out of the wall and built the sides up. It was a great job. After a chat between them, they decided not to put a door there, just bamboo curtains.

This man, John Thomas, was a genius. He had found a large coal range cheap and by Thursday morning they were baking in it. they were using wood and it was going great guns. Most of all, the smell of the baking was wafting up and down the lane all day. It was the talk of the town.

CHAPTER 7 – MAGGIE

A month had gone by and the extension to the Tearooms was in full swing. It was getting so busy that we had to talk about having another hand in to serve, as the customers were not supposed to be kept waiting.

Every morning about eight o'clock, a young girl would stand in the lane as if she was waiting for someone. One minute she would be leaning up against the wall, a little higher up than the Tearooms, then Annie would look again and she was gone. This had been going on for weeks. They all had noticed her, she had such a sad face, no-one knew who she waited for or where she went later.

The next time I see her, Annie thought, I will go out and ask what she's about. It was three days later that Annie saw her again. She motioned to Auntie and out she went.

The poor girl didn't know what to do. She didn't realise that Annie was coming out to her or she would have run off earlier but she was trapped. Annie just caught hold of her arm gently and asked her what she was doing there all the time.

The poor girl got into a state and protesting all the time said, "I'm not doing anything Miss, honest I'm not."

"But why are you waiting here?"

She was crying now. Annie didn't want to make a scene, so she walked the girl down to the Tearooms, took her straight into the scullery to Auntie and put her to sit down on a chair, shut the door to the Tearooms and asked her once again what she was doing there.

Eventually she said, "I was just standing to smell the backing because I have never tasted a cake ever."

Annie was shocked and let the girl's arm go. She looked at Auntie, then looked back at the girl. "Where do you live?" She asked, "and what is your name?"

"I live down on the quay in a room by myself. I am fourteen years old and my name is Maggie."

"What about your parents?"

"My mother died four years ago and my father went to drink. He went out one day and I haven't seen him since."

The two women were flabbergasted and just looked at each other. Annie asked, "Where do you get food from?"

The girl said, "I go around the back of the ale houses and get some scraps, some always leave something for me."

There was a lull in the Tearooms at that minute so Annie did no more, went upstairs to her cupboard, got some oatmeal and made a large bowl of gruel for her. Cut a big chunk of bread and put some cheese on her plate. Maggie couldn't believe her eyes. She really thought that the lady was going to fetch the constable, but instead she ate a hearty breakfast. The first proper food she had had for ever such a long time. As she was eating she stopped and said, "I won't be able to pay you."

"Don't worry about that," Auntie said.

Things started to get busy now so Annie told Maggie to go home to her room. "Tell me where you live and I will come down to see you after the Tearooms are closed."

Maggie looked scared and said, "I wasn't doing anything wrong Miss. I was just smelling the cakes baking."

"Don't worry about that," said Auntie.

"I'll come to see you later," Annie said, "when things are quieter here."

Maggie protested once more but Annie said, "get home with you now and wait in for me to come. Don't worry, it will be to your advantage."

As much as Maggie understood the conversation, she thought that perhaps they were going to give her more food. Maggie was quite happy with what she had this morning. It was the best and the most food she had eaten since her father had gone.

In the Arms of Merlin

It was very busy in the Tearooms that day. Every table was full. Annie's venture was definitely taking off.

The customers started dwindling about ten minutes to six and by six both rooms were empty, so Annie and Auntie rushed around and cleared everything. Laid all the tables again with snow-white cloths. They did not put the crockery on the tables because it would get dusty as Annie would have to clear the grate out in the morning in order to light the fire again. All the dishes were washed and put away and covered with tea towels.

Everything done, they both sat down to a steaming hot cup of tea. They were both very tired but happy. Both of them loved their jobs so they didn't mind how hard they worked. It was different when they worked in the Infirmary. They were working for themselves now in any case. That made all the difference.

"Auntie," Annie said, "the time has come for us to have help."

Auntie looked up and across to Annie and said, "Do you know, I think you are right and if I am thinking on the same lines as you, you have found the one to come to work here. Am I right?"

"You must be a mind reader. The only thing I am bothered about is where she is going to live."

Auntie chirped up and said, "What about our house? She will be earning money here so she can give me a few shillings to fill Uncle's eyes. Not that he would mind but it will be good for the girl to learn how to live."

It had been in Annie's mind to have the young girl to stay at the Tearooms, but she thought better of it because before long she would be looking for her son. "God only knows where he is, but I am going to have a good try to find him."

Eight years had gone by since the child was born. She tried to put it out of her mind because it was hopeless thinking about having her son to live with her. She didn't have any idea where he was. He could be anywhere in the country. She had promised herself that if she saved a little more money, she would pay for someone to look for him. She had been told that it could be done.

She always kept calm when she thought of the boy, perhaps it wouldn't be long before they would be together. Annie would be having her 22nd birthday on 11 August. She felt much older than 22 years, she actually felt 42.

She was working quite hard in the Tearooms but it didn't show because the work at the Infirmary was drudgery. How poor Auntie had done it for all those years she would never know.

It was only the other day Annie realised that Auntie wasn't that old. She was only 45. Now they said hard work doesn't kill anyone, I'm sure that is not right.

With the front door locked, Annie and Auntie parted company. Annie made her way down to the quay. She wasn't very happy going down there, especially on her own, but go she had to. She had to walk right down to the end of the quay, over the bridge and up a little lane.

She arrived at the number that Maggie had given her. It was nothing but a hovel. Maggie came to the door and that wouldn't close. It got worse when Annie saw the inside and the smell was terrible. It must have been coming up from the river. This poor girl. It must have been a nightmare for her to live in such squalor.

She asked Annie to sit down, apologised for the state of her home and said that what she wanted was to get out from there.

Annie thought that she had had a hard life but the workhouse and gaol was not as bad as this.

"Have you got any clothes?" Annie asked.

"No Miss," she said. "Only what I have got on."

In the Arms of Merlin

"Don't worry," Annie said, "we will find something for you."

They got to Auntie's about half an hour later. The table was laid and a delicious smell coming from the kitchen. The poor girl was bewildered because she didn't know what was going on. Annie took her upstairs and showed her her room and told her to wash her hands. They came downstairs and Annie said "we will talk later."

Maggie was worried; she had no idea what was going to happen. She did what she was told, washed her hands, which took ages because she had not washed them for weeks. She did her best; they looked a bit better but not much.

She arrived in the kitchen just as Auntie was dishing up the meal. Maggie sat down and tucked into the food. She had never eaten food like this in her life and she just threw it down her throat. She ate every morsel and was just going to lick the plate when Auntie put her hand on her arm and said, "no, no my girl, you must not do that. If you want more you ask and if we have some you can have it. Is that clear?" Maggie nodded and looked very sheepish.

Auntie was sorry that she had done what she had done but thought that we must start as we mean to go on.

After they all had finished their food, Annie asked, "Maggie would you like to work for me at the Tearooms? It would be hard work but you would get paid and you could stay with my Auntie and Uncle but you would have to give them lodging money."

Auntie chirped up, "we wouldn't be taking too much from you, just enough to cover your food. That is fair enough isn't it?" Maggie nodded once again.

"I don't think she is taking any of this in, Auntie." Perhaps we had better talk to her later on in the evening.

Auntie went to the scullery to get the water ready for them to wash the dishes. Annie showed Maggie where the tray was kept and asked her to clear the table. She did without any hesitation. She did it quickly and tidily and put them on the table in the scullery.

Annie said, "Do you think you could do that for me every day in the Tearooms?"

"I think so, Miss" she said awkwardly, "but I wouldn't be able to wear these clothes in the Tearooms."

Annie knew that but thought that she would leave that until later, but seeing as it had been mentioned Annie said, "Don't worry, we will find clothes for you somewhere."

Maggie seemed pleased and thanked the trio very much.

After the dishes had been done and put away Annie told Auntie that she was going to slip home to see what she had for Maggie to wear. She didn't have a lot but she was sure that she could find something tidy.

An hour later Annie came back with a long black skirt and a cream blouse. They were very old but they were tidy. The girls went to the kitchen. Auntie got the big zinc pan in from the yard and started carrying water from the boiler on the side of the fire.

"What are you doing?" uncle asked.

"Getting the bath ready for Maggie."

"I was wondering how you were going to work that in."

They didn't want to scare Maggie or embarrass her but everything fell into place. Maggie was only too pleased to have a bath. It was going to be her first; she told them.

"And not your last!" they both said.

They gave her a piece of Uncle's flannel shirt and a bar of red soap. Showed her what to do and left her to finish off and get herself dried.

Maggie had never felt like this in her whole life. She felt alive for the first time in her young life. Her skin was tingling and shining all over. Her hair was gleaming. Maggie wondered how she had gone all these years being dirty like she was. It was no fault of her own. She didn't even have cold water, leave alone hot water.

She dressed in Annie's clothes and Auntie had some bloomers and a bodice that had gone too small for her. The only things missing now were stockings and boots. "I've got some stockings here somewhere," Auntie said. "Will, you can go down to the market first thing in the morning, to the seconds stall and get her a pair of boots."

"Right you are," said Uncle, "I had better go to bed so as to get up first thing." Off he went and Annie made her way home because it was getting rather late.

After a good night's sleep, Annie got up, went downstairs, lit the stove and got the kettle boiling in a short time, ate her breakfast and started laying the tables, when a knock came at the front door and there were Auntie and Maggie. The latter was all excited and it showed.

"Now Maggie, I will show you what I want you to do. Every time people finish their teas don't rush to clear the table, just wait until they pay me and get up from their chairs. As they are going out through the door, you come with your tray and clear the table. Take the tray into the scullery, put them on the table, wipe the tray and bring the clean crockery and cutlery back to the table. Lay the table up ready for the next customers. I want you to do that as quickly as you can so that everything is ready for the next people. Is that clear, Maggie?"

"Yes," she said.

It was so busy that day it was closing time before they looked round. They did all the jobs that had to be done every night, then sat down and had a cup of tea and a bun and talked about the day behind them.

"Well, Maggie," Annie asked. "How do you think you are going to like working here?"

"I'm going to love it," said Maggie. "I will do my very best for you, Miss. Do I go home with Mrs Evans now?"

"Yes, and after you have eaten your food, you have a good wash all over and you will be nice and clean for another day's work tomorrow."

"I will, Miss" Maggie said and they put their coats and hats on and off they went.

Annie didn't feel much like tea by the time she went upstairs to her room, took the takings up with her and put it under the mattress. She put it right down the bottom of the bed because it would be too lumpy anywhere else. The bed was hard enough without coins under it.

After that was done, Annie thought perhaps she would go for a walk. It was quite a nice evening, so she went by the Church. She might even go as far as the Infirmary to see how things were going on. There were quite a few people walking that evening, no-one that Annie knew, only those she knew by sight.

She was passing a shop window and saw her reflection, her clothes were still shabby but she still looked acceptable. Perhaps one evening she might put on her new outfit. She had had it a few weeks and hadn't put it on her back. "Never mind," she thought, "I will wear it one day."

As the church came into sight, Annie could see the vicar coming out of the Church. She quickened her step and arrived at the lychgate. He saw her and stopped, "Annie," he said, "where have you been keeping? I thought you would have been around before now."

She felt embarrassed and tried to explain that they had been very busy.

She told him about the Tearooms, he knew nothing of them. He thought that she was still at the Infirmary but as he said, he might have been told about her new venture but it must have gone out of his mind. He confessed that he was very absent minded.

"Are you busy now?" He asked Annie.

"No," she said, "as a matter of fact I was making my way up to see if I could see you. I feel so guilty that I have not been sooner but while working at the Infirmary it was impossible to go anywhere. It was from bed to work and work to bed. I don't know how my Aunt, Mrs Evans did it for all those years."

"That's how it goes my dear, when you have got to do something, you do it. I knew that Mrs Evans had left the Infirmary, but didn't realise that you were also connected with the Tearooms. I got to hear that Mrs Evans is very happy in her new situation. I am very pleased for her and it was you who gave her the chance. That is the best news I have heard in a long time. What gave you the idea of opening a Tearoom then Annie?" the vicar asked.

"Well it was like this," she said. "I met Doctor Morris when I was scrubbing one of the wards. We had a long chat; I used to help in the sick ward in the gaol. He thought that I was wasting my life scrubbing in the Infirmary. I told the Doctor that I would love to be a nurse and I had started to put my mind on it too. Doctor Morris approached the Governors and gave me a glowing reference, told them that I could read and write. They were very impressed until they found out that I had been in gaol. Doctor Morris thought that they would change their minds but deep down I knew that they wouldn't, so I went all out and rented a cottage from Mr David Jones. I stayed on in the Infirmary until I had saved a little money and went all out for it.

I wouldn't have been so lucky if it wasn't for Mr and Mrs Evans, John Phillips and the second hand dealer down the lane. I must also mention Letitia Phillips, John's sister. She came in the first day we opened. I think she came in to have a laugh at me but was so impressed with our cakes and snacks that she told all her friends and we haven't looked back since. I suppose you know that I have rented the cottage next door and opened the downstairs room as an extension.

Everything is rosy at the moment and Mr and Mrs Evans are happy and have got a little put aside. She doesn't have to work half so hard so everyone is happy. Although my happiness has got a shadow over it."

"Well well, my girl," the vicar said, "what is marring things with you?"

"Do you remember when I was in the workhouse the first time we met?"

"Yes," he said.

"Do you remember what you did for my friend and I?"

The vicar scratched his forehead and thought for a minute. He couldn't for the life of him think, so Annie helped him on. "Don't you remember christening our babies? They were two little boys. Think, vicar."

All of a sudden he started smiling, "Yes, he said, "it was the Matron who asked me to do it as I happened to be there for a funeral. One of the elderly inmates had died and Matron thought that she would catch me. I didn't go to the workhouse very often. So how does this affect you so badly?" the vicar asked.

"Well," Annie said, "you knew why I was sent to gaol?"

"Not really," he said.

Annie took the bull by the horns and told the vicar everything. The vicar gave a long sigh, put his hand on her shoulder and said, "You poor girl, no wonder you feel sad but why are you seeking my help? How can I help you?"

"I was wondering if you could find out where my son is. He was put in an orphanage straight after I was put in gaol. I am now in a position to have him with me where he should be, so do you think you could do something for me?"

He nodded his head, "I will start this very afternoon."

It took Annie quite a while to explain why she had left the baby on the doorstep of the Big House but he seemed to understand her logic.

In the Arms of Merlin

It was getting late by now so Annie thought that she had better make tracks for home. The vicar walked with her as far as the main street past the Church because it was a bit lonely around there. As they came to the beginning of the main street Annie told him that she would be fine from here, as there were only a few people around, so they parted company. Annie said "goodnight," thanked him and off home she went.

That was the first sleepless night she had had since the first night before she opened the Tearoom. The dawn was breaking and it was then that she could have gone off but it was her turn to do the baking so up she got and in her mind, as she started the baking, was the thought of going to bed early.

It was market day and the place was busy, all through until five o'clock. Nobody grumbled and Maggie was taking to her job like a duck to water. She had been with us a month now and looked really presentable. Auntie had gone to the shop that sold materials, bought some remnants and made an outfit for her. Auntie was very good with the needle. She didn't have time to do anything while she worked at the Infirmary. She deserved everything she got because she was so kind and helpful to Annie and now to Maggie.

Maggie was as clean as a pin now. Auntie didn't have to keep on to her; she enjoyed being clean, which was a Godsend.

There was no early bed for Annie that night. About three o'clock a little boy came into the Tearoom and asked for Annie. She went over to him and he handed her a note in an envelope.

Annie was puzzled until she opened the envelope. It was from John Phillips. Her heart started to race as she read his strong handwriting. It was a request from David Jones for her to go to his home to talk about the situation of the cottage.

Annie's jaw dropped. Here's trouble, she thought to herself, I wonder what the matter is. She took the note out to the scullery to Auntie. She was as puzzled as Annie was. John was to pick her up the following evening if she didn't have a previous engagement. This meeting was at a very short notice, for which he apologised profusely.

Panic bells were ringing for Annie and she didn't know what to do about the situation. The worry about what he wanted to say about the cottages was bad enough but the thought of her going to his home and him talking to her in those surroundings was making Annie feel faint.

"Come on with you, girl," Auntie said, "he can't kill you, he is only a man!"

"That's the trouble," Annie said, "I am so shy. If he was a woman I wouldn't worry at all."

"Yes," said Auntie, "he's not a woman, he's a man and you will have to get a grip on yourself or he will think that you are a weak individual and not worth being in business with."

"I know you are talking sense, Auntie, but I think it is going to be too much for me. I know I have come out of my shell since the Tearooms have been opened, but this is different."

"Well, Annie, you have just got to get on with it and think what you have got. What you didn't have before. If you lost it all, where would you be then?"

There was a silence. Annie, nearly in tears, swallowed hard and said; "All right, I will do my best."

Auntie smiled and said; "That's more like it, think of the years ahead, when you and your son will be together. You may even have another family of your own; you are a good looking girl. You also have good prospects. You will have all the young men of the town coming to call on you before long." That last statement made Annie worse, so Auntie thought that she had better not tell her any more.

In the Arms of Merlin

Annie got into bed. She was so tired and was longing to go to sleep but it was impossible. She just lay on her back thinking about the following evening. Dawn arrived and she thought that she dropped off for about half an hour, then woke up with a start. Everything was all right; it wasn't her turn to do the baking. She took her time, did all she needed to do then came downstairs and went right into the work that she had to do.

Maggie and her worked well together. The younger girl thought the world of Annie but respect her as her employer. Annie didn't act as a boss but Maggie didn't take any advantage of anyone there. She was so grateful for what they were doing for her, as Maggie wouldn't have survived another winter. She would have either frozen to death or she would have started to death.

The only other alternative was to go to the whorehouse on the quay that served the sailors when their ships docked. She had never been there but she had heard others talk about, when they were all trying to keep warm behind a very large wall which was the bake house. They spent quite a bit of time there and nobody bothered them either.

Things started to wind down about five o'clock so Auntie said to Annie, "why don't you go upstairs now and get yourself ready for this evening?"

Annie gave a shiver, made a face to Auntie and left them to tidy up and prepare for the next day. As she was leaving the room to go upstairs, Auntie shouted after her, "Don't forget to wear your new outfit."

"What?"

"The time has come," said Auntie, "for you to make the most of yourself, so off you go and give those cheeks a pinch or two for you to have a bit of colour."

"I won't have to do that," Annie said, "because I will be like a beetroot all the time that I shall be there."

CHAPTER 8 – VISITING THE PLAS

It was six o'clock when Auntie called her from downstairs. "Mr Phillips is here," she said.

Annie had just been standing waiting for the call, she just couldn't sit down; she was on pins and was really glad to hear that John had arrived.

When she got downstairs, Auntie and Maggie gave a smile, didn't pass any remarks about her attired, just as if she went out looking like that every day. There was pride in Auntie's eyes as she saw Annie make her way over to John Phillips. He offered his hand to her, she shook it, turned to Auntie and said, "we are off then" and away they went.

It was a Governess' cart they got into; he took her hand and helped her to sit down. Annie felt like a princess as they made their way along the street. He was talking to her the whole time.

As they were getting to the outskirts of town he explained about the lateness of the meeting. He said, "David knew that you wouldn't leave your business to meet him, so if you don't mind, after the meeting you are to be invited to stay to dinner. He didn't mention it in the note in case you had other things to do."

Annie's mind was in turmoil. Eat food there! That would be impossible. She wouldn't know how to go about eating with the gentry. The only thing in her favour was, that when she had worked in the dining hall in the Big House she knew about the place settings and what to use but it would be different sitting down at a table with a man who affected her so strangely.

John could see that she was deep in thought, so he said; "if it is going to be a problem, don't worry about it. My sister and I will be there. It won't be all that bad and David is not an ogre. So relax, you might get to enjoy the evening."

In the Arms of Merlin

Would she by heck, Annie thought.

It took twenty minutes to get to the drive of the house. They turned off the road. Now there was no turning back. Annie was so nervous that she didn't even answer John. He could see the pressure she was under so he didn't say anything to her until they stopped outside the house.

As he helped her out of the trap, David Jones came into sight. "Here we go," Annie thought. "Now's the time to shine." She walked up towards him as if she had met him many, many times before.

Her confidence impressed him. "Good evening, Miss Owens," he said.

"Good evening, Mr Jones."

He smiled. "Would you like to come this way?" They walked up a large flight of stone steps and entered the main hall. The house was much bigger than the Big House that she worked in, down in Pembroke. There was beautiful furniture in the hall and leading off it was a very wide staircase. It was very impressive.

The butler came, took her jacket and her little sailor hat that Auntie had made from a bit of velvet she had bought cheap on the market.

David Jones took her elbow and led her into the study, showed her to a high backed chair and he went around to sit behind his desk.

By now Annie was feeling sick and wished that she was in a dream and would wake up any minute. But this was real enough.

"Now then," he said, "let's get down to business. I hope you don't mind my doing things like this but I thought it would be a good way to get to know you. I feel I owe you an explanation. You must have been wondering what I was about; we haven't had a chance to talk on our own. I hope you didn't think that I had an ulterior motive in asking you here, but Letitia is here and John and you know the both of them, they speak highly of you.

Now I know this is going to bring back bad thoughts into your head, but these things have got to be said. I know all about the trouble you had in your first job. I know about it from beginning to end, don't fret now, I know what sort of a girl you are and were. You see, Lady Barbara was my sister and she told me everything. She took a liking to you. You were very kind to her and your actions saved her from more degradation. You also put your life at risk and you bore the brunt of that animal's action. Miss Owen there is nothing that I wouldn't do for you.

My sister asked me to look for you after you got out of gaol. I did try but it was by accident I found you scrubbing the floors at the Infirmary. I promised Barbara that I would help you as much as I could. You were in her thoughts until she died. It was a blessing when she went. That man had undermined her. She just lay in bed from one day to another, not eating or drinking anything. She just lay there waiting to die; he had ruined her life and her soul.

You don't know about this as you were in gaol, but my sister tried to keep the baby, to care for it herself, with help of course, but he went absolutely berserk and beat her nearly to death. After that, she didn't get out of bed. The servants told me all about it. James the butler, wrote me a letter telling me everything. The whole staff were shocked.

It makes me mad when I think about him. I am not a violent man but if I ever saw him, I would land in gaol myself. He went to America straight after that incident and later his Solicitor sold up everything and he will never be seen again.

Someone from the North of England bought the estate and kept all the staff. They have all settled down with their new master and mistress but things didn't change for you or my sister. I can't do anything for my sister, but I will do my very best for you."

Annie was flabbergasted, she blushed. To think that he thought so much of her. Annie had sacrificed herself for her Mistress and she would do it over again because she thought so much of Lady Barbara. Poor thing, she had been dead all this time and Annie didn't know.

She was glad that she knew everything; she was beginning to worry what was going on.

David Jones got up from his chair, moved over to one of the cupboards, opened it and proceeded to pour two glasses of sherry. He turned around and brought her a beautiful crystal glass full of sherry. The glass was so fine that Annie was afraid to hold it too tight, considering this was the first time that she had ever held a glass like this empty, leave alone full of sherry.

She would be lying if she had said that she had never tasted sherry, because if Mrs Brodie and James, the Butler, were in a good mood, they would give the young ones a sip in a thick old cup. Thinking back, this sherry tasted much better than the one they had from James.

"Are you feeling alright now, Miss Owens?"

Annie nodded and took another sip of sherry. They had been talking for about an hour. He leaned down to the bottom drawer of his desk and brought some papers out. Annie was really puzzled now.

He looked at Annie and said; "I have got a property in the main street of town and it is going to become vacant. It would make an ideal Tearoom. From what I hear about your business it is booming, so what do you think about moving to the new premises?"

Annie stuttered and stammered, saying "Oh no! I couldn't possibly afford that sort of money. It would be too great a step for me to take."

In the Arms of Merlin

"I know you are right to think this way, but you do not know all the circumstances yet. You see, Miss Owens, my sister told me to look after your interest. She also left you a legacy."

Annie thought this must be a dream.

"Now I shall show you it." He passed a document to Annie. Her hands were shaking as she read it. She started at the top, saw the date and then read on until she came to the sum. She couldn't believe her eyes. Lady Barbara had left her £2000. What an enormous amount. Annie looked up at him in amazement and couldn't bring out any words.

David could see the state she was in, so he said; "Drink that down and I will get you another one. All right?"

Annie let the document drop into her lap; he came around the other side of her and gave her the sherry. She took it from his hand and absolutely threw it down her throat. She was a bit ashamed really but she had to do something or she might have made a real fool of herself.

"Enough for now," he said. "Are you composed enough to go into dinner?"

The sherry was beginning to do its work. Annie wasn't used to it.

"Yes," she replied, getting up and feeling a little unsteady as he escorted her through the large hall and into the dining room where Letitia and John were seated already. As they approached the table, John got up and pulled her chair out for her to sit down.

In a matter of seconds the butler was there with two young girls dressed in black and white. Very nice, the hovered around all through the meal. The food was delicious. How Annie got through the meal she never knew. It took hours.

When the men later had a brandy, Letitia and Annie removed themselves to the large sitting room across from the dining room. They sat down on deep red high-backed chairs and chatted about nothing really of any importance. Letitia didn't want to quiz her but she was dying to know what this was all about. She would have to wait; it would all come out in the end.

Conversation was nil by the time the men arrived. They sat down and David asked; "Did you enjoy your meal, Miss Owens?"

Annie nodded. "Yes, it was lovely."

He seemed pleased with her answer and her state of mind. She seemed to have composed herself by now.

David said; "do you think it would be in order for us to call ourselves by our Christian names?" The brother and sister were all for it but Annie said; "I could never call any of you by your Christian names."

Don't be silly," Letitia said, "you can call me Letty and I shall call you Nan. How does that feel?"

Annie thought that she had better agree, so that was how it went.

David, John, Letty and Nan. Everyone was relaxed after that and they had a great evening.

It was getting rather late and Nan looked at the grandfather clock, she could just see it from the corner of her eye, as it stood in the hall. David caught her doing that and promptly suggested that they call it a day. "I realise that you have to get up much earlier than these two, so John, you can drop Nan off after you take Letty home."

"Yes, certainly," he said. David rang the bell and the butler came and helped the ladies on with their coats.

David turned around and told Annie; "I hope I haven't startled you too much. I will get word to you later in the week, so you can come to my office to talk some more. I will see that my Solicitor will be there too."

Annie thanked him once more and made her way towards the hall and the outside world.

In the Arms of Merlin

She couldn't wait for the morning to come to tell her Aunt and Uncle. They were going to have a shock. John stopped the trap at the bottom of the lane and insisted that he come right to the door. He waited until she opened the door and said "goodnight".

Annie thanked him and he strode down the lane back to the trap and off he went.

They lived the other end of town in a very big house. Auntie knew all about them and she thought that they had servants too. David and John had been brought up like brothers and Letty a sister.

Annie thought about them. She knew that they were very nice people and would make good friends in the future.

All night Annie tossed and turned, she still couldn't believe what had been said this evening.

Now it was sinking in with Annie. She had been left a fortune. She was a wealthy woman; from rags to riches. She thought of her son and said to herself, "Now, William, I can definitely find you." With that last thought in her mind she dropped off to sleep.

She didn't wake up until five o'clock. After glancing at the clock, she jumped out of bed, did her ablutions, dressed and came downstairs as Auntie was coming in through the front door.

Annie said, "You've made a mistake, Auntie, it's my turn to get the baking done, not yours."

Auntie took no notice of her and carried on taking her coat and hat off and said, "I know that but I couldn't wait any longer to find out what happened last night and what is going on up there?"

Annie said; "You had better sit down, you are going to have the shock of your life like I have had."

"Right," Auntie said, "get on with it girl."

After Annie had given her all the details of last night, she just sat down in a heap. "My dear girl," she said; "I know you have been through the mill but you are made for life." She got up, hugged and kissed Annie until they were both crying.

There was a knock at the front door startling the two crying bodies. When they opened the door, there stood Maggie. It was getting very late and they hadn't even started the baking. Now it was go ahead, all hands on deck. Even Maggie was having a go at the baking.

They had a terrific few hours, really going for it. Laughing and crying together. It took a while for Maggie to get the gist of what was going on. It sounded good to her and she was very pleased that such a good thing had happened to Annie, as she had definitely saved Maggie's life.

How they got through that day they never knew, even Uncle was doing a jig.

Half way through the afternoon, a boy came into the Tearooms with a note for Annie. She opened it; it was from David, he said he had more news for her about the property in the main street and for her to call at the office as soon as she could.

Annie was puzzled, she thought that he had changed his mind about renting it to her – not that she would have been bothered, she wasn't a greedy person. She was quite happy with what she had already got. She had a chat with Auntie and they worked it between them when she should go to see David.

The following morning, Annie dressed in her working clothes, made her way to David Jones' office. They were all cross that she wasn't dressing for the occasion but Annie told them, "If he can't put up with me like this, he is not the man I thought he was."

It took Annie ten minutes to get to the office. The receptionist was at her desk, as dry as usual.

"Good morning," Annie said.

The receptionist looked up with a look of disdain that freaked Annie a little, to the extent that she failed to notice that John had come into the room.

"Hello, Nan," he said; "come into my office." She took her gaze from the frozen maiden and walked towards John's room.

He closed the door behind her, offered her a chair and went around the desk and sat in his chair and pulled some documents out of one of the drawers.

"David has asked me to show you this document. He is very sorry that he couldn't show it to you himself but he had a very important meeting in London, that is why he is not here."

Annie felt a little disappointed that he wasn't around. Perhaps he didn't want to do the dirty work himself. Stop it now Annie, she thought to herself, this man has been very good to you so give him the benefit of the doubt whatever it's all about.

John passed the papers over to Annie. She started reading. First of all the address was a London one. Annie didn't have a clue, she carried on reading some more and couldn't believe her eyes. John was looking intently at her reactions and certainly got a huge one.

Annie's face was a picture, she just looked at John with tears streaming down her cheeks. She passed the papers back to John and just said; "I just can't accept anything like this. The family have been more than good to me already, this is ridiculous and impossible."

"Now, Nan," John said; "don't talk like that in front of David or you will really hurt him. David's mother is showing in her own way her gratitude to you for what you did for Barbara. If you hadn't acted as you did, things could have got worse. Not that they didn't for you and her. It must have been terrible for the both of you, that man is very lucky that he left the country. David would have run him with his horse, then he would have been in trouble. Thank God that he went on his own bat. That is the cleverest thing he ever did, the devil must have been looking after his own at that time. You must now go home and talk things over with your relatives. I am sure that they will be delighted with your extra good fortune."

Half an hour must have gone by. Annie got worried about the time and John could see that she was starting to fidget. He had never met such a girl in all his life. She was such a genuine person, no side with her and everything was on the table with her.

He got up, came around the desk and handed the documents back to her and said; "Go home, Nan, and David will get in touch with you tomorrow. Will that be all? Right?" he asked.

Annie just nodded and made to turn away from John. She looked so pathetic in her working clothes and sad that he just wanted to take her into his arms and keep her there forever but now that was going to be impossible. John could say goodbye to the sweet and lovely Nan.

While David had been in London he had called to see his mother. She lived in a very smart place in the middle of London. She had another home in Wales too but spent most of her time in the city where all her friends were. Perhaps if she had been closer she would have seen what was going on in her daughter's home.

David's mother had not been very well since the death of her daughter. It had been a bitter blow to now find out what sort of man she had married. Everybody had been pleased that Lady Barbara was marrying this very rich land owner from Scotland, now living in Wales. Nobody knew much about him but because he was very wealthy they all said he was all right, but now after all that had happened everyone was saying that they knew what he was from the beginning.

David was the only one who didn't like or trust him. He couldn't say too much, he didn't want to hurt Barbara who was desperately in love with him at the time. Even David thought he was crazy about Barbara too, but obviously he wasn't. He just wanted a son from someone of good breeding and a well-known wealthy family.

It was too late to think about things that had gone wrong if that is all David could think every time her face came to him. Now all he could think of was the young girl who had saved her from degradation and pain. David would be in her debt for the rest of his life. It wasn't much consolation for Nan; she had gone through hell by helping his sister, where he should have been in command of the situation.

After hours of thought wrestling with himself, he came to the same conclusion. What is done is done and no-one can do anything about it, only do what they could for Nan and that is what they were trying to do.

He arrived home the following day and asked John how the meeting had gone. John told him everything, how quiet Nan had gone; "she hardly spoke to me after I gave her the documents."

"Do you think she will accept?"

"I don't know," said John. "She is a very proud girl. You will surely know tomorrow as I told her that you would go to the Tearooms to see her. Did I do right?"

David nodded and walked out of the room.

When Annie got back to the Tearoom it was so busy; she had just enough time to take her coat off. She was glad now that she hadn't worn her best clothes or she would have had to work in them and Annie wouldn't have been happy with that.

The clock was striking six when everything went quiet. Annie said, "Come on girls, let's make a cup of tea and have a sit down. I have got more news to tell you."

They both looked puzzled and had no idea what had happened now. Annie looked very serious, so it could be anything.

Auntie cleared a table. Maggie made a pot of tea and Annie fetched a piece of sponge each, she thought that they hadn't had time to eat as they had been one helper short, so sit down they did.

Auntie said, "Come on then, girl, tell use the worse. We can take it."

Annie went to the kitchen to get her bag, sat down and pulled out this very important looking document and started to read it out. Their faces were a picture, the more Annie read, the more their faces changed. Annie finished reading, looked at Auntie and said, "What do you think?"

Auntie was struck dumb and couldn't answer for a few minutes, then the questions came. Annie answered a few.

"Auntie what am I to do?" she asked.

"Do?" said Auntie, "accept of course, what do you think?"

"I feel that they have given me enough."

"But," Auntie said, "the legacy was from Lady Barbara herself. This is from her mother who lives in London. She hasn't been too well since she lost her daughter, poor thing; it hit her very hard. Your children are not supposed to die before you are they?"

"No," Annie said. "I will have to have someone to advise me. We will have to have more staff, more furniture, crockery, cutlery and goodness knows what else and I don't know if I am capable enough to deal with all this."

"Well," Auntie said, "I never thought I would ever hear you of all people, saying anything like that. Has all this gone to your head and made you weak minded? I don't think so Annie Owens, so get your best bib and tucker on first thing tomorrow morning. Go to see Mr David Jones, tell him that you have no doubt at all and that you accept his mother's offer and thank her very much and give him a big hug from me."

"And me," said Maggie.

They all had a good laugh and Auntie said, "Will will have to do the dishes tomorrow. He will be pleased!"

CHAPTER 9 – THE TIVOLI

It was five thirty in the morning and Annie got out of bed. It was a little early but she didn't want to rush. She hated rushing and might spoil her day. Since they had rented the cottage next door they had made the upstairs into a living room with a sofa and one armchair and a small table. It looked not too bad. It was somewhere for Annie to sit, other than on the bed. She had found some dried flowers on one of the days off that she had gone to the market, and arranged them quite sweetly on the table. It gave a bit of colour to this dull room.

She finally got dressed and went downstairs to see the others. They were getting on fine without her. Uncle came on to her, gave her a big hug and congratulated her on her good fortune.

As she was walking down to the office, she was met by John. He held her elbow and guided her down to the Governess' card, opened the back for her to get in and explained that he was taking her to the Plas.

That upset Annie straightaway. She thought that John would be seeing to her like the last time but it wasn't to be. She was more nervous than she was the last time she went out there. It was a good job that she didn't know that David's mother was going to be there as well.

John knew better than to tell her. He was getting to know her ways a little now. All the way to the Plas they talked about everything under the sun, except business. John was leaving that to David. They arrived at the gates and Annie was back as she started. Nervous.

John helped her out and as they walked up the stone steps to the house David appeared. He came forward and took Annie's hand and said, "how are you my dear? It is nice to see you again. I am sorry that I missed our last meeting but don't worry, we can make up for it today. I hope you haven't got to rush away this time because now my dear, you must learn to delegate. You are in a position to hire more staff and it will make your workload lighter. I know from what I have heard from different people that you work harder than the people that work for you and that will never do but this is by the by, come along in and meet my mother, she is patiently waiting to see you."

Annie's legs went like jelly as she was escorted into one of the large rooms off the hall. His mother was sitting in one of the high back chairs. Annie was taken aback really, because she was an older replica of Lady Barbara.

David's mother saw the look on Annie's face and tried to make the girl at ease. She got up and held her hand out to her and said, "How are you my dear? I am very pleased to meet you at last. I have heard so much about you from my son and John."

It was John's turn to colour up a little now.

"Sit down," she said, "just let us have a little chat." She looked up at the boys and said, "I am sure you have something to do somewhere the two of you." They were both reluctant to leave her there on her own. Not that the older lady would have been anything but kind to her but they knew that she wanted to hear about what had happened to her daughter and that this was going to be another upset for Nan, but off they both went like two little school boys.

Lady Elizabeth, David's mother had remarried after David's father had died. She had grieved deeply for a good few years and was advised to go to London for a holiday because she wasn't picking up at all. She hardly wanted anything to do with little David, so her doctor insisted that they both go away somewhere and that is what they did.

They were staying with a cousin of Elizabeth and while they were there, her cousin entertained as much as she could to try and buck this poor girl up.

In the Arms of Merlin

Elizabeth would 'hum' and 'ah' before going downstairs to meet these people at the dinner parties that were given in her honour really. Finally she succumbed and went to join the party.

After the first two she started to enjoy herself and really looked brighter and better. At the third party she met George. He was a handsome Cavalry Officer with a brilliant future in front of him. Elizabeth fell in love with him as soon as he looked into her eyes and the same happened for him. They were the ideal couple and six months later they were married and lived in London.

David was also happy. His mother was back to how she used to be when his father was alive. He was only young but George must be a good man to make his mother feel happy, so he thought, "I shall love him too."

They were all ideally happy until one day there was chaos in the house. David couldn't see his mother anywhere, nor George. By now he had started calling him Papa.

David's Nanny tried to keep him in the nursery but the little boy was making excuses to get away from Nanny but she wouldn't let him. He was getting quite worried when all of a sudden the nursery door flew open and in strode Papa with something small in a shawl. He looked so excited, David ran up to him and said, "what is it Papa?"

He kneeled and showed David what was in the little bundle. David was taken aback and gave a gasp. Papa heard it and said to David, "this is your little sister, her name is Barbara and I want you to promise me that you will look after her."

David was thrilled to pieces and running his small finger down her tiny cheek tears came into his eyes and he said, "I will Papa, I will."

David did look after his little sister until she married that monster. He couldn't do anything about it really, as they didn't get to see one another as often as they used to but that is all behind them now.

Lady and Elizabeth and Annie chatted for ages. The older woman asked questions, heard the answers but didn't push Annie too far. She realised that Annie was going through as much pain as she was, so she got up from her chair and said, "I think we have talked enough my dear, so perhaps we should go into dinner. I am sure you appreciate how much we owe you for what you did for my daughter. From now on it shall not be mentioned ever again but you do know what we all think of you. Come along my dear."

They went into the dining room; David and John were already there. David gave a sign to the butler and they all sat down to a delicious meal.

Annie thought that she could get used to this ...

On the way home, John was very quiet, so was Annie. They had exhausted themselves with all their talking. It was nerves on Annie's part but she did not know about the others.

John stopped the Governess cart at the bottom of the lane, tethered the horse to a rail and started to walk Annie up the lane. She protested and said that she would be fine but he wouldn't have any of it. He took her to her door, she thanked him very much and he said "goodnight".

She had a look around and saw that everything was all right. She made her way up the narrow stairs and into her bedroom, sat on the bed and thought about the happenings of the day. She should have been the happiest girl in Christendom but there was something missing. "I suppose everything will work out before long." She pulled the clothes back and went to bed, more tired than if she had worked all day long.

The morning came all too soon. Annie got up, washed, dressed, ate some breakfast, then started her work.

She must have been working for an hour when the girls arrived. They wanted to talk about what had happened the day before and when Annie told them that his mother was there and that she was a Ladyship they couldn't get over it.

After talking things over with her Aunt and Uncle, Annie decided to ask John for advice. Everyone was in favour; he had so much experience in business matters. Annie decided to send a message down to the office. She couldn't take more time off; she didn't want to impose on her friends, so she asked John to come to the Tearooms after they had closed.

Auntie asked her if she was doing a wise thing but Annie reassured her that John was all right. She was surprised to see John in the Tearooms around three o'clock. He had come to make proper arrangements for the evening.

Annie told him that they would be finished about 6.30pm.

He said that he would be on time.

To make sure, Annie told him it would be better if he ate before coming. Making a meal would be time consuming for Annie, as she was up first in the morning. She didn't think that he took offence with her suggestion. Even if he had, he was too much of a gentleman to show.

He arrived at 6.30 on the dot. Annie had just enough time to wash her face and hands and give her hair a good brush. John passed a remark about the freshness of her face and that her hair was shining.

It was the first compliment that Annie had ever had, so she just looked up at him and said "thank you".

He sat on the chair and Annie sat on the sofa. Annie had a little note book with her and was ready to jot down anything that John might say to help things get off the ground.

"First of all," he said, "you must go up to see the premises and then we can go from there. Do you mean to expand or are you going to stop still?"

"Well," Annie said. "I would like to make it into a bigger concern. I have got enough money haven't I?"

"Of course you have," John said. "Start writing, you will need new tables, chairs, linen, cutlery, some sort of stove and you will need more staff. How is that for a start?" John said.

Annie was getting really excited, she knew what she wanted but had to have someone to lead her.

The following evening she took the lamp from her living room and they made their way to see the new Tearooms. Auntie and Uncle were waiting outside the door when they arrived. Excitement filled the air. John opened the front door and in they went. It was very dark; John lit a match to light the lamp. A warm glow filled the hall. It smelled damp inside the door but that could be cured. Uncle said a few days of good fires and that smell would go. They turned to the right and there was the most wonderful room that Annie had ever seen. It was massive. It must have been four times as big as her two little rooms. Annie fell in love with it straightaway and knew that this place had been meant for her.

She was delighted and it showed. They went right back to the kitchen and that was a delight. In the corner was a huge stove. Uncle pounced on it straightaway. He asked John to bring the lamp closer for him to have a look. "By golly," he said, "this is a good 'un."

Annie crossed 'stove' off the list. There was a back door. John found the key and opened it. There was a large yard, a garden and a lawn. This place was a surprise a minute. They made their way back to the hall and went up the stairs. They came to a large landing which opened out to five rooms. They had high ceilings and big windows, something neither Annie nor Auntie had ever had. They were all more than pleased with the property.

"Wait a minute," John said, "there is more." They couldn't believe it. They made their way up another staircase, a narrow one this time, and landed up in the attic. It covered the whole of the house. It was huge.

"Well, well," Auntie said, "you certainly have been a very lucky girl, you are made. All the hard work and someone to point you in the right direction. You are going to go very far as far as business is concerned."

"Not only me, Auntie. All of us."

"Now my dear," Auntie said, "this is yours; you might want to be on your own. You can now hire as many staff as you want."

Annie was shocked to think that they thought like that. "Look," she said, "you took me off the street after I came out of gaol. Where do you think I would have landed if you hadn't? So please don't think about anything like that. I am now in a position to look after you both. You know me, I won't squander any of the money that Lady Barbara left me. I will buy what I have to buy, work hard again, perhaps not so hard as before. I will be the same girl that came to you with nothing. You took me in and what is more, I think of you both as my parents and I love you both dearly."

Auntie started crying and Annie put her arms around her and said, "Does the truth always make you cry, Auntie dear?"

Auntie just sobbed and shook her head.

They had seen all they wanted to see. John didn't think that the rooms needed decorating. It all seemed to be fine. The only thing he said was, "You will have to come to see it in the day and then we will really know what's needed."

They all parted company. Annie ran upstairs, undressed and jumped into bed, forgot how hard her bed was and had hurt on her bottom. As she pulled the clothes up she said under her breath, "The first thing I am going to buy is a new bed, a nice feather one. What a luxury." She put the light out, lay back and went to sleep.

In the Arms of Merlin

From then on it was all go. Annie hadn't decided what to do about the old Tearooms but an idea was forming in her mind. She had also decided that she was going up market in the new Tearooms. She was going to keep the old one and perhaps ask Esther her friend to run it with Auntie and Uncle.

Once Esther had finished her housework there was nothing to do. She had told Annie that she was getting a little bored. She would have to clear things with her father but she didn't think it would be a problem.

Annie had words with Auntie and she was pleased. Annie didn't think that Auntie wanted to go to the new Tearooms, so everything would be resolved like this.

Next thing was to get in touch with Esther and her father. Annie went to see them after she closed the Tearooms. It was really too late for visiting but she explained to Mr Evans that time now was valuable to her. He understood but was fine, he thought the world of Annie.

She had been such a good friend to his daughter while they had both been in gaol and now he understood that Esther was also going to have a share in the profits. His small business kept them floating but what would happen to Esther after his days?

This offer was a Godsend to John Evans and had taken a load of worry off his shoulders, now knowing that Esther would be all right after his days.

Things now were getting to place. Everyone knew where they were standing. Annie even had Auntie to take a share in the profits.

By the weekend, John was going to have some papers drawn up regarding Auntie and Esther. For their benefits, not Annie's.

John couldn't get over the way Annie coped with everything. She was such a dynamic person and he thought more about her every day.

In the Arms of Merlin

John and Letitia had their own money. They were quite well off but not in the same league as Annie was now. It saddened John, he thought that he was falling in love with her. He knew that nothing would come of it because she now was a very wealthy businesswoman and would get wealthier as her new business venture would go ahead.

Another thing John thought. David was sweet on her too. He wasn't quite sure but he had never heard him talk so much about a girl before.

CHAPTER 10 – GOING TO THE BALL

The day the new Tearooms were opened, Annie went to the Emporium to get a new outfit, nothing elaborate, just something good and tidy for her to wear to work.

She made arrangements with Auntie and off she went, walked in through the front door with far more confidence than she had the first time she went there. A lady came on to her as she walked in and asked her if she could help her. Annie thought that it was the same one as before, if she was she was far more attentive than she was the last time Annie came there.

"Never mind"! she thought, "I know what I want and no-one will make me buy anything that I don't need." By now the woman was fussing all over Annie, she knew who she was but it didn't rub off on Annie at all. The woman could see she was wasting her time, so went to soft soap someone else who enjoyed it.

The young assistant who was looking after Annie was a very nice girl, she also knew about Annie's new venture and her new fortune. Annie didn't realise it but the whole town must know. It didn't worry her, she just bought what she wanted, the assistant packed them and Annie was out of there.

It took a week to open the new Tearooms. They had found a name for it. The Tivoli Tearooms and it was really up market.

There were palms dotted here and there Aspidistras in lovely china plant pots. Whiter than white net curtains so nobody could see in, white wall lights, which were gleaming by the time everything was finished.

They opened on the Monday morning and they didn't look back. It was a success from the word go.

In the Arms of Merlin

Annie took Maggie up with her to the new Tearooms and she settled down right away, considering that she had never been used to a higher class of people, but Annie kept her in the back but did send her in to help when they got really busy. Annie thought that this was the way to go about it with the girls.

There were three waitresses, girls that auntie had known. They were all excellent and moved like lightening. Annie had been very lucky all round. Another little lady that auntie knew came to do the washing up and some of the rough work, but now you couldn't call it rough as there were carpets. The only scrubbing was in the kitchen and Annie, Maggie and Mary shared that between them.

Annie had to dress very tidy now as some of the customers used to ask to speak with her. She was becoming quite a topic of conversation in the town. Annie didn't mind one bit as long as they came to eat and drink at her Tearooms.

Even down in the old shop business was good. Uncle, Auntie and Esther were going great guns. They were all happy. Things were at an even keel.

One afternoon one of the girls came to the kitchen and said that Annie was wanted in the Tearoom. Annie washed her hands, tidied up her hair, put her skirt straight and walked out to the Tearoom and there sitting at one of the tables was Lady Elizabeth, Letitia and David.

The waitress was taking their order as Annie got to the table. They all looked up at the same time. It was funny really but Annie wasn't laughing.

She greeted them as politely as she could. Lady Elizabeth showed how pleased she was to see her and said "have we caught you at a busy time? Are you able to come and have a chat?"

"No," Annie said, "there is nothing that won't wait."

David loved that comment. This girl bewitched him every time he met her. The only thing was, that he couldn't get to really meet her.

His mother's talking interrupted his thoughts as she said "We have all been away my dear, that is why we haven't called with you sooner. That's right isn't it Letitia?"

"Yes, Auntie" she said.

Annie had wondered why they hadn't called to see how she was getting on but she thought that their class didn't bother with the likes of her. It was one thing to give her the money but another to socialise with people in her circle. Annie couldn't be more wrong, it wasn't like that at all. They had all been away to the South of France as David had property there, as Annie was told later on in the conversation.

Rose came with the order. Annie could see that they were impressed. Annie wouldn't join them, she thought it wouldn't be fitting, so she sat and listened to what they had to say. She was amazed with their way of life and their conversation, until they came to the last bit. "Would you like to come next Thursday to the Plas for the evening? I am giving a charity ball and we would all be very pleased if you would come as my guest?"

Annie didn't know what to say so only stuttering and stammering came out.

"Come on, my dear, you can do better than that!"

Annie pulled herself together and sailed on with the conversation as if they had asked her to go down the market to fetch some cockles.

She swallowed hard and said "Thank you, Lady Elizabeth, I would be delighted to come."

David couldn't believe his ears. His mother hadn't even mentioned it to him, not that he minded not knowing, but it came as a bit of a shock. He wondered if Annie would come. He had heard her accept the invitation but if she came was another story. It would be a big step for her to cope with anything like this. She had certainly been thrown into the deep end.

Poor Nan, as he called her. David wondered if he should have a word with her on her own. He wasn't sure of his mother's intention, whether it be good or bad, but David didn't think that she was like that.

David went up to the counter and settled the bill. While he was there Lady Elizabeth told Annie once more "don't forget now. I don't suppose I will see you until the night of the Ball."

They all got up in turn, said their goodbyes and went out through the door and out of sight. Annie turned around and made her way back to the kitchen to work, to take her mind off the problem because that is what it was, until she saw Auntie or Esther so that they could tell her if she should go or not.

They closed up as usual. Annie took the takings upstairs with her, put them away until the following morning when she would make a detour down to the old Tearooms to have a word with her confidante, Auntie.

She slept after a while and woke up very dull and sluggish. She went about her usual chores. Half way through the morning just before she was going to the bank one of the girls came in from the shop and said Annie was wanted. Annie thought "whoever is there now?"

"Say I won't be minute," she told Rose, "I might as well go straight down to the bank after seeing who wants me. All right girls?"

She had tidied her hair and was now putting her coat on. She thought that she had better wear her tam, it wasn't ladylike to walk about the town without a hat, so on went the tam and out through the door she went.

Lo and behold, there stood David. If she had realised it was him, she would have come out sooner. She apologised for keeping him waiting.

In the Arms of Merlin

He smiled and said, "don't fret, I happened to have got plenty of time today, tomorrow it might be different. You are on your way somewhere I presume?"

"Yes," she said, "I am going to the bank, then I was going down to the lane to see my Aunt."

"I'll escort you."

"Oh there's no need," she said; "I usually run down there."

"Now Nan, what did I tell you before, you have got to learn to delegate. When are you going to start? Never by the looks of things but there you are, who am I to dictate to you? You certainly know what you are doing, so you carry on."

As David walked Nan to the bank he asked her if she was happy about coming to the Ball. Nan said that she hadn't made up her mind properly yet but would like to go as it would be a new experience for her.

David was in agreement with her and said, "don't be offended now if I make a suggestion."

Nan replied, "carry on."

David said, "shall I ask Letty to give you a hand?"

Nan thought for a minute and said "why not?"

David then added that Letty thought a lot of her and would give expert advice. Nan was glad that he had suggested Letty, as Auntie wouldn't really be able to advise her but they could have chatted about it.

It was arranged that Letty would come to the Tivoli soon after opening, before the rush, so by nine o'clock, Letty was waiting in the shop for her. She was as excited as Nan, so like two big school girls they went arm in arm down to the Emporium.

It was a different kettle of fish today. As they went through the door, the Manageress sailed down towards them and was all over them. Annie didn't take offence, she realised that when someone like herself came in dressed like she was, she supposed they did hold back a little.

In the Arms of Merlin

Now Nan was the cat's whiskers. She swept them upstairs and had two assistants seeing to them. Nan was a little embarrassed but when she saw the Ball gowns she forgot about everything.

She tried about six gowns on. They were all beautiful and as she looked in the mirror she couldn't believe it really was her.

In the end she chose the white one. It was heavy white satin with rosebuds here and there on the skirt, a plain tight fitting top with a few more rosebuds around the neckline.

The assistant went off for a minute and came back with a small spray of rosebuds. Nan was puzzled. The girl sat Nan down, undid her hair, got a brush from one of the drawers and gave her hair a good brushing and put it up from her face and pinned the spray on the side of her ear.

"You may not like this, madam," she said, "but I am only trying it out for you. The choice is yours. Perhaps you don't feel like putting anything at all on your hair, you have got good hair and a lovely colour."

Nan said to Letty, "what do you think?"

"I love the flowers," she said.

"All right," Nan said, "I'll have the spray."

"What about slippers?" Nan looked at Letty and she said "Bring a few pairs to see how they look."

It was a good job that Letty had been with her or she would have been going to the Ball with her boots on and that would never have done.

Nan came out of the shop loaded with parcels. She had white satin slippers, the Ball gown, a silk set of lingerie and a silk handkerchief.

They both walked back to the Tivoli. Nan had a look about her as if everything was going to be all right and made her excuses.

She looked beautiful. She was going to turn a few heads on the night of the Ball. Letty wondered who was going to be the lucky man that night. She had a good idea whom he was going to be.

After Nan had put all the clothes away, she dressed and they made their wan downstairs. Letty ordered a pot of tea and some scones with clotted cream and jam. She sat and guzzled them all down and sat for a while delighted with herself, full of scones, clotted cream and jam and had kitted Nan up for the Ball.

She suddenly thought, "perhaps I should buy a new gown for myself. I haven't had a new one for a long time. I shall ask John when I go home."

Nan wouldn't think of taking money for the tea. She was taking Letty to the door. Letty asked Nan if she would like to come with her to buy her gown.

As much as Annie would have loved to, she thought that she had better not push her luck. She didn't like to impose on her girls too much, not that they would have complained, but Annie didn't think that it would be fair on them.

In the middle of the afternoon, Annie sent Maggie down the lane to ask the girls to come and see her clothes after the Tearooms closed.

Even Auntie was thrilled with the Ball gown. They had never seen anything like it, it was a wonderful thrill just to be able to touch it even.

Everything was going fine. Auntie and Uncle were having things that they had never had before and Annie was living in a different world but she was so sensible and her two feet were firmly on the ground.

The week went oh, so slowly. Even though they were very busy. Annie thought the night of the Ball would never arrive but it did eventually.

It was exceptionally busy that day, it was all go until they closed. Annie started to help with the clearing up. All the girls said, "now leave everything to us. You go and have a bath and get yourself ready for tonight."

Annie didn't have to be told twice, she was off like a shot. She took the stairs two at a time. She had a boiler by the side of the fire in her kitchen and the water was always hot. She got the big zinc bath out and used all the water from the boiler. It took ages to fill the bath, then it took ages to fill the boiler. She couldn't leave it empty because the fire was still going.

All was done that had to be done. Annie undressed, slipped into the bath and wished she could stay in it all night. Being able to bath like this was one of the luxuries that she enjoyed since she had come into her money. She had never had a bath before and if she had time she would be bathing every day, but that was an impossibility.

She came out of the bath, dried herself, put a robe on, went into her bedroom and lay on the bed for a few minutes. Her thoughts were racing. She hoped she wouldn't make a fool of herself. She couldn't really dance but as long as her partner could dance she would be able to follow him.

Annie had washed her hair the night before. She would never have got to the Ball otherwise as her hair was very thick and took ages to dry but that was all done. It just needed a good brushing and then she would go from there. Annie was lucky, she had a kink in her hair and she was quite good at putting it up.

Annie got up from the bed, looked around the room and hugged herself. Nearly everything was all right with her world. Just one thing was missing and God willing, she would find her little son before long.

She put those sad thoughts from her mind and made herself a cup of tea. She didn't sit down to have it, she took sips as she was doing her hair. It came the first time. Annie was so pleased as usually whenever you want things to be nice they aren't, so this must be a good omen she thought.

Hair done, she had just put a tiny touch of rouge on her cheeks but took it off because she didn't need it, her cheeks were flushed with excitement as it was.

She did something that she had never done before; she didn't put her vest on. It worried her for a minute or two but she couldn't wear it with her low cut gown. She hoped that people didn't think that she was a hussy but this is how the upper crust dressed all the time. She put her slip over her head and it slid over her body. The feeling she had was something that she had never had before. The silk clung to her. She looked in the mirror and got quite a shock. She certainly had all her curves in the right places. Her stay for her waist was next, then her silk stockings, her slippers, then her gown. She put it over her head, it slipped down. She just managed to catch hold of it before it went to the floor.

She was stuck now, it was a good job that the girls hadn't gone home. She took the dress off, put her robe on and went to the top of the stairs and called for someone to come and help her. She was so glad that she had gone earlier or she wouldn't know what she would have done.

Rose came to the bottom of the stairs and asked her what was the matter.

Annie said; "can one of you come up to give me a hand?"

"Certainly," she said. She went to tell the others where she was going and then went up to Annie. The young girl followed Annie into the bedroom, picked up the gown and put it over Annie's head, caught it before it fell and started putting the hooks into the eyes.

Annie pulled herself to her full height, took a deep breath, looked at herself and gave a small sigh.

Rose was so excited to see her Mistress looking so beautiful, she went to the top of the stairs to call the others up.

In the Arms of Merlin

They all stood around Annie, admiring her, without one bit of envy. It was so nice.

"There you are," said Hannah, "you would be going to the Ball half dressed."

Annie turned around and said; "what do you mean?"

Hannah started to smile, "it's nothing serious, but you have forgotten your spray of rosebuds and that is going to be the final touch to your elegance."

"Don't be silly Hannah," Annie said, "you are making me blush." She went to the drawer and took out the spray of rosebuds and secured it to the hair, on the side over her ear.

Jane said, "you were quite right Hannah, that has put the finishing touch to everything."

"John, you can come whenever you like, I am ready."

Annie thought that she had said that with too much bravado. Letty had lent her a small silk shawl, they had forgotten about something over her shoulders in case it was a little cool. Letty saved her life again.

It was seven o'clock. Annie had but the takings away and they were waiting for John to come and pick her up. The front door bell rang twice. Rose went to open the door for John.

Annie had come down the stairs and was coming through the hall when she stopped in her tracks. Standing there was David, not John, as they all thought. It shook Annie for a few seconds but she thought, "am I going to be like this all night, I can't control myself."

She pulled herself to her full height and went forward to greet him.

He was certainly taken aback by her beauty. She was perfect, he knew she was a good looking girl, but he didn't realise how good. She looked as if she had just come from a Paris Fashion show, she was absolutely gorgeous.

Annie could see it in his eyes that he was shocked by her appearance.

"Come along then," he said, "you are going to cause enough disturbance without being late."

Rose opened the front door and there was a coach with two white horses and a coachman. He held her hand as she got into the coach and got in behind her after she had put herself tidy. He sat down beside her. As they drew away, Annie waved to the girls, saying under her breath, "I hope they lock up properly."

"Pardon?" David said.

"It's alright, I was only thinking aloud" and off they went into the darkness towards the country.

Anybody who was anybody was going to the Ball. Annie wasn't really looking forward to the evening but she was committed now and there was no turning back.

David didn't talk much during the journey. He couldn't help thinking how wonderful she looked. She was certainly going to turn some heads tonight. The way he felt he would have liked to whisk here away somewhere on their own and dance with her all night. The only consolation he had was that she would be in his arms when they danced together.

At last they turned up the drive to the Plas and it was all lit up. They got out of the coach and walked up the wide stone steps into the hall, which was full of people. David guided her through the crowd upstairs to their private quarters and took her into Letty's room. She was just putting the finishing touches to her hair as they walked into her room.

Letty looked absolutely gorgeous. She wore a pale blue gown, slippers to match and two little diamond ear-rings in her ears and no other jewellery.

David passed a remark by saying that he had the two most beautiful girls in the County. "Come on you two or the Ball will be over before we get there."

They made their way downstairs and made a grand entrance. All eyes were turned to the wide door leading to the

Ballroom. Annie was in a daze. All she could see was a sea of faces, all in shimmering gowns and men all in black.

David walked across the dance floor with the two girls, one on each arm. His Mother was sitting on a chaise long and John was standing behind.

He said to David "where on earth have you been?"

"Blame your sister," he said, "she took ages to get ready."

"Don't listen to him, I have been ready for a long time, I have just been waiting for them."

Annie coloured a little and said, "it was my fault I think. I'm so sorry."

Lady Elizabeth interrupted and said; "don't worry child, you are here now. In any case you have other things to do before getting yourself ready. I just want you to relax and enjoy yourself. By the way, you look most charming."

Annie was quite flattered with Lady Elizabeth's compliment.

Just as Lady Elizabeth patted the space next to her, David asked Annie to dance.

Now this was going to be the test. She lowered her eyes, then looked up and him and said, "thank you" and went straight into his arms and just danced. He was such a good cancer that she just felt as if she was floating on air. He was so easy to follow, she was amazed at herself.

He looked down at her and said, "you dance quite well Nan. I am pleasantly surprised."

Annie didn't tell him that after supper in the big house, Mary, Billy and her used to practice the dances. Her mind went back for a few minutes until David interrupted her train of thoughts. She didn't want to think of those days, especially tonight.

The dance was over and they went to sit down by Lady Elizabeth, Letty, John and another two ladies, who David introduced Annie to. They were relatives of his mother. They were quite nice but they were dying to know more about Annie and where she came from and who had brought her to the ball.

David put them out of their misery and told them that she was with him.

John looked a little peeved but then he came around to Nan and asked her to dance.

Annie got up and danced the next three dances with him. He also was a good dancer and very easy to follow.

By the time they went to have refreshments Annie had danced with half the men in the room. She was really enjoying herself and she didn't think that she was making a fool of herself either. Every man who danced with her complimented her. Annie really felt like a princess.

The evening was going along nicely. David came up to her and asked her to dance. As they were moving off he said, "I had better watch you or you will be slipping through my fingers."

Annie was surprised to hear his comment.

He added, "I don't want to lose you now that I have found you." He felt Annie shiver when he said that. "What's the matter my dear?" He said, "am I being too presumptuous? If so, please tell me because I don't want to frighten you away from me. I intend to see a lot more of you if you are willing?"

Annie didn't realise what his intentions were. She thought that he was being kind to her because of his sister but his last remark stunned her. She went very quiet.

He asked her if he had upset her.

She shook her head and said, "no, I didn't think you would even look at me as a poor working girl with a trail of disasters behind me."

He said, "don't think like that. I bet nearly all the men here tonight would give their eye teeth to court you but I will give them all a run for their money. What do you make of that my dearest dear?"

Annie felt like giggling like a school girl, tried to suppress it and almost failed.

The dance ended. David took her arm and they went out to the veranda. On their way out, he picked up two glasses of champagne and sat outside in the moonlight. He offered the glass to Annie and said as he clinked her glass, "here's to us."

They both drank the liquid on their heads. They laughed as they both finished the drinks together. They put the glasses on the wrought iron table and he took her in his arms and gave her her first kiss.

It was incredible, she had never been kissed like that before. She was absolutely melting in his arms. They kissed a few more times. Annie just wanted to stay outside and let him kiss her forever and ever.

David suddenly said, "we had better go in or I won't be responsible for my actions and that will never do."

Annie was quite disappointed but took his arm, tidied her hair and walked into the Ballroom.

The dance was in full swing as they arrived where his mother was sitting. Annie went to sit down but was whisked away to the dance floor by John. He could see that her cheeks were rather flushed. He asked her if she was alright.

Oh! Yes," she said, "I have never experienced anything like this in my life. I wish this night would go on forever."

John was touched with her innocence and would love to have taken her into his arms and told her that he was in love with her but John thought that he was a little late. He thought that David was also in love with her but he had decided that he wasn't going to give up, because all is fair in love and war, so as he whirled her around the dance floor he thought of nothing but love for her.

John thought to himself that he had plenty of opportunities to talk to Nan but he was afraid that he would scare her off. Tonight he realised that he had missed the boat but he wasn't going to give up until he was sure that David had won her heart.

Annie sat down for the next two dances while David danced with his mother. John sat next to her, chatting about everything under the sun except his love for her. He wouldn't have blamed her for choosing David, he was a great chap and he had far more money than he had. Not that he was poor by any means. Their father had left them quite well off but John didn't think that Nan was interested in money. She was not a poor woman herself.

Nan was introduced to more men than she could remember. She really was the belle of the Ball.

Letty and even David's mother were glad for her. They knew this was the first time for everything that happened to her this night.

It must have gone midnight when the orchestra tuned up and everyone stood still while they played the National Anthem. The whole Ballroom was buzzing, groups of people were coming up to Lady Elizabeth to thank her for the lovely evening. Lady Elizabeth thanked them for coming and also thanked them for their donations.

Later Nan was to find out from Lady Elizabeth that they had had a wonderful response from everyone, every bit of effort that had been put into the evening had been worth it.

Nan was herself thanking Lady Elizabeth for her enjoyable evening and John chirped up and asked, "how is Nan going home?"

"Oh!" Letty said; "David has arranged that ….."

John, deep down, knew that this was going to be the answer. He was disappointed but hoped he didn't show it. His sister Letty saw it and her heart went out to him. She knew

John of old. He didn't push himself anywhere but he must have been kicking himself for leaving things too late.

Letty loved the two men dearly and couldn't fault one of them, so all she could say was let the best man win.

By the time they said their 'goodnights' and 'thank yous' it must have been one o'clock. Nan was quite pleased that Lady Elizabeth had put her arms around her and kissed her on her cheek and said "goodnight my dear, I hope this occasion will be the first of many."

Nan lowered her eyes and said, "thank you and goodnight everyone."

By the time they got outside it was a bit chilly. Nan pulled her shawl a bit tighter around her. David put his arm on her shoulder and pulled her closer to him. They got into the coach and he put his two arms around her to keep her warm. That was his excuse and he smiled as he told Nan.

She didn't smile, she just giggled. The champagne was beginning to work. They both laughed all the way home. He kissed her cheeks until the carriage stopped.

He got out and took her hand. She fumbled for the key. David took it off her and opened the door. Nan stopped but David took her through the hall and up the stairs into her bedroom, gave her a long lingering kiss and said, "now go to bed and I will see you tomorrow."

Nan was on cloud nine and didn't want him to leave her but she didn't tell him that or he would have thought that she was cheap. She thanked him, he turned on his heel and walked out of the room, down the stairs, locked the front door with Nan's key, then put it through the letter box. He got into the carriage and off home he went with his head in the clouds.

CHAPTER 11 – WILLIAM

Nan was trying to keep awake to mull over her thoughts of the evening but the champagne was taking effect and she went into a deep sleep and didn't wake up until Rose came into the room with a cup of tea for her.

"Well," Rose said, "this is the first, never been known before!"

Nan was full of apologies but Rose said, "we don't mind, we all are surmising that you had such a good time, that is why you have overslept."

"You have hit the nail on the head Rose, "Nan said; "it won't do for me to do this too often will it?"

Rose smiled, "you deserve a little of the good times, let us hope that the bad times are behind you."

Nan didn't rush; the girls had everything in hand. By the time she got downstairs everything was in full swing.

Nan has just gone into the kitchen for something. In the corner of her eye she saw the vicar. She wasn't surprised to see him here; she did what needed to be done in the kitchen and made her way out to see him.

He took off his hat and Nan offered him a seat at one of the tables. As Jane was passing, Nan asked her to bring a pot of tea for two and a plate full of some confectioneries. The vicar protested for a few minutes but soon changed his mind when he saw what was on offer.

Nan poured the team and offered him the cup and saucer. She then passed the plate over to him. He looked and said, "well, well, I had been told about your fare here. Now I realise how your business is flourishing."

"Now down to business. Since I saw you last I have been in touch with at least two dozen orphanages with no joy, but this morning I received a letter from one near Cardiff. It seems it is not a very big one, only ten children." The vicar kept talking, "one of those children is your son."

Annie had to hold on to something. It was the table. She felt all the blood draining from her face, then she had a sinking feeling and she knew that she was in trouble. She was going to faint. Suddenly she remembered when she was in the sick ward in the gaol and they used to say take deep breaths. She took massive breaths – from her boots.

The vicar didn't know what to do so he kept his cool and was just going to get help when he saw that Annie was taking control of the situation. " Thank goodness," he said; "are you alright Annie?"

"I feel better now," she said, "but was I dreaming or did I hear right?"

"No my dear," he said; "you heard what you have been waiting to hear for a long time."

Annie couldn't help it, but she was sobbing.

One of the girls could see what was going on and went to Annie's side, took her arm and led her into the kitchen. The vicar followed her. By then there was chaos there.

Rose took control of the situation and ushered Annie and the vicar upstairs.

"This is what you should have done in the beginning," Rose said. Annie was still crying and trying to get out that she had no idea what the vicar was going to tell her. "Never mind," said Rose, "no-one can hear or see you up here."

"Thanks Rose," Annie said and wiped her eyes and her face. She started asking questions. The vicar couldn't keep up with her.

In the meantime, Rose had sent Maggie down the lane to the Tearooms to get Auntie. "Annie needs family at a time like this."

By the time Auntie arrived Annie had composed herself a little, but as soon as she saw Auntie, she started to cry all over again.

In the Arms of Merlin

Auntie took hold of her and hugged her. "Don't cry now," she said, "this is what you have been working and waiting for all these years. Come on now love, dry your eyes again and give your face a little swill.

By the time Annie came back from the kitchen she was more composed and Auntie was asking the questions.

"First of all when can we see him and where do we see him?"

Annie chirped in, "what does he look like? Is he big or is he small?"

"Now Annie," the vicar said, "hold on. You have to write a letter to the orphanage and tell them that you are the boy's mother and you wish to see him and then you will want to bring him home with you. That is what you want, isn't it?"

Annie said, "yes, yes. That is all I have been longing for since the day I left him."

"Right", said the vicar, "have you got writing paper? I will draft a letter out for you, then I will post it for you."

"It's quite alright," Annie said, "I can do that myself."

The vicar was surprised that she could write, but there you are, she must be able to read and write to run two businesses.

There was nothing else the vicar could do now, so he excused himself and as he was going down the stairs Annie followed him put her two arms around him and gave him a big hug. The vicar was a little embarrassed. He didn't think anyone had done anything like that to him before.

She thanked him once again and told him that she would let him know when she heard from the orphanage.

He made his way down the stairs and thought about the hug that Annie had given him and he felt very pleased with himself. He also gave himself an imaginary pat on the shoulder and made his way back to the Vicarage.

Around tea-time a messenger arrived with a note for Annie. It was from David. He was enquiring how Annie was and was she tired after the Ball. If she was, he would send a messenger tomorrow and 'we will go from there', the note said. Annie was too excited to think of anything but William, her son.

She thought for a few minutes. They might not even call him William. She truly hoped that they had, but if they hadn't she would just have to put up with it.

There was no way that she could go down to help them in the Tearooms but they said that they could manage, so Annie did no more, she sat down at the table and wrote a letter to the orphanage telling them who she was and all her details. She put her shawl and her tam on and ran to the shop to get a stamp and posted the letter. She sighed a sigh of relieve as the letter fell into the box.

More than a week would go by before she would hear from them again, so patience was going to be the next thing she had to learn. It seemed to be the slowest week in her life. She had another note from David but sent a letter back saying that something had cropped up and it would be impossible to meet for a while.

David was very puzzled when he received the letter. He saw to all his meetings and then made his way to the Tivoli. When he opened the door his eyes swept around the room for Nan. She wasn't anywhere in sight. David panicked for a minute; he thought perhaps he had rushed her too much, but if that was the case, she wouldn't have written to him.

Hannah saw him sit down at one of the tables and promptly went to serve him. He ordered a pot of tea and the usual cakes. She went to the kitchen with his order and told Rose that Mr David was here.

"Has he asked for Annie?" she asked.

"No, not yet," Hannah said, "but I think he's going to. What shall we do?"

"I'll just go upstairs to tell Annie that he is here."

Annie was a little nervous when she heard the news. She told Rose to send him up in a few minutes, "let me titivate myself, because I must look a wreck."

"You are not too bad," Rose said as she was running down the stairs. She went over to David and told him what Annie had said. He finished his team, didn't eat any of the cakes and made his way upstairs.

Once he saw Annie he knew immediately that there was something wrong. He went forward and kissed her on her forehead. She smiled at him and offered him a seat on the sofa. He sat down and said, "what is the matter Nan?"

Nan knew that David knew that she had a child when she was raped, but neither of them had spoken of it. I suppose it was as hurtful to David as it was to Annie.

Now Nan had to put her cards on the table. She started from the beginning. The time that she had come out from gaol and had met the vicar. How he had promised to help Nan find her son.

David listened intently and didn't interrupt.

Nan ended her story with the news that the vicar had found her boy and that she was awaiting correspondence saying when and where she was going to meet him. Nan covered her face as she finished telling David.

He was quiet for a few seconds, then he took her in his arms and kissed her gently on her forehead, then her eyes, then her lips and drank the sweetness from her.

It was four days later that Nan heard from the Orphanage. It was a very polite letter, saying that as far as they could see, William was her son. Tears were now flowing as Nan read further. They asked her if she would be able to come to Cardiff to see the boy, as there was no way that they could bring him down to West Wales. "Fair enough," Nan thought. "Now which way to Cardiff?"

David called the day after she received the letter and asked her how things were progressing. Nan showed him the letter and David said, "there is no problem here, I will take you up. I don't want to hear another word."

Nan gave a deep sigh, all her problems were solved. She had found a way to get up to Cardiff and David didn't mind about her having her son back to live with her.

It took three days to organise the trip to Cardiff. Maggie had to go down the lane to the Tearooms and Auntie had to come up to the Tivoli. There was no problem for David; he gave Nan another two days to write to the Orphanage so that they would be ready for them.

Wednesday morning, David was at the door with his carriage waiting for Nan. It was 6.00 am. Nan got into the carriage, David put her bag on the opposite seat and put his next to hers.

Nan looked at David and thanked him. David said, "let's go." He rapped the side of the carriage with his cane and off they went.

It wasn't a boring journey; David talked to her all the way. He had such a lovely voice and he was such a well read and learned man. Nan could have listened to him all day and all night.

Just on the outskirts of Cardiff they stopped at an Inn. It was very pretty and looked well kept.

"Why are we stopping here?" Nan asked.

"We always stop here on our way to London, even Cardiff is too far to go up and back in one day.

Annie hadn't thought of that and David didn't think to tell her either. He didn't realise that Nan had never travelled before. "Does it make any difference?" he asked her.

"No," she stammered, "I didn't tell the girls about staying away overnight, perhaps they will get worried."

"They are bound to try and get in touch with my family and they can put their minds at rest, they know that we always stay here. I am so sorry," Nan, he said, "but I didn't realise, please forgive me."

Annie just said, "I am sorry if I panicked but if you say that everything will be alright, it's bound to be, so let's make the most of our time together."

He was surprised at her last comment. He then ushered her in through the door of the Inn. As they walked past the door leading into the bar the Innkeeper came to meet them and greeted them warmly. "It is a pleasure to see you again Sir," he said. "What can I do for you?"

"We need two rooms."

"Yes Sir," he said. He called for one of the chamber maids, gave her instructions and she scuttled off. The Innkeeper ushered them into the room opposite the bar and asked them what they would like to drink.

"We could have a little premature celebration drink, what do you think Nan?"

Annie had never drunk anything in her life until the charity Ball. "I don't know," she said.

"Come on now," David said, "let us be joyful."

Annie was pleased that he was happy with the situation. She agreed to have a drink with him.

"Innkeeper we will have a bottle of your best champagne." David helped Nan off with her coat; she left her hat on and put her gloves in her bag. The champagne arrived. David opened it and poured a glass each. He raised his glass and clinked it on Nan's and said, "here's to everything that you wish yourself my dear and I dearly hope that I am part of that wish."

Nan coloured a little and said, "thank you David, I will never forget what you have done for me and I will never turn my back on you. I will always be grateful to you for the rest of my life."

"Nan, it is not your gratitude I want."

Nan looked up and he said; "it is you I want. I have loved you since the first day that I saw you scrubbing the floor in the Infirmary. Your hair was hanging down and your face was dirty, you didn't have beautiful clothes but I fell in love with the girl who looked as if she had all the worry in the world. I didn't even know who you were then. After I came home from the Infirmary, I started to find out about you and that was the biggest shock I've ever had in my life. It seemed more natural that I got to know you then, so Nan, I am not going to babble on any more. Will you do me the honour of being my wife?"

Annie knew that David liked her but she didn't realise that he wanted to marry her. She couldn't contain herself any longer but couldn't say yes until she had made things clear about William, that she wanted him to live with her.

When she told him he said, "silly girl, of course I realise that you want the child with you. What mother does not want to look after her own flesh and blood even though your circumstances were a trifle bizarre. Get those lines from your forehead. Smile and tell me that you <u>will marry me</u>?"

They both stood up and Nan said "yes."

David grabbed her and Nan thought that he was going to squeeze the life out of her and he was kissing her all over her face. Then he came to her lips and he gave her a long and lingering kiss. "Now our fates are sealed," he said.

Another second and the Innkeeper would have been in the middle of it.

"Are you ready, Sir, Madam?"

They both looked at each other and said, "yes."

He took David to his room and the chamber maid took Annie to hers. Annie was full of excitement. The door closed after the chamber maid and Annie sat on the bed hugging herself. What a wonderful day. She couldn't believe all this was happening to her but it must be, she thought as she pinched herself really hard.

She got up, went to the wash stand, took her blouse off and gave her face a wash then her hands. Looked in the mirror and thought, "you don't look too bad my girl." She tidied her hair, put a fresh blouse on, straightened her skirt and pulled her stockings up and waited for David to call for her, as the Innkeeper said that there would be a meal laid on for them in the Innkeeper's private kitchen. Annie was delighted.

Another ten minutes went by, then there came a knock on the door. Annie got up to answer it and there was David, as handsome as ever. Her heart gave a little somersault when she saw him.

"Is everything all right Nan?" he asked.

"Oh yes," Nan said, "everything is marvellous."

"It has taken me a few years to get on track but I know", she thought, "that I am on the right one at last." She put her arms around him and kissed him full on the lips.

David was delighted and was looking forward to their life together. There was only one thing that he thought could change their future and that was her son. David felt a bad feeling when he thought of the child, how it was conceived and the involvement of his sister but if he was going to make a life with Nan, he had to put all those thoughts aside, a little boy, an innocent child should be the least of his worries. But worry he did.

They ate their meal and enjoyed every mouthful. Nan commented about the food and David passed the message on to the Innkeeper.

The Innkeeper said, "now I know why you always use my Inn."

David smiled and thought "I shall always remember this place but not for the food, but where Nan accepted to be my wife."

They were both very tired, so after a glass of port each they went to their respective rooms. Annie was very surprised that David didn't come into her room but she was very glad that he didn't.

In the Arms of Merlin

Annie woke as the dawn was breaking. She didn't get up straight away, she just lay there, looking up at the ceiling, hoping against hope that the young boy would like her and David and later get to love them both. She got up about 6.30 am, did her ablutions and sat in an armchair in front of the window until David knocked the door. She opened it and stood aside for him to come in. She left the door open as she was a little embarrassed.

"Good morning my darling," he said.

She couldn't get over that she wasn't shy with him and went up to him and kissed him with a little peck. David caught hold of her and drew her into his arms and it was no peck he gave her. She thought that he was going to squeeze the life out of her. He just couldn't help it. He had had a very bad night, first of all thinking about the child that might put between them, then thinking about Nan lying in bed in the next room. It was as much as he could do to contain himself. He didn't want to frighten her and spoil things for them, so he just lay there, thinking about everything under the sun. He went to sleep eventually and dreamed about the most stupid things. Just like a child's dream. He was glad to wake up.

They ate their breakfast and the happiness was plain to see. The Innkeeper came to chat to them just as they were finishing and asked them if they would be staying another night?

"I am not quite sure," David said. "It all depends what happens when we get to Cardiff. Will you have the rooms if I leave the booking until later?"

"Oh don't worry Sir, it is very quiet here at the moment so if you want to stay it will be fine."

David was glad. He hoped that they would be able to stay for him to enjoy another few hours with Nan.

The coachman was waiting outside for them. The door of the coach was open and David helped Nan in, got in behind her. The coachman got up to his seat and off they went. To happiness or disaster.

"We will soon know," David thought.

They got to the gates of the Orphanage about 9 o'clock. A young lad about 12 years old opened the big gates. He just looked up at them and didn't utter a word, let them through and closed the gates behind them. The carriage stopped right outside the large front door, they both got out and David knocked the door and as soon as he did, a very large man opened the door and invited them inside.

There was a small hall and four doors leading off it. The man introduced himself and said that he was the Master.

"My goodness," Annie thought, "he looks a nasty big of goods." He offered them a seat each to sit on and made his apologies, said he wouldn't be long and left them alone.

A few minutes later, a lady walked into the room; she introduced herself as Mrs George, the Master's wife. David now introduced Nan as William's mother and he introduced himself as Nan's fiancé. The next thing, a young girl came in with a tray of tea. Mrs George poured the tea and talked about their journey, but didn't mention the child.

Annie had nearly finished her tea; she couldn't stick it any longer, sat up and asked straight out, "where is my son?"

Mrs George was taken aback a little with Nan's forwardness. She didn't make an issue of it, just said, "he won't be too long, my husband has gone to the dormitory to fetch him. There has been a little upset there this morning but we can talk about it later on."

Nan and David were puzzled but had to wait to see what the problem was. Annie's heart was pounding in her breast, she was glad that the woman was talking to David and not to her. She didn't think that she would be able to keep up a conversation with her. At last the door opened and a small boy was pushed in, in front of the Master.

In the Arms of Merlin

Nan and David could see that there was a problem by the way the boy was acting.

Nan got up and made her way over to the boy and tried to take his hand but he would have nothing to do with her.

Annie felt as if someone had put a knife through her heart and stifled back tears, which had been on the way since they had left the Inn. She stood back and tried another tactic.

She went back to her chair, smiled at him and asked his name.

He looked up eventually, saw the face of this woman who wanted to take him away again. This had happened to him a few times and he didn't like it one bit. He was used to making such a scene every time someone came to adopt him, that he frightened the couples so much that they left without him every time.

He was quite a smart little chap; he knew how to go about things so that he could stay here with his friends. It wasn't great here at the Orphanage but it was all he knew, so now he had to work out what he was going to do to put these people off.

He was still standing in the middle of the room where the Master had left him; his head was hanging low. From the corner of his eye he could see the feet of the woman coming towards him. He hadn't made up his mind what his next move was going to be but by this time the feet had arrived right in front of him. Now he was stumped. He waited for her to make the next move.

She took his chin in her hand and rose it up so that he was looking straight into her eyes. He was surprised. She had very dark blue eyes and they looked full of love. He didn't move a muscle, or blink an eyelid. The softest voice he had ever heard came out of her mouth and she whispered to William. "I am your mother and I have come to take you home. I have been looking for you for years, so here I am. Are you willing to come now without any fuss?"

In the Arms of Merlin

Annie felt so sorry for the child, it must have come as a great shock to him. Little did anyone know that the boy used to say his prayers every night and at the end, he would say, "please God, let my mother come and get me."

William just couldn't believe his ears, he thought that he must be dreaming. This was one of his regular dreams. He was only eight years old but life had been quite hard on him. The helpers at the Orphanage used to talk about William's circumstances.

They didn't think that he could understand but he was quite an intelligent boy. He didn't understand everything that they said but he learned enough to know that as far as they knew his mother was alive and really he wasn't an orphan.

"Now," William thought, "what am I going to do? I am not going to make a scene like I would have usually done. Put your thinking cap on."

Master and Matron were pleasantly surprised at William's attitude with this woman.

Annie turned around and sat back on her chair. She raised her cup and took some tea. She didn't take her eyes from William's. She was willing him to come over to her. By the time she had finished her tea, he was standing by her side, just looking at her.

David turned to William and said, "I am David" and offered his hand to him. William took it and pumped it up and down. David was impressed with the grip he had in his hand and gripped him back.

Master and Matron got up, made their way out of the room and as they were going through the door he turned to David and said "perhaps you would like to come into my office to sign a few papers, then he will be all yours."

Nan was in tears by now and the boy could see that she was upset.

In the Arms of Merlin

Williams asked her, "why are you crying? Have you changed your mind and you don't want me now that you have seen me?" William was starting to work himself up.

By now and Nan realised what was happening, she dried her eyes and said, "no my dear, I am crying because I am happy that I have found you at last."

That was enough for William, it would do for him.

David told Nan, "I think that you should go into the office, I'll stay here with William, so off you go."

In the meantime Matron came back with a little flour sack. "These are a few items of clothing, not many, but if you don't think you will need them, perhaps you would leave them with me for another boy. I would be very grateful."

Matron could see that they were well breached and that William would have all new clothes when he got to his new home. As a matter of fact Matron was glad that William's mother had turned up, he was the longest inmate that they had. Most of the children were adopted as soon as they arrived, that is if they were babies. There were two other boys William's age but they had only been there for two years and they were brothers. William was quite a nice boy really, she had a soft spot for him and would have adopted him herself but her husband wouldn't hear of it and now he would be going to a loving home.

Matron knew he would appreciate it, as it was getting harder for William when his friends were being adopted. If the two brothers would leave, he would be on his own until someone else came.

Matron gave William his jacket, he put it on and stood waiting for the next move. Nan came back into the room, thanked Master and Matron and told William to say thank you to them as well. He went up to Matron, offered his hand and she took him into her arms and gave him a big hug, turned him around and guided him towards his mother and they all went out through the door and didn't look back.

In the Arms of Merlin

Their carriage was still waiting for them in the courtyard. William had never been in a coach before and he was hoping that the others were watching him through the window. He sat opposite his mother and David sat next to her. The coachman flicked his whip and off they went.

They hadn't made any arrangements before they came away from the Inn in the morning. David was a little worried. It was a long journey all in one go, so he asked Nan if she thought that it would be a good idea for them to stay the night and make a very early start in the morning.

Nan said, "perhaps it would be a good idea." They would have to stop for food and that would take more time. Nan also thought it would be nice for the three of them to get to know each other in a neutral place. After all they were all on strange territory and she wanted to make the most of having David to herself but she wasn't on her own anymore. She had a son and she prayed that he would settle down and be happy.

They drove for half an hour and arrived at the Inn, the Innkeeper's wife was in the bar as they passed the door. "Oh," she said, "you're back."

"Yes," David said, "we wondered if you had another small room, we have an extra guest?"

"I don't see any problem," the Mrs said, "I'll go up and make his bed. Your beds are like you left them this morning. My husband thought that you might come back this afternoon. No point making work for myself is there?"

David turned to William, "you will be alright sleeping in your own room won't you William?"

William nodded and thought to himself, "it will be my first, a room to myself, even a bed to myself." It wasn't too bad sleeping with another boy. It was great in the winter when it was cold, as long as he didn't wet the bed, then it was worse. It could get very smelly in the summer.

In the Arms of Merlin

William said, "yes I will be fine" and up the stairs they all trooped, each to their own rooms.

David brought Nan's bag to her room and they both went to see William in his room. Nan knocked the door and walked in and there was William stretched on the bed enjoying every minute. He was just thinking to himself as the knock came on the door, "if the life I am going to have is going to be as good as this bed, I think that I shall be alright."

Nan looked at David and he looked at her and they both smiled, "come along my boy," David said, "we shall go down to have some food, then we will have an early night. We want to make an early start in the morning." Down they all went and sat down to the most delicious meal that David had had in any posh hotel.

After the meal David lit a cigar and had a brandy, while Nan had a glass of sherry. She was getting quite used to the little tipple now and again. As she was sipping the sherry, she thought of her mother. Poor thing, she had never tasted sherry in her life. Annie had come a long way from those days and she was sorry that she couldn't call them <u>the good old days</u>.

It must have been nine o'clock by the time they finished everything. They got up and made their way to the bedrooms. Annie took William into his; asked him if he needed help to go to bed.

William went all shy and said, "I'm fine thank you. I have always put myself to bed since I was small."

"Alright," Annie said, "don't forget if you want anything in the night. You know where I am, or if I won't do, you know where David is."

"Thank you," William said, "I shall be fine."

Annie closed the door and left the little boy thinking quite hard about the life ahead of him.

As Annie went over the landing to her room. David came out of his room and said, "I was just coming to ask you if you would like to come for a little stroll before we retire?"

In the Arms of Merlin

"Yes," she said, "that is a good idea. I don't think I would be able to sleep with all the things that have happened to me in the last few days. I still pinch myself to see if I'm dreaming. I won't be a moment, I just want to get a wrap to put over my shoulders."

She got her shawl from her bag and as she passed the mirror, she took a swift glance at herself and was very pleased to see how good she looked. She thought of David, her cheeks flushed a little more and he was only the other side of the door.

How was she going to be when she would be in his arms later on? At least she hoped that she would.

She gave a little giggle as she came out of her room. David caught the end of it and asked he what was so funny.

"Oh," she said, "I will tell you one day." They walked downstairs out of the Inn, hand in hand.

David was quite quiet as they walked around the back of the Inn. They found a gate and walked up the field behind. They got up to the top of the hill, stood and looked back. They could see for miles. It was a beautiful sight, as the sun was setting and everything had a rosy hue.

David asked; "Nan are you happy now?"

Nan nodded, and said, "everything is good, too good. I hope that things don't change. Nothing has ever gone as good as this for me before."

"Look Nan," David said, "from now on your life will always be as good as this. I will see to that."

David told her what he was thinking about while they were walking up the hill. "It seems that it's my life being liver over again. The only difference is that I wasn't in an orphanage. The man my mother married treated me like his own son and I will do exactly the same for William. Trust me."

Annie knew that he meant every word. He was such a sincere and genuine man and that made her love him the more.

"First think I am going to do when we get home is to get him a horse. I'm sure he will be a good horseman."

"Poor William, I bet he has never touched a horse with his hand, leave alone ridden one."

"All the better, " David said, "he will be fresh, will listen and won't have any other influence with bad habits. Come on then Nan, we had better make tracks or it will be dark."

They called into the bar, there were a few old boys having a chat and a few tankards of ale. The Innkeeper was serving.

David asked Nan what she would like. She had decided to have a cup of cocoa if it was possible.

"Certainly," the Innkeeper said, "I will tell my wife."

He gave her a shout, then turned to David and asked what he would like.

"I'll have some ale and perhaps you could put the poker in it and warm it up?"

"Right Sir, I won't be a jiffy."

David turned to Nan and said "I feel quite chilled."

Nan said, "I hope you haven't got a cold coming on."

"Well if I have, this hot ale will do the trick."

They finished their drinks, said their goodnights and made their way upstairs. David didn't want to leave her on the landing, he wanted to take her into his bed and have her lie in his arms all night but he was afraid to suggest it in case he would frighten her off. He realised that he would have to be very gentle and tactful when things came to that stage. Little did he know that Nan was longing for him to come into her bed, but she didn't show him anything in case he thought that she was a bold slut.

In the Arms of Merlin

Annie had never talked to anyone about the facts of life. What she knew about life had been forced on her and it frightened her. She knew that it wouldn't be anything like that with David. Even though she was scared, she was yearning to feel David's body close to hers. She also knew that David would not ravage her like that monster did.

Annie gave a little shiver, carried on undressing and went into bed. They were both thinking of each other as they dropped off to sleep. David called William at five o'clock, then he called Nan. They had eaten breakfast and David had settled the bill and were on their way home.

William was very quiet for a few miles. Nan asked him what was the matter. He said, "nothing, I think I'm a bit tired."

"You shouldn't be tired," David said, "you went to bed quite early."

"Didn't you sleep?" Nan asked him.

"No," he said, "I was awake for a long time after you went to bed."

"Oh." Nan said, "I didn't come to say goodnight to you as I thought that you would be asleep."

"No," he said and he started to cry quietly.

Annie got up and took the seat next to him, put her arms around him and kissed him on the top of his head. "You were tired last night, I noticed," Nan said, "are you worrying about something?"

William was a bit slow with his responses and eventually he brought it all out. He was sobbing now and was trying to tell them in his own little way.

Nan let him be. Eventually it all came out. He was only eight years old but realised that they were wealthy people and he was a scruffy common boy. He thought that he wouldn't fit into their lives and would have to be sent back to the Orphanage.

In the Arms of Merlin

Nan was in tears by now and held him tightly in her arms and told him, "I have been looking for you for years and now that I have found you I will never let you go. When David and I get married we will all live together. You will then have a mother and a father like any other boy. That's all we have got to do is to get to know each other, with a little give and take because things are not all going to be rosy. Not one of us really knows one another, so we will have to learn as we go along. Are you happy now?"

He dried his eyes and said "yes Mama, even if it's only for me to say that word."

Nan looked at David and she thought that David had a little glistening in his eyes.

William fell asleep in Nan's arms and slept until they were nearly home. He stirred and opened his eyes and asked, "are we home yet?"

"No son," David said, "but we won't be long."

William rubbed his eyes and straightened his clothes to try and make them a bit more presentable.

At last the carriage stopped outside the Tivoli. They all got out. Nan opened the side door and they went straight upstairs to Nan's private accommodation.

Nan had seen to William's bedroom before she went to fetch him, so all she had to do was show it to him. Nan could see that he was thrilled with his room. It must have been a lovely feeling to know this was his very own.

She kept him home for a week. He seemed to settle down but he was a very deep little boy and could hide his feelings if he wanted to.

Nan sent Maggie down to the Emporium to get some boy's clothes out on approval. She wrote his age and measurements and told the assistant to use his own discretion with the colours.

Maggie came back with a load of parcels. William was playing out in the garden. He came flying in to see what his mother wanted. When he saw all the parcels Annie thought that he was going berserk. She called to him to calm down and after a few minutes he did. He had never had new clothes in all his little life. Bless him, no wonder he was excited.

Annie opened the first one and there was a smart suit in light grey. The next one had a white shirt and a grey tie. Annie asked him if he would like to go to his room to try them on. He was off before Annie could ask him again. He came back in ten minutes all dressed up. He actually was unrecognisable. Annie couldn't believe it was him.

"You have to have a haircut next. I shall take you tomorrow, then we will go to Mr Evans to have him make you a pair of shoes."

Annie took hold of him and put him tidy, straightened all the seams and the tie. After we get your shoes and your haircut, we will ask David for his opinion on how you look. Perhaps you can wear these to our wedding. What do you think of that?" Annie asked.

I think he was taken aback a little when his mother talked about the wedding.

"Anything wrong?" she asked.

"No." William said, "but will I still be living with you when you get married?"

"Of course you will, where do you think you are going to then?"

"I don't know," he said, "but things have been going so good for me lately, I thought that a change must be on the way."

"Don't be silly," Annie said, "you are mine and you are with me now until you want to leave me, or should I say us, because David will count soon."

William thought it over for a few seconds and asked if he could look at the rest of the clothes, so Annie started to cut more string and William opened the brown paper. He had pants, vests, shirts, socks and jumpers. He didn't bother to go up to his room to change, that took too much time. Everything was in a heap on the floor by the time he had tried everything on. He was so excited; his face was as red as a beetroot.

"Now calm down, William," his mother said, "or you will make yourself sick and we don't want that now. Help me tidy these things up, then we will take them to your room and put them away."

After all the clothes were put away, Annie asked William to put his coat and cap on and they made their way down to the barber's shop in the main square.

The weather was starting to get cold. Annie pulled her collar tighter around her neck and told William to do the same. He obeyed her straightaway. There were three old men in the shop. They were all smoking pipes and the room was full of smoke. Extra smoke was coming from the fire too as the barber had just put some wood on to get some more warmth in the shop. As soon as someone came in they let all the warm air out. The old boys didn't seem to mind. It was the chat they came to the shop for, not really to have their hair cut, so when one of them offered to let William go before him Annie accepted immediately. William needed an overcoat because the hard weather was coming in fast.

William sat on the chair and the barber asked him his name and William said, "William Owens."

"Oh," the barber said, "that is a strong sounding name and where are you from?"

"I am from Carmarthen and I live in the Tivoli Tearooms with my mother."

"Now then," Annie thought, "put that in your pipe and smoke it." She gave William a wink. With William's hair finished, Annie paid the barber; put on William's coat and his cap and off they went back to the Emporium to get him an overcoat.

They weren't two minutes fixing him up. He looked quite good in it, so Annie said, "we'll have that one. Can you take the ticket off then he can wear it home, it is quite cold outside?"

The assistant agreed with her.

"Will you put it on my account?"

"Yes certainly madam.2 They all knew who she was now.

They left the shop and made their way to Mr Evans' shop. He was busy at his last making a pair of shoes. As the bell went he looked up and was overjoyed to see Annie. He got up from his bench, walked over to her and put his arms around her and gave her a great big hug.

Annie said, "it's so nice to see you. I don't get to see you often enough these days. I know you are busy and you have extra things to do."

He let Annie go, turned to William, caught hold of his hand and said, "I presume that you are William?" He shook his hand up and down a few times then he caught hold of the boy, put his arms around him and gave him a great big kiss on his cheek.

William went all red and looked at his mother. Annie smiled and said, "William this is Mr Evans, a very good friend of mine and if you are lucky enough, he will be a good friend to you too."

William looked him straight in the eyes and said, "I am very pleased to meet you Sir."

Annie was very pleased with his manners and proceeded to tell Mr Evans what she wanted.

He put William to sit on a chair and he kneeled down and measured William's foot, said something under his breath and proceeded to a shelf behind the counter and brought a beautiful pair of soft leather boots over to William. He took the laces loose and put the first one on, then he put the other one on and tied the laces on both the boots and told William to stand up.

William stood up like a soldier. He couldn't tell that he had got boots on, they were so soft, and a lovely brown colour.

"Do they feel good?" Mr Evans asked.

"They feel great." William said, "I have never had anything like this, ever before."

"Right," Annie said, "he can keep those on. Have you got a black pair exactly like those?"

"Yes," Mr Evans said, "I will fetch them now. I only finished them yesterday, so you are lucky."

William was delighted and came over to his mother and put his arms around her and showered her with kisses. "Thank you, thank you, Mama," he kept saying.

Annie said, "who else do you thank?"

William turned to Mr Evans and thanked him also.

Mr Evans took a liking to the boy straight away, he thought he was so open and a well-mannered boy. That must have been thanks to Mrs George, the Master's wife. It could have been so different and Annie realised that every time she said her prayers at night.

One pair of boots was packed up in brown paper and William wore the other pair home. Annie asked if Mr Evans could do anything with the other pair. He said he thought he could, he knew a little boy who would be glad of them.

"Good," said Annie. She shook hands with him and they made their way to the door, gave one more smile and went outside to the cold afternoon.

They had to pass the bottom of the lane by the Tearooms to get home, so they made their way up the lane and went into the shop. It was all so cosy and the smell that came from here was lovely.

Annie felt a little pang as she went right into the old Tearooms. Auntie came running towards her and gave her another hug and one for William.

William chuckled and said, "Auntie, that's all we have today, hugs and kisses."

"Never mind," Auntie said, "what about a nice cake from your old Auntie? Come on loves, you both look perished. Is it that cold out there?"

"Yes it is," William said and he proceeded to stand in front of the fire like an old man.

Auntie and Annie chuckled at the sight of him standing there. Annie had a pot of tea and William had a cup of chocolate and two pieces of Victoria sponge.

CHAPTER 12 – CHOOSING A SCHOOL

William told Auntie where they had been. He also told her what they had bought, all the clothes that he needed, he was so excited.

Auntie was smiling when the boy was telling her all about his day. She looked at Annie and said; "Christmas is coming early this year is it?"

"Oh," Annie said; "he only had the clothes that he stood in and he will be going to school before long. I'll have to make time to go to see about him going next week. He had to have this week home for us to get to know each other. Tomorrow morning I will make my way up to Priory Street. They have built a new school up there and it's not too far away."

They finished their food and started to make their way back home. Annie went in through the Tearooms to see if everything was all right and everything was. They made their way upstairs. As they were going into the parlour, William looked up at his mother, "have I got to go to school Mama?" he asked.

"Oh yes darling, or you would not be able to make a living, get married and have a wife and a son of your own, will you?"

"I don't want any of those things, I just want to stay with you forever."

Annie patted him on his head and said, "you will, when the time comes, don't you worry."

William gave a deep sigh, already worrying about going to school. While he was in the Orphanage they didn't go to school. A man came once a week and tried to teach them. The children were so unruly that the poor man didn't have a chance. William did pick up some things. He was able to count and do sums; no-one would do him out of a penny. He could read a little, but he couldn't write.

He kept sighing for three days.

On the fourth day Annie took him to the new school to see what they could do for him.

They landed at the school around ten o'clock and were ushered into the Headmaster's room. He was a very large man with a lot of hair and a big beard. He looked more like a pirate than a school master.

Annie could feel William's hand shaking in hers. She looked down at him and gave him a sweet smile, squeezed his hand and proceeded into the small room.

"Good morning," the man said.

Annie answered him politely. He motioned to the chairs and asked them to sit down. As soon as they were seated, he asked her what he could do for her.

Annie took the bull straight by the horns; she introduced William as her son and said that she wanted him to attend this school as soon as possible.

Mr Griffiths then asked what school William had come from.

Annie flushed up and stuttered a little.

Mr Griffiths realised that he had embarrassed her. He got up from his chair, came around the desk and took William by the hand and took him out of the room. He was talking to him as he was walking across the small hall. She couldn't hear William answering, then she heard a loud clang when he opened the huge door leading into a classroom. "Miss Lewis," he said; "look after this boy until I come to fetch him. His name is William."

Next thing he was back in the small room and sitting down and said, "now, let's talk."

Annie started to tell him some of the story.

In the Arms of Merlin

He stopped her and said, "you are Miss Owens and you own the Tivoli and the Tearooms down the lane, is that right?"

Annie said, "yes. I am sorry about earlier but I didn't want to tell you about William's circumstances in front of him. He has been through enough as it is, so thank you for taking care of the situation.

William was brought up in an Orphanage outside Cardiff. I have been looking for him for four years. I found him about ten days ago, so as you can guess, he has come from the Orphanage with nothing. Now he has got a mother and will have a father in a few weeks. On top of everything else, he has got to go to school."

"Oh, I understand now. I wasn't very sure who you were. I know now. My wife and I have been in your tearooms many a time and I remember seeing you. Not to be too personal, you are going to marry Mr David Jones. I have met him a few times in my capacity as a school master. Mr Jones has been very generous to us at the time we were starting to build this school. I don't think you will have a problem bringing your son to this school."

After he took William's details down he started talking about the school. "There are only twenty children here, yet the parents are a bit wary about sending their children to school but before long it will be compulsory to send them.

Most of the men around here work in the tin works; they work hard and don't get much pay. Most of them are heavy drinkers and there is hardly any money left for the wife and children. There are loads of them and when the time comes for them to have to come to school, the school will be overcrowded, then perhaps they will build another school. There is a rumour that they are going to build more into the town. Let us hope that this is right. I am really looking forward to having a full school.

It has been good for William that he picked up something at the Orphanage; it will be in good stead for him when he starts here. When would you like him to start Miss Owens?"

Annie had thought it over before she came this morning and hoped that he could have another week for him to get used to his mother and David. She explained to Mr Griffiths, "David has been away in London on business since we brought William back from Cardiff. He hardly knew David at all."

"Right," the master said, "when is Mr Jones coming home?"

Annie said, "at the end of the week."

"It is now September the 14th, I'll give him until the 1st October. How does that sound?"

"It sounds very good Mr Griffiths and thank you very much. The next time you come into the Tivoli ask the girls to call for me."

"No, no," the man answered, "there is no need for that, my wife loves to come there. She hasn't got to be enticed to your Tearooms."

"Well, we will see," Annie said.

Annie was quite pleased to hear the man complimenting her Tearooms, Auntie would be proud of her and what she had achieved in her few years of business, but she would never forget that it was David who had made it possible. Thinking about him sent a shiver down her spine.

While Annie had been day dreaming, Mr Griffiths had gone to fetch William from the classroom. He looked quite happy, took his mother's hand and said; "Mama I like it here. Am I going to come to this school?"

"Yes." Mr Griffiths bellowed.

William's eyes blinked with the roar the man gave. I'm sure William was shaking in his boots.

In the Arms of Merlin

So as not to frighten him anymore, Annie turned and offered her hand to the Headmaster, thanked him and said, "we will see you on 1st October" and out they went to the playground, up to the school gates and onto the road.

As they walked, William danced by the side of her. They crossed the road half way down the street and there was a little candy shop. William stopped and looked in the window and asked his mother if he could have some candy.

Annie stopped, looked into the window and said, "why not?"

They walked into the tiny shop and looked at their wares. Everything was home made. He picked a black and white 'bull's eye'. Annie asked for two ounces, she didn't want him to eat too many candies.

William was very pleased with what he had. They were the first sweets he had ever had.

When they got out of the shop he stuffed two into his mouth.

Annie was shocked and worried, "now take one out of your mouth William, what if you choke? You wouldn't want that would you?"

William obeyed and stuck the second one back in the bag. It stuck to the others like glue.

CHAPTER 13 – OLD FRIENDS

They walked briskly back to the Tivoli as it was starting to rain. They walked through the shop entrance and Esther was waiting for her.

"What's wrong?" Annie said.

"Oh, nothing's wrong, just there are two people asking to see you. I put them in the corner and gave them a tray of tea. I also gave them some cakes. I hope that I have done the right thing."

Annie turned around and there was Auntie May, her next door neighbour and sitting next to her was Jack.

Annie could not believe her eyes, as she was making her way over to the table. They both looked up at the same time. They both had a shock when they saw this woman, who after a few seconds, they realised, was Annie.

Auntie May met Annie half way, they put their arms around each other and both were sobbing on each other's shoulders. It was a few minutes before Jack could get hold of Annie. He hugged her as much and as long as Auntie May.

After the initial shock of seeing each other, Annie said, "come on upstairs, we have made enough of a scene here already, so let's finish it upstairs" and off they went.

Annie took them into the parlour and asked them did they want something to eat or drink. They both declined and said that they had tea downstairs with the girls.

"By the way," Jack said, "we haven't paid for it either."

"Get away with you," Annie said, "to you think that I am going to charge you for that? After we finish our chat I will make you the best spread that you have ever had but we talk first" and talk they did.

They were at it for about two hours. After Annie found out what they were doing up in town, she asked them would they like to stay the night. They were both delighted, because they would have to find a lodging house, as they would have to drive back in the dark and Jack's pony wasn't too keen on being out at night. That problem was solved.

They had no idea how to go about finding Annie. The first place of all was the workhouse. They said that she had a Teashop in one of the lanes in the town, so they went from there.

They spoke to Auntie and she knew who Auntie May was, as Annie had talked about her when she went to live with them. She had also told them that she had heard of Jack. That made him smile too.

They thought that perhaps she had forgotten about them all down there but obviously she hadn't

There was no way that Annie was able to go to visit them, for one thing she never had a day off. She couldn't have written to them as Auntie May couldn't read or write. They were here now. Annie was as excited as a child would have been. She couldn't come down to earth. She knew that she would have to before long, so she took deep breaths and counted to twenty and knew now that she was in control.

Annie had told her story to them and they were both very upset. Annie said; "we have to forget all that now, it is all in the past. I would like you to meet someone." She got up and beckoned to them to follow her. She took them into William's room; he was sitting quietly on the bed looking at a picture book. He looked up as they came in and gave them a lovely smile and got up and went to stand by his mother. Annie said; "Auntie May, Jack, meet my son, William."

They were both flabbergasted. Jack shook him by the hand but Auntie May took hold of him, hugged and kissed him until William was squealing for help from his mother.

Auntie let him go at last and they all laughed. They all sat down again and Auntie May asked Annie if she had any more surprises up her sleeve?

In the Arms of Merlin

"Well," Annie said, "if you can wait until this evening, I will have another one for you."

"I can't wait," said Auntie May.

There were three bedrooms in Annie's home. She didn't feel that William should be taken from his room, after all he had only just got used to it.

She asked Jack if he would mind sleeping on the sofa?

He said, "don't worry about me, I will sleep on the floor."

"No indeed you won't," Annie said, "will the sofa do?"

"It will be fine."

"Auntie May, you are in the guest room, so everything is fine. What time did you arrive in town?" Annie asked.

"It must have been about ten o'clock, we started at the crack of dawn, so that I could finish my business, then we could come and look for you."

"Did you have business here as well Auntie?"

"No," she said, "but Jack called the other day and we were talking about you. He promised me that if he had more trips up to Carmarthen he would bring me with him."

"How wonderful," Annie said, "you have found me and we will never lose touch with each other again."

Annie then asked Jack what sort of business did he have in the town.

"Well," Jack said, "you remember my father died and I had to leave the Big House? I had to go to another farm to work to help my mother. I worked there for two years. I saved every penny that I could, then my mother was taken ill and in a few weeks she died. After everything was over, a solicitor called me to his office to tell me that the smallholding that I had been brought up in had been owned by my parents for the last ten years. I didn't know anything about it until after my mother died.

I am rather tired of working for other people, so I have been to the bank and put the smallholding up as collateral to

In the Arms of Merlin

start my own business as a haulier. I have bought a cart horse and a large, flat, heavy cart. I am going to haul timber and coal. They are crying out for people like me, so I am on my way Annie. I hope that I end up like you have."

"I hope you will Jack, you were so good to use when we worked together. I have a friend who has a coalmine, that's the boy for you to get to know. You shall meet him this evening."

Auntie was sitting on the sofa getting to know William. She had certainly won him over in her own right.

Annie had given Jack a glass of brandy; he was sitting on a chair at the kitchen table, watching and talking to Annie.

There was a large chicken in the oven and Annie had just finished cleaning the vegetables and they all were simmering on the top of Annie's new stove.

Auntie was a little guilty because she wasn't doing anything to help but Annie reassured her that she could manage everything herself. Auntie gave in and made the most of it.

Annie went into the dining room and laid the table for six.

Jack said; "how have you laid up for six people?"

"Oh," Annie said, "I have got a surprise for you all. To make the numbers up I have invited Esther my friend, who runs the Tearooms for me, to have a meal with us. Is that all right with you?"

"I don't mind," he said, "but as you know I am not much of a talker. Can you explain and tell her that I am very shy?"

"Get on with you Jack, you are not a bit shy, you can talk the hind leg off a donkey, you'll see."

"Who is the other guest?"

"Well the other man is David Jones. He is the man that I am going to marry. Does that shock you?"

"No indeed it doesn't, I thought that you would have been married ages ago. If you weren't courting, I was going to ask you myself."

Annie chuckled, he also chuckled half-heartedly.

Annie changed the subject, she thought that he really meant it and that would never do. She was hoping that he would like Esther, that is why she was asking her to dinner.

Esther had no idea, she thought that it was just an ordinary meal, with just Annie, William and her. She didn't even know that David was going to be there.

The Tearooms were closed at 5.30 on the dot. They cleared everything in double quick time and prepared everything for the morning.

Esther locked up after the girls and made her way upstairs, went into the kitchen to Annie and asked if she could have a wash.

Annie said "yes," off she went.

Esther's hair was quite blonde; she gave it a good brush. It actually sparkled, it shone so much it was like spun gold. It wasn't only her hair, she was a very pretty girl with a beautiful figure.

After the had finished titivating, she made her way into the parlour and was asking Annie a question when she came across the visitors.

Esther had a shock, she thought that the visitors had gone out of the side room. She didn't dream that they were staying the night as Annie had informed her.

She gave one good blush and then she didn't have time to blush any more. Jack didn't give her a minute to even think of blushing.

Auntie couldn't get a word in edgeways; they were just having a glass of sherry when the front door bell went.

Annie excused herself and went downstairs to answer the door. It was David. Her eyes shone as she saw who it was. He swept her into his arms and nearly smothered her.

In the Arms of Merlin

She had to pull away from him in case Auntie came to the top of the stairs. She wouldn't have in any case, but Annie was shyer than she made out to be.

"Come on," she said, "come and see who is here." They are staying here with me tonight.

David was puzzled. They made their way upstairs. David was introduced to Auntie May and Jack.

Annie explained who they were. David was pleased to meet them, he had heard all about them. He knew how good they both had been to Nan.

Annie passed a glass of sherry to David and they all sipped and chatted together until Annie said that dinner was ready. They all made their way to the dining room, sat down and ate a very pleasant meal together.

Annie didn't have time to make a dessert, so she had taken a gooseberry pie from the larder in the kitchen. She also got some fresh cream.

Neither auntie May nor Jack had eaten a meal like this before. Auntie couldn't get over it. She couldn't stop talking about the food and how good a cook Annie was.

Annie owned up about the pie but said the first course was her own.

David was very thrilled with Annie's cooking. None of the women in his family could cook at all. They didn't need to in any case, but that was beside the point.

After the meal was over, the men moved into the parlour and William went with them. He was a very good boy, he only spoke when he was spoken to, so while Jack and David were talking about Jack's new business, William just sat there and listened.

David gave Jack a lot of good pointers regarding the haulage business but one thing he needed to do was get another horse. One horse wasn't going to be strong enough to pull timber and carry coal.

He told him to go to the bank in the morning, David would get in touch with the Manager and he would give him an extension to the loan that he already had.

Jack was a little apprehensive about the extra loan but David reassured him that there would be no problem regarding the extra money.

Jack was over the moon; it really was his lucky day today. David also gave him instructions as to how he get to the coal mines.

"When you get there, ask for me. Don't let anyone put you off."

Auntie had insisted that she helped with the dishes. Annie did not refuse, she wanted to get in on the conversation, the night would fly and they would be on their way home again.

Annie thought that she would be able to see Jack more often now if he had business with David.

While David and Jack were finishing their chat about Jack's new venture, Auntie May and Annie went to take Esther home. It was a lovely night with a full moon but it was very cold.

They walked quite briskly and arrived at Esther's house in good time. Her father answered the door and Annie introduced him to Auntie May. She also explained that Jack and David were talking business at home, so they could leave William in.

"I was wondering why you were leaving him there on his own."

"You know I wouldn't do that."

"How is the young man? I haven't seen him for a while now. You must bring him down the next time you come."

They left Esther's and made their way back home.

Jack was quite flushed with excitement by the time they got home, with the thought of the good things that were going to come. He knew that he would have to work hard, but he was used to hard work and hard masters, which he promised, that if he ever had anyone to work for him, he would never be a hard taskmaster.

Annie made a pot of tea and got out the brandy for the boys.

Auntie didn't stop talking until she was exhausted, then asked Annie if she could go to bed.

Annie took her to her room, lit the lamp and told Auntie May to leave the light on; Annie would turn it off when she came to bed.

By the time she got back to the parlour, Jack had drunk his tea and brandy and was ready to go to bed.

Annie showed him his room, lit the lamp for him and said goodnight, then went back to David.

CHAPTER 14 – PREPARING FOR THE WEDDING

This was the first time they had been on their own since before they went to Cardiff to fetch William.

She asked him if he wanted more tea of anything.

"I don't want anything, so come and sit here by my side for me to hold you in my arms. I have missed you so much. I can't believe that I could need somebody so much. I have been on my own for a good few years and it has never bothered me before, so Annie I think the time has come for us to get married. That is if you still want me. Do you?"

Annie's shyness had gone out of the window since she had met David. She answered with a deep kiss that made him shudder down to his boots.

They talked for a while about the wedding. The date was set, the place and time.

"Now I will leave all the arrangements to you and my mother. She is going to be overjoyed when I tell her in the morning. I shall ask John to be my best man. What about your side?"

"Well," Annie said; "I shall ask Esther to be my maid of honour and Uncle Will can give me away. Does that sound alright?"

"Yes," said David.

He thought that he had better make his way back home, he couldn't contain himself any longer.

Annie was quite peeved that he was going so soon but she didn't tell him. She thought he must have been up early that morning. It was quite a cold night and it was a long way home for him, especially on horseback.

Annie went into Auntie May's room to put her light out. She was still awake so Annie gave her the good news.

In the Arms of Merlin

She was so pleased. Annie asked her if she could come up to stay a week or so before the wedding. She agreed immediately, they said their goodnights.

Annie put out the lamp and went to see William. He was fast asleep, so she went to her own room, got undressed, went into bed and thought about David until she went to sleep.

It was 6.30 am when she got up and started to prepare the breakfast for her guests and William. They got up at 7 o'clock and they all ate together.

William was quite at home with them, it was as if he had known them all his life.

Auntie May was very impressed with the little boy. He was a credit to Annie but as Annie said, it was Mrs George who had brought him up. He was lucky that she loved him and had taught him as if he was her own.

As soon as they had finished eating, Annie told them about the wedding.

William was so excited. "Now," he said, "I will have a mother and a father."

"Yes," Auntie May said. "You are a very lucky boy and I hope you appreciate it. When you are older, you will realise what your mother has been through. I hope that you will look after her and respect her all of her life. She has been to hell and back."

The little boy didn't have any idea what Auntie was talking about but he would one day.

To change the subject Annie asked Jack what he thought of Esther.

He thought she was a very nice girl, but not for him.

He surprised Annie greatly and said whom he really fancied. It was Rose, one of the waitresses.

Annie couldn't get over it but as Jack said, Esther was on a higher plane than he was, whereas Rose was more of a working girl.

"Esther is a working girl too."

"No," Jack said, "she's different."

"Never mind," she said, "you will have enough time to get to know the two girls when you start working up here with your haulage contracting."

By lunchtime they were all ready to move off.

The last thing Annie was telling them was that she would be sending the wedding invitations in due course and for Jack to keep in touch with her Auntie.

Annie gave them both another hug and kisses. They did the same to William. Annie waved to them until they were out of sight. She was glad that she had given Auntie May a large quilt to put over her knees as it was a very cold day.

In the next few days David's mother and Letitia came to visit Annie. They were both pleased about the wedding.

Annie didn't think about Letitia when she said about her maid of honour. She had been a good friend to her as well, so she asked her if she would be her maid of honour too.

Letitia was delighted and started rabbiting on about what they were all going to wear.

"Right," Annie said. "I have found a seamstress who is a tailoress. She is very good but does not have a very large clientele, so perhaps we could go and see her one day this week. Do you think you could come up here again this week? We could have a chat with her and she could show us what she can do for us."

"That will be wonderful," Lady Elizabeth said. "Perhaps I won't have to go to London to get my clothes."

They were like three little children, so excited.

They left a little later and Annie went down to the Tearoom to break the news to the girls.

Annie said, "I have decided that we will close the Tearooms all that day so you all can come to the wedding. They were all delighted.

In the Arms of Merlin

The following day, Annie made her way up to Miss Davies. She had heard about her from one of her customers, who thought that she had found a treasure.

It took Annie ten minutes to get up to the top of Priory Street. She was glad it was in the daytime as there were loads of children around. Some of them looked quite menacing.

She got to Miss Davies' door, knocked and in a few seconds the little lady was standing there in front of Annie.

Annie explained what she wanted from her. She seemed pleased as she ushered Annie into her front room. One corner of the room was full of materials; another corner had a table with hundreds of paper patterns and a large treadle sewing machine. The floor was littered with bits of material and bits of cotton. It was a typical dressmaker's room.

She offered Annie a chair.

Annie told her exactly what she wanted. She also told her about Lady Elizabeth. The poor women couldn't believe her ears and asked Annie if she thought that she was good enough for her Ladyship.

"Well," Annie said, "if what I have heard about you is correct, then I would say yes."

The little lady was beaming.

"There is one problem."

"What is it?" Miss Davies asked.

"You know that I am in business. I won't be able to come up here whenever you ned me. Do you think that you could bring your machine to my home? You would have a room to yourself, then whenever you wanted me I could come up to you and go back to work straightaway. Do you think you could manage that?"

"Of course."

"I would feed you as well."

"I wouldn't worry about food," Miss Davies said, "but how will I get the machine down to your place?"

"That is no problem," Annie said, "my Uncle has got a hand care, he will get it in a jiffy. I will need you to make my wedding gown, two gowns for my maids of honour, a suit for my son and a rig out for my mother-in-law, Lady Elizabeth. By the way, the wedding is on the 21st December. Do you think you can do it all in ten weeks?"

"Certainly I can, but we will have to start as soon as possible."

"When?" said Annie.

"Today." Miss Davies said.

Annie smiled. This little lady knew what she was about and from now on, Annie would have her any time she needed anything new.

When she got back to the Tearooms, she took over from Maggie and asked her to go to Uncle Will's and ask him to bring the handcart up to Tivoli, as Annie had an errand for him and it was very important.

Off Maggie went and Uncle Will was there before Annie turned around. She gave him the address of Miss Davies and asked him to collect the machine. William wanted to go with him. Uncle Will was quite willing, so off they went with William sitting on the cart.

An hour later Miss Davies was sat at her machine and going great guns. She had taken William's measurements, gone down to the Emporium, back at the table, cut out the garments and was merrily sewing when Annie went to give more instructions. She didn't stop sewing until Annie took some food for her. She was reluctant to stop and eat it but Annie insisted, or she said she would be ill and she wouldn't be able to do anything.

She stopped and took her food. She had tacked the jacket, fitted it on William and now was sewing it on the machine.

Annie went upstairs to see if she wanted anything but she said that she was finished. She was just putting the finishing touches to it. The jacket was now complete apart from putting on the buttons and doing the buttonholes. This had all taken Miss Davies just three hours.

Now for the trousers. She went downstairs to see where William was. One of the girls said that he was playing out the back. Miss Davies went to fetch him. He came straightaway, went up the stairs and stood straight and quietly to be measured again.

"He was as good as gold," Miss Davies later told Annie. "I shall stay now until the suit is finished. Obviously I will put the buttons on and do the buttonholes when I am home. There will be no more measuring."

"Now before we go any further Miss Davies, you must not kill yourself. Is that clear?"

Miss Davies looked up and tried to protest but Annie stopped her.

Miss Davies stayed upstairs for another hour, made her way downstairs to the Tearooms and explained to Annie that she was going home, taking the suit with her to finish it off properly.

"If that is what you want, you must do it your way."

"It is," Miss Davies said, "then if you have time tomorrow we will go and shop for the material for your gown. Will that be alright for you?"

"Certainly," Annie said.

Annie couldn't get over the quickness of this woman. She remembered an old lady doing dressmaking when she was a little girl. She used to take ages to do things but this woman was definitely a find.

David came to see her after she closed. He hadn't been home; he had come straight from the office. They had a meal together about 8 o'clock. William had eaten earlier and now was in bed, tired out after his long day of playing in the garden. "He was no trouble at all, bless him," Annie thought as David and her were eating.

In the Arms of Merlin

David wasn't willing that Annie was making a meal for him after she had been working all day.

"Don't be silly," Annie said, "how are you going to eat after we are married?"

David was taken aback at her remark, "what do you mean Nan?" he asked.

"Aren't I going to cook for you after we get married?"

"Certainly not," he said, "I have got two cooks, one butler, three chamber maids and God knows how many maids down below stairs. No certainly not, you are not going to cook for me or anyone else."

They hadn't talked beyond the wedding day, the night he asked her to marry him. Annie was under the impression that he would come to live here at the Tivoli but that was the furthest thing from his mind.

William and Nan were coming to Plas yr Arad to live, to his home.

After Annie had heard all this, she told him that she thought Plas yr Arad was his mother's home and that he was going to move in with them at the Tivoli.

"Do you remember a while ago I told you that you must delegate? Well that is what I had in mind. You won't be working here after we are married. I really don't understand what made you think that you would be staying here."

Annie understood what he meant but really wasn't very happy about it.

"We should have talked more than we did Nan. I don't want you to have to slave from six in the morning till late at night. You might have had to do it when you started the Tearooms but now you are going to be my wife and I intend to look after you and William for the rest of your lives, or should I say, the rest of my life."

"Oh David," Annie said, "I know you mean well but I have only just got used to having a business of my own. I think I have run it well too, don't you?"

"Yes," he said, "you have, but that doesn't mean that I want you to come all this way every morning by six o'clock. You will have to get up at four every morning and Annie, that will never do. Please think hard about. Do you still want to marry me Nan? Please don't say no, it will break my heart if you do."

Nan said; "I'm sorry, I wasn't thinking clearly when I mentioned the Tivoli after we were married. I have got an idea forming in my mind."

You are still going to marry me aren't you Nan?"

Annie nodded and said "yes."

David was so relieved that a great big sigh came from his boots. "You didn't realise that my mother lives in London most of the time. She comes down here when she's had enough of the high life. Letitia and John have been brought up with me. Their father was my father's best friend. He was killed in my father's mine; my father took the children in because they had lost their mother in a hunting accident. We have been brought up as brothers and sister.

When John gets married he will leave for a place of his own, so will Letty. They have an inheritance after their parents, so they are pretty well off.

My Mother will be in London for Christmas. John and Letty will be with an aunt and cousin who live in the South of France.

We will be having our first Christmas on our own. What do you think of that?"

Annie was quite pleased with what David had told her. All of a sudden she wondered why she wanted to work instead of looking after her darlings, David and William, the two people that she loved most in the entire world.

After David had gone, Annie started to think more about the idea that had started forming in her mind. She could put Esther in complete charge, let her live on the premises and give her a percentage of the takings. She would confer with David tomorrow.

Annie had a word with Esther when she arrived the following morning. Esther was quite thrilled to hear Annie's proposal but suddenly thought about her father. She would have to leave him to live alone.

Annie hadn't thought of Esther's dad. "Perhaps he would come to live here as well," Annie said, "it is far more comfy here than in your house. No disrespect now Esther," Annie said. "It is a much warmer place and your father could use the shop as a lock up shop and rent the upstairs. That's a good idea isn't it? I will come to see him this evening if you like, perhaps David might even come with me."

They didn't talk anymore on the subject, just got on with their work.

Annie had to go out with Miss Davies to choose the material for her wedding gown so she thought that she had to work a little extra today.

Miss Davies had brought William's suit back this morning. It was absolutely delightful; it fitted him to a tee. What a wonderful woman. Her talents were certainly wasted here. Perhaps Lady Elizabeth would do some good for her when she made her clothes for the wedding.

Annie made dinner for William but took none herself. She wanted to slip down to the Emporium to get a few things for William. He would be going to school next Monday, so by going today for half an hour, she would have a little more time to choose her material.

Esther closed the shop, brought the takings upstairs to Annie. While they were talking, David came up.

Esther went home as soon as David arrived. Annie made some food, then they talked about the shop, Esther, her father and the living quarters.

David thought it was a good idea.

"Now," Annie said, "we have got to impress Mr Evans."

It was still quite early, so they took William with them, because he couldn't be left on his own.

By the time they arrived as Esther's they had eaten and were just having a cup of tea. Esther got up immediately to get them some tea but both refused, as they had already had one, so the talks started in earnest.

Mr Evans wasn't too keen in the first instance but as David talked about the pluses, Annie thought that he would come round to their way of thinking.

By the time they left, all had been arranged.

Annie would be getting married from the Tivoli. They would stay overnight at Plas yr Arad. Letty would look after William and Lady Elizabeth would drive up to London with Annie and David, to save two carriages, then the bride and groom would drive to Dover, take the boat across the channel, then on to the South of France. David had a villa just outside Nice.

After the wedding Esther and Mr Evans could take their time and move over to the Tivoli.

It happened to be very busy when Miss Davies came to call for Annie. She had to wait a while until things got quieter. Annie called her into the kitchen and told her to help herself to whatever she wanted.

She landed up with a glass of cordial and sat quietly in one of the corners of the shop, like a little mouse.

Things got a little quieter. Everything was under control, so Annie flitted off to get it over with.

She felt really guilty about leaving the girls on their own while she went swanning about the place. It was a good job that David couldn't hear her thoughts, or he would not be too pleased.

Annie put her coat on and went to get something to put on her head, flew back down the stairs, dropped William in the back garden, gave him a quick kiss and went to get Miss Davies and off they went.

The Emporium was very busy too. The elite of the town were there.

Annie didn't know half of them but they all knew who she was and they knew all about her. Annie could see them all wish-washing and giving her sly glances but she didn't care. She just went on with her own business.

As they got to the counter, Annie thought, I bet I could buy and sell the lot of them. Half of them were, as they say in Wales "shabby genteel".

The assistant, who had got to know Annie by now, came to tend them. Annie told her what they wanted. The young assistant was thrilled and gave them all her attention.

She must have brought every roll of material down on the counter to show them. They brought the choice down to three. The first one was a pure white heavy satin. The second choice was a pearl grey heavy satin and the third choice was a pale gold brocade.

Annie looked at Miss Davies and she looked at her. The assistant put the fabrics up over Annie's shoulder in turn to see which of the colours suited her.

Annie didn't say anything but the two ladies had made up their minds. The pale gold was the one for Annie. Annie had that colour in her mind also, so it must have been the right one for all three to think the same.

Miss Davies gave all the measurements.

They worked it out how much material they wanted and where to deliver it. That was another job done.

"Now," Miss Davies said, "we would like to see veils, head-dresses and slippers."

"Upstairs please and ask for Miss Walters, she will see to you. I will bring a pattern of the brocade for her to match everything for you."

"Thank you," Miss Davies said and off they went.

In the Arms of Merlin

Annie didn't think Miss Davies had it in her. Little did Annie know that Miss Davies had owned a high-class gown shop in London. As a matter of fact, she had been a very wealthy woman, had fallen in love with a man who gadded about with the rich set and met Miss Jane Davies.

She fell for him, hook, line and sinker. He turned out to be a cad and took her for every penny she had.

Her so called friends dropped her but one true friend took her in until she was able to scrape enough money together to get back home to Wales.

Jane Davies came back to Carmarthen a broken woman. Nobody in the town knew why she had come home. She just stayed in her mother's house, cleaning all day long, never going out anywhere.

Her mother didn't know how to handle the situation; so she just left her to do what she wanted. She was obsessed with just cleaning.

She was like that for a year, then her mother was taken ill and Jane had to nurse her for three months, then she died. Jane was very sad about the death of her mother. She was a very sprightly lady and not that old.

She mourned for four weeks, left the blinds in the front of the house down day and night. She didn't go out of the house for two of those weeks, until she was eating scraps covered with mould.

She ran upstairs sobbing, she had now come to the end of her tether. She just slumped on her bed and sobbed for hours. It was getting dark, she must have sobbed herself to sleep.

She turned over on her back, looked at the ceiling and tears started to roll down her cheeks again, when all of a sudden, she heard her mother saying, "Jane pull yourself together, or you are going to end up in the asylum."

Jane couldn't believe her ears. She sat up in bed and looked around the room. There was nothing to be seen. She

In the Arms of Merlin

got up and lit the lamp. As she passed the wardrobe, she saw her reflection in the long mirror and had such a shock when she saw herself. She had aged ten years. She had huge bags under her eyes and her whole face was swollen through crying.

"This will never do," she said to herself, "now you have got to pull yourself together, you are on your own now, so Jane just you go downstairs, have a good wash, get some clean clothes on and go next door to get some food in."

There was a little shop next door that sold everything. Mrs Edward, who owned it, had a bit of a shock when Jane walked in. She had been worried about her for weeks but didn't like to interfere. There was nobody in the shop as luck would have it.

Mrs Edward said, "well Jane fach, how are you? I have been thinking about you but I didn't like to call in case you would think that I was being nosy. You look awful. Come around to my kitchen and let me make you a cup of tea and something to eat. You look as if you haven't eaten for days."

"I don't know when I ate last Mrs Edwards," Jane said.

Mrs Edwards picked the top of the counter up and opened the door to let Jane in. There was a lovely fire in the grate; everything was looking nice, warm and homely, like her mother's kitchen used to look.

Jane started to cry again, Mrs Edwards put her arms around her and held her tight. "There, there," she said, "come on, you have had nobody to help you to grieve after your Mam and that is what the matter is with you."

Jane then told Mrs Edwards about her mother's voice coming to her.

"There you are, your Mam can't rest because you are worrying her. Now every morning you must come in here. We can have a little chat and you have got to get on with your life. You are a young woman with a living in your fingers, so get on with it."

In the Arms of Merlin

From that day onwards, Jane got on with her life. She put a notice in her window which said, 'Alterations, Dressmaking and Tailoring to order'.

That was a good few years ago. It was a miracle that her mother had come to her in her hour of need and Mrs Edwards had pushed her on some more to get her going.

Many a suitor called on her but she would have nothing to do with them, more's the pity. It was too late now.

Miss Walters took them to the counter and placed a few glass drawers in front of them. By now the assistant had come up with the roll of gold brocade, to match with the head-dress and veil. One was a coronet of gold leaves, another one with autumn flowers and another one was a tiara, gold coloured with a Celtic design with little diamond-like stones here and there.

Annie fell in love with it as soon as she saw it and asked Miss Davies if she thought that it would be fitting for her to wear a tiara. Miss Davies didn't think that there was any problem at all. They then chose a pale gold veil and slippers to match.

Miss Davies asked Annie if she was ready to go home but Annie wanted to buy some under garments for her honeymoon.

Miss Davies said, "if you don't mind I'll go downstairs to get the cotton and everything that I am going to need."

"All right," Annie said, "whatever you need, put it down on my bill and I will settle up when I leave."

"Good," Miss Davies said, "I can start this morning. I have got all your measurements so I will see you later."

"Thank you very much," Annie said, "tell the girls that I won't be long."

Annie went across to the lingerie counter, told the young lady what she wanted and they went from there. Annie was delighted with what she had bought, she had never owned such things before. She had bought a lovely slip to go to the Ball but she had excelled herself today. She felt like that cat who'd had the cream.

She went to the cash desk and paid for everything she had had in cash. She was given a very good discount and the manager was hovering around her and wished her and her husband all the job and good wishes for their future. He added that he hoped she would continue to buy at the Emporium after she got married.

"Thank you very much," Annie said, "I certainly will. Everyone has been good to me from the first time I ever bought here."

"That is very nice to know," the manager said.

Annie scuttled back to the shop. She drew her coat around her as it was getting quite cold. However, by the time she arrived at the Tearooms, she had warmed up and her cheeks were quite flushed.

She opened the door to a warm and friendly atmosphere. The girls were very busy so Annie went straight into the kitchen, took off her coat and went straight to work, talking about nothing, as no-one had time. "It will wait, I suppose," Annie thought.

Once Annie arrived, it seemed to ease a little. One extra pair of hands made all the difference. While Annie was serving and doing any other jobs that needed doing, she thought that she had better find someone sooner, rather than later, to take her place.

They all took it in turns to have a snack. At about five o'clock, things cooled down. By five thirty it was dead quite.

Annie said, "close the door Hannah, let us sit for a minute and have a chat."

Rose made a pot of tea and they all sat around the table.

The first thing on the agenda was to have someone to work here instead of Annie.

Jane said her cousin had just left school and was looking for a job.

In the Arms of Merlin

"That's another thing," Annie said, "William is starting Monday. Someone will have to take him until he gets used to going on his own. Where does your cousin live Jane?"

"Up the road from me, Miss," she said.

"Do you think she could start straightaway?" Annie asked.

"I don't see why not," Jane said, "her father hasn't long died and they need the money."

"Right," Annie said, "I can have her to work here on your recommendation."

"Yes Miss." Jane said.

"When you go home tonight, go and see her and ask her if she would like to work here. Tell her it is quite hard work but it isn't dirty work is it?"

"No Miss." Jane said.

"If she is interested, bring her with you in the morning and I can have a chat with her, see what she is like and what she can do."

The girls started to clean up, as the time was getting on.

Annie caught Esther by the arm and asked her if she had discussed her proposition of the other night.

"Yes," she said, "I am giving him another week if that is alright with you?"

"Yes, that's fine," Annie said, "I would hate for him to do something like this and not think deeply about it but I honestly think it is a marvellous idea for everybody all round."

Esther took Annie to one side and whispered in her ear, "I have been invited out tonight."

"Have you?" Annie said, "may I ask by whom?"

Esther blushed and said, "John Phillips."

Annie was delighted and put her two arms around Esther and said, "my two favourite people in the world and they are going to get together."

In the Arms of Merlin

"Annie," Esther said, "don't marry me off. This will be the first time I have gone out with him."

"Well, if he's wise, like I know he is, he will snap you up straightaway, then we will have to look for somebody else again to take your place."

By the time Annie had made a meal, eaten it and cleared up, it was eight o'clock. She then took William to bed. She kissed him goodnight, closed his door and came out to the living room.

There was a nice fire and the room looked lovely and cosy.

Annie sat down in an armchair and started thinking about all that was going to happen and had happened. She certainly had come a long way since those days in the Big House. It all seemed years ago but it was only nine years.

She realised that she had had to go all through that bad time to get where she was today and have what she had. She could never wish that it had never happened.

William was fast asleep when she peeped into his room a little later. She then decided to have a cup of tea.

While she was boiling the kettle, the front doorbell rang. She wondered who it could be, as it was getting late. She went to the parlour, opened the window and looked out and there was David.

He looked up and saw Annie, gave her a lovely smile and said, "good evening, may I call on you?"

Annie laughed, closed the window and ran down the stairs to open the door for David.

As soon as she opened the door he came inside, put his arms around her and showered her with kisses as if he hadn't seen her for months.

"David," said Annie, "hang on, let us get upstairs."

"But William will be there."

"No," Annie said, "he has long gone to bed."

In the Arms of Merlin

David gave a smile and chased Annie up the stairs two at a time.

"Careful now," she said, "or you will wake William up and you don't want that do you?"

"No my darling," he said, "I want you all to myself. As a matter of fact, I would love to stay the night with you and hold you in my arms all through the night."

Annie blushed a little and said, "David, you know that William is here and he has some idea what is what."

David went all quiet, "as a matter of fact," he said, "I was going to ask you if I could stay the night to save me going home? It is late and I have to go in early in the morning.

"You little devil David, why couldn't you have said that in the beginning?"

David smiled, "I just wanted to see the look on your face. It was a picture. I can see that I am going to have to wait for my bride until our wedding night."

Annie thought to herself, "why don't you come clean with him and tell him that you want to jump into bed with him and be in his arms forever?"

David was starving, so Annie made him a quick fry up. That was all she was able to do.

After he had eaten he said, "come and sit here by me and we can talk."

"I have got to make a bed up for you, it is getting quite late and if you have to be up early in the morning you had better go to bed."

David said, "I will help you with the bed."

"No, it's quite alright," Annie said, "I can manage."

David gave another smile and said, "I love to see the look on your face when I make suggestions to you. You are such a sweet innocent darling and I love you more than anything in this world."

Annie had no doubt about that. She let him help her make the bed up and in the middle of it, William came from his bedroom wondering what was going on.

"It's quite all right darling," Annie told him, "I am only making a bed up for David. He was late at the office and has to be there early in the morning for some meeting or other."

William rubbed his eyes and said, "all right, " said goodnight to them both and went back to bed.

Annie was convinced that he was sleep walking.

"Perhaps he was," David said.

At six o'clock Annie got up and started breakfast for David. Halfway through, she went into his room and gave him a little shake. He was awake when Annie came in but he waited for her to come to the bedside and while she was trying to wake him he caught hold of her and brought her down on the bed.

She had such a shock that she gave a little scream.

"Oh!" David thought, "I've gone too far this time, she will never forgive me for this," but instead of making a fuss she just lay there in his arms laughing. She didn't even move when William came in to see what was going on and in two shakes of a lamb's tail, William was joining them.

It was so natural and lovely and after the 21st December they would be a real family. That thought stayed with David all day.

Miss Davies was sewing all over the weekend. She was no problem; she just sat there sewing. Every now and then she would accept something to eat from Annie. Annie didn't know how she did it. She didn't stop.

Monday morning came. William was the first up. He had washed and dressed before Annie had come down to the kitchen.

He was so excited he wouldn't eat any breakfast. Annie was getting worried, he couldn't go until midday without any food. In the end she persuaded him to eat some bread, butter

In the Arms of Merlin

and jam. He drank a cup of milk which was better than nothing, his mother thought.

It was twenty to nine. Annie put her coat and hat on. They went downstairs and he said goodbye to all the girls. They all gave him a hug and a kiss before he went out through the front door and as he was going out of their sight, he was wiping all the kisses off, just like a little boy of his age would do.

It was very cold, there had been a hard frost the night before and everywhere was white. People were toing and froing, all going about their business.

Annie was quite tired, having to say "hello" and "good morning," to everyone who knew here. Even as they got by the Church, the vicar was coming out through the gate and a few words were passed to Annie and more so to William.

The vicar added as he was leaving them, "I may come to see you later William. The older children are having a religious exam this morning."

Annie was glad that she had bought an overcoat for William. It worried her to see the other little boys with just a scruffy shirt and an old coat, that a brother or even his father used to wear, but Annie could do nothing about it in any case and, "but for the grace of God, go I," she thought.

They eventually got to the school. They went through the main gates, down the playground and down to the infants' part.

Annie walked into the tiny cloakroom. It was full of children – what a noise! Miss Lewis came from somewhere and took them into the babies' classroom, out of the way of the other children, where they had a little chat.

Annie said that she or one of the girls in the Tearoom would come and fetch William to take him home to have his dinner.

In the Arms of Merlin

"Right," Miss Lewis said, "it is quite new to him, yet once he gets used to school and the way home, he can go home on his own."

"We'll see," Annie said, in a very protective sort of way.

William took his coat and cap off and they went back to the cloakroom. Miss Lewis showed William which way he was to put his coat and cap on the peg. It was peg number 6 and William was to remember that number and to use that peg every time.

William nodded, turned to his mother, waved his hand to her and went with his hand in Miss Lewis's hand.

Annie turned away, the tears were flowing down her cheeks. She could not help it, she knew that she had only known William for a short while, but the bond was there, no matter who his father had been, or the circumstances of his conception. He was hers until the day she died. Annie thought that the little boy thought the same about his mother too.

The tears were getting less as Annie made her way home to the Tivoli.

CHAPTER 15 - THE TAILORESS

She was now looking forward to her wedding day and her life with David, the only man she had any sort of relationship with. The minute she entered the front door of the shop she thought the world and his wife would use the Tearooms all day today.

As it got nearer to lunch-time, it started to ease off a little, so Annie made her mind up to get William herself. She told the girls, put her hat and coat on and ran upstairs for a scarf, as it looked much colder than this morning.

Off she went, all wrapped up. She landed at the school as the bell was ringing and made her way down to the cloakroom where William was waiting with his cap, coat and scarf on.

"Come on sweetheart," she said.

William felt a little uncomfortable as the other children were looking on.

Annie didn't realise this until she was outside the main gates and William told her about it. "Mam," he said, "if you do that to me again, I will have to come home on my own."

"What do you mean?" she asked him. After he told her she realised that she had made him feel a little foolish.

"All right," she said, "I promise that I won't do it again."

After the first week, he was coming home on his own but every trader in King Street was keeping an eye on him.

From the first day he started in school, William loved every minute and he caught up with the other class in a few weeks. He never looked back and was a very happy and loving child.

On the fifth day, Miss Davies finished Annie's wedding gown. It was absolutely gorgeous and it fitted Annie like a glove.

Miss Davies had completed all the finishing touches to it, she called Annie upstairs and asked her if she had a few minutes to spare?

Annie said, "yes, what is it Miss Davies?"

"Oh," she said, "I want you to try everything on before I put it all away."

"Miss Davies fach," Annie said, "I have been working since seven this morning, I need a good wash, my hair is terrible. Can we make it another time?"

"I'm sorry," Miss Davies said, "I didn't think, I just want to see you all dressed up in all the rig-out."

"Don't worry Miss Davies," Annie said, "we will work something out for tonight – that is if you will stay to dinner with William and I?"

"Oh, there's no need for that," she said, a little flustered.

Annie wouldn't take no for an answer. When she got downstairs, Esther asked her what was the matter?

Annie told her and thought that she had upset the little lady, so she had asked her to stay to dinner this evening, then after Annie had washed and changed, she could dress up in everything. "Do you think your father would mind if you had dinner with us as well?"

"Can't see any problem," Esther said, "as long as I go home and make something quick for him."

"All right," Annie said, "that will be fine."

Annie had prepared a meat pie the night before, so she only had to do some vegetables and put them on the stove while she had a good wash and changed her clothes.

Miss Davies had also slipped home to feed the cat and to let it out.

Esther had gone to see her father and they all got back the same time.

Everything was going to plan. They all sat down to a lovely dinner, didn't waste much time after they had finished

In the Arms of Merlin

eating. They took all the dishes into the kitchen and stacked them on the table.

"Don't forget," Miss Davies said, "I will help to wash the dishes as soon as I have seen that everything is all right, promise?" Annie said, as she went into her bedroom, got her lingerie from the drawer, stripped off, then put them on and called to Miss Davies and Esther in for her to get the dress on.

Esther passed remarks about her underclothes, complimented her really. Annie was pleased and smiled.

Miss Davies came with the dress. How she had managed it the whole time she had been making it, Annie would never know. Esther had to help her. It was so heavy to handle. She got a little worried but once it was on the weight was evenly distributed. It just fell over Annie's figure.

Esther held her breath for a few seconds. "It's beautiful Annie," she said, "I have never seen such a creation."

"Don't be silly girl," Miss Davies said.

While Miss Davies was hooking all the eyes in the back of the dress, Annie said, "you are quite right Esther, I haven't seen anything like it before myself."

Miss Davies was overcome, "I thought that I would never hear those compliments again," she said.

"My dear lady," Annie said, "you are wasted where you are. You wait until my future mother-in-law finds out what you can do, she will have you sewing for half the county.

"Oh dear," Miss Davies said.

The dress was hitched up, so Miss Davies had set the tiara onto the veil. All that was left was to put it on Annie's head and let the veil flow.

Esther said, "you look like a princess Annie."

"I feel like one," Annie said, "I never dreamed that I could ever look like this."

"Well," Miss Davies said, "you have got a good figure, lovely hair and a great face, so this dress just compliments you my dear, not the other way about, you understand?"

Annie thought, "this must be the biggest blush of my life."

Esther caught hold of her in her arms and gave her a great big hug and said, "Annie you are wonderful."

Annie was really looking forward to the wedding now. She still couldn't get over how she looked. She wished that her mother was here to see her but there we are, that could never be. Auntie May and Auntie Sal would be there for her though.

Every day that arrived was a day nearer to their wedding day.

Miss Davies had made Esther's dress and was half way making Letty's. This woman was certainly a find. There were quite a few dressmakers and many tailoresses in and out of town but this woman was a gem.

Annie was waiting for Lady Elizabeth to see what she could do for her.

After Letty's dress, there was only her future mother-in-law's.

"I don't think she will come here Miss Davies. If it came to the crunch, do you think you would go to Plas yr Arad?" Annie asked.

Miss Davies said, "I don't see why not but how would I get there and back?"

"Well," Annie said, "someone will have to fetch you and take you back, if that is what they want, they have to abide with you. You have been very fair with me and I expect that they will be fair with you. I hope so, but in any case we will worry about that when the time comes."

The time did come.

Annie got word to Lady Elizabeth, telling her about the situation. Word came back from Plas yr Arad, saying that if

Miss Davies wanted, she would be fetched in the morning and taken back every night. So that was that.

They were collecting her at eight o'clock and bringing her home when she wanted.

When Monday arrived, Miss Davies was waiting on the doorstep with all her paraphernalia ready for the off. Lady Elizabeth had already bought her material in London when she first heard about the wedding, so Miss Davies was picked up and made her way to Plas yr Arad.

When she arrived at the house they took her up to Lady Elizabeth's room. She was sitting in one of her armchairs in her negligee ready for Miss Davies to measure her.

The maid knocked the door and Lady Elizabeth said, "come in" and in Miss Davies went.

Miss Davies said, "good morning."

As Lady Elizabeth answered her, she stopped and said, "don't I know you?"

The question startled Miss Davies for a minute and she said, "I don't know my Lady, should you?"

"Well," Lady Elizabeth said, "did you used to do all my clothes for me when I lived in London? I would have known you anywhere."

Miss Davies put her glasses on and looked hard at the other woman, "yes indeed, I do know you."

Lady Elizabeth told Miss Davies that she had been looking for her for a long time and "here you are on my doorstep. I can't believe it. My friends and I really missed you. Where on earth did you get to?"

"That's a long story. I might get round to telling you one day."

"Before we start Jane, I must offer you a hot drink, it is quite nippy out there."

"Thank you," Jane said. The maid was summoned and they had a little chat with their drink.

In the Arms of Merlin

"It's no wonder that Nan is over the moon with what you have done for her, now I know why. You are the best tailoress and dressmaker that I have ever come across. You can be ready for all my friends to start coming back and forth to you again. I just can't believe it and you have been here all the time." Lady Elizabeth was really pleased that she had found Jane.

After all the measuring had been done, Lady Elizabeth took Jane downstairs to a room alongside the kitchen. The material was on the table. It was a heavy satin in rich burgundy. It was beautiful.

"Oh!" Jane said, "it is going to be a joy working for you again my Lady. You always chose such lovely colours and materials. After all that excitement, I must get started."

"Carry on my dear, when it is time for lunch, one of the maids will bring you to the dining room and we will eat together. Is that all right?"

"It's quite all right my Lady, I will have a snack in the kitchen."

"No indeed you won't," her Ladyship said, "I feel as if I have found a long lost friend, so no more talks of snacks. If you need me for anything, just ask one of the maids."

Jane just got on with her cutting, she certainly was a wizard with the scissors. She cut that satin as if it was butter. All was cut out in double quick time. She didn't have to have patterns to make anything, it just flowed from her head and down through her fingers. She certainly was good.

As she started the stitching, her mind went back to the good old days, when she was a top notch in London. She had all the rich set as clients and perhaps they would come to her again.

Jane was getting excited thinking about it. She would be able to make her way. Lately, she had been juggling to make enough just to live on. She had no luxuries at all.

Everything was hard going, she lived a very frugal existence. Jane hoped that things would change a little for the better.

At five minutes to one, the door opened and one of the maids entered the room. She said her Ladyship was waiting in the dining room and luncheon was being served now.

Jane dropped everything and made her way to the dining room.

The maid opened the door and ushered Jane in. Lady Elizabeth was already seated and said, "come on in my dear, it's just us two today."

When the maid got back into the kitchen, she asked the cook what was going on. She had never known a tradesperson to ever eat at the same table as her Ladyship. The cook didn't know all the details but thought it was something to do with London and left it at that and told the girl not to gossip about her employers.

Sal, as was the maid's name, went back and forth to the dining room and kept her ears open the whole time she was in the room, so she caught a few snippets, but couldn't make head nor tail of them. She supposed it would all come out one day.

As the days went by, Jane started opening up to Lady Elizabeth. She wasn't prying, just wanted to know how she disappeared without trace.

By the time she had finished the outfit, she had bared her soul to Lady Elizabeth and Sal the maid.

Lady Elizabeth was so upset to think that this poor woman was in London on her own and not a penny to her name. "Why ever didn't you think of getting in touch with me, or any of my friends? One of us would have helped you."

Jane said, "I could not go to my own friends, I was so ashamed that I had been taken in by that man. I must have been so soft. I cringe sometimes when I think how gullible and naïve I was. I don't think anyone would be able to do anything like that to me again, for one thing, I shall never let another man into my life again."

"You. Silly girl," her Ladyship said, "you are still quite young and there is someone good waiting out there for you."

Jane just tut tutted and tried to change the conversation.

Sal had nearly all the details of Miss Davies' life, she felt quite sorry for the woman. She had got to know her by now, while she was sewing. Sal would go in to have a chat with her, not for too long, not for her to get distracted.

Jane Davies had made a friend of Sal, who was a nosy parker really but now had formed a different opinion of Miss Davies. The lady that nobody knew about.

It was going to be the last day for Jane at Plas yr Arad, the outfit was nearly finished.

Lady Elizabeth was delighted and couldn't praise Jane enough. They had their last luncheon together, before Jane started to pack up her things. They talked for more than an hour after they had finished eating.

Jane had told Lady Elizabeth that about four of her friends had already left messages at her home and that she would be busy for quite a while.

"I am so glad for you my dear, things will start to look up for you now."

As the coachman came to the hall to tell the staff that he was there, Lady Elizabeth caught hold of her and kissed her on both cheeks and said, "see you at the wedding."

"Oh," said Jane, "but I haven't had an invitation."

"Well you have now."

Sal and the coachman carried Jane's stuff into the carriage. She thanked her hostess once more and got in. As they were moving off, Lady Elizabeth said, "you will be back before you know it, I will be wanting clothes to go on my holidays before long."

Jane smiled and raised her hand to give a final wave. She gave a sigh as they got onto the road from the drive. She had worked very hard but had enjoyed every minute of it and was looking forward to going over there again.

As the carriage stopped outside her house, about four people came out of the shop next door and just stood gawking at poor Jane but she didn't mind now. she seemed to have gained her confidence since being with Lady Elizabeth.

She opened the door and the coachman helped her inside with her things. She thanked him very much and closed the door behind her. She turned around and leaned against the door hugging herself and smiled.

There were two more messages waiting for Jane on the hall lino. She hastened quickly to read them and knew the two people who had sent them. She put everything away, put the kettle on and made herself a cup of tea, then she sat down and started answering the letters from Lady Elizabeth's friends.

The sooner the better she got on with the rest of her life. After she had finished her letter writing, she went down to the Post Office and posted them all at the same time. She then called in the shop with Mrs Edwards to give her all the news.

Mrs Edwards could already see the difference in Jane as soon as she came through the door. "Now tell me all about it," she said, "you really look as if you have got something good to tell me."

They went into the kitchen behind the shop and Jane had another cup of tea. Mrs Edwards had noticed these carriages stop outside Jane's house in the last few weeks but didn't realise what it was all about. She felt so glad for Jane, who was such a nice person. She had magic fingers that could be put to use again.

The following morning there were two very excited people in the Tearoom, one was Letty and the other was Lady Elizabeth. Not only was she happy with her outfit, but the thought that she would have Jane for the rest of her life to

In the Arms of Merlin

make her clothes. One of Lady Elizabeth's pleasures now was clothes, so she made the most of it.

She had decided to go to London for a few days and she could get a hat made to match her ensemble.

Annie gave a quite thanks. One would think that Lady Elizabeth was the bride. I suppose this was how she was and there wasn't anything anyone could do. Annie could put up with it all because she really was a lovely person.

Everything was going smoothly on the wedding front.

Annie had sent Auntie up to Miss Davies to measure for her outfit. But as you can guess, it wouldn't be anything like Lady Elizabeth's. I bet Miss Davies would run it up in a couple of days.

All the girls had new clothes for the wedding except Maggie. She was having a hard time money-wise, as she was catching up with debts she had before she started working and it was taking a long time but she was getting there quietly.

Maggie was the same size as Annie, so Annie did no more. She called Maggie out of the kitchen and asked her to come upstairs with her. Maggie couldn't make out what she wanted but followed her like a lamb.

Annie said, "go into the kitchen and make us a cup of tea, I want to have a word with you and I want to show you something."

Maggie went into the kitchen, the kettle was simmering on the hob. She fetched two cups, two saucers and two spoons and made a pot of tea. She let it steep and said, "it's ready now Miss.

By this time Annie had come into the kitchen and over her arm was the suit that she had bought to go to Plas yr Arad the first time to meet David's family, and the little pink tam to match.

Maggie's face was a picture.

"Would you wear this Maggie?" Annie asked.

"What do you mean Miss?" Maggie asked.

"Well" Annie said, "would you like to have this suit to wear for our wedding? Afterwards it would be yours."

Maggie was overwhelmed and started to cry.

"Why are you crying Maggie?" Annie asked, "have I upset you in any way?"

"No Miss" Maggie said, "you are more than kind to me. If it wasn't for you I would be dead."

"You must forget about that Maggie, that is in the past, you are alive and well. I have been thinking things over. I am going to send you down to the Lane Tearooms after I get married. Esther will be coming up here to take charge, then they will be one short in the Lane. You know what to do by now, don't you?" Annie asked.

"Yes Miss" she said, "I am good at washing dishes. I do them all clean."

"No, no" Annie said, "after the wedding you will be a waitress, with more money in your pay packet. How's that?"

Maggie was flabbergasted and didn't know what so say but in the end she realised that the only thing that she could say was "thank you."

Annie said "think nothing about it, you have worked hard for me since you started here, so this is your reward."

They finished their tea. Maggie insisted on washing up the dishes and down they went. On the way down she asked Annie if she could tell the girls?

Annie smiled and said "yes."

CHAPTER 16 – LOVE FINDS ITS WAY

It was quite hard for Annie to prepare for the wedding and Christmas. They would be living in Play r Arad by then and David had been talking about their honeymoon in the South of France. If the weather was as bad as it was now, how was it going to be by the 21st December?

Annie wasn't all that keen on going all that long way and leaving William for the first time since he had come to live with her. That wasn't the only reason, as David said, it could be disastrous if the weather changed for the worst by the time of the wedding, so the next time David and I will see each other, we will cancel and go over in the spring.

Everything will have settled down by then. Worst of all, it would be William's first Christmas with his mother and she wouldn't be with him, so that is the answer, we will go in the spring.

Annie couldn't wait for David to come that night. She had put William to bed and was sitting down for her first rest of the day. She was also going to discuss the possibility of her coming now and then to the Tivoli, just to keep her hand in, in case she was needed. She didn't know what he would have to say about that but there was no harm in asking.

David arrived, he had eaten, he had been working at home all day. He took her into his arms and kissed her deeply and thought to himself, "here I go again," drew away from her and said "how are you my darling, you look ravishing, poor Annie."

She thought it didn't take a lot to please him. She had had a good wash all over and changed to a clean skirt, blouse and cardigan and given her hair a good brushing.

He also passed a remark about her hair, saying how it looked good. "You will have to please me one day after we get married. I would love you to wear your hair down, I bet you look stunning with it loose."

Annie paused and stammered a little.

He wondered what he had said and asked "what is it Nan?"

"Oh!" she said, "it is something I should have told you, I can't wear my hair down, not in public at least. I had an accident while I was in gaol."

"For goodness sake Nan, tell me, was it something terrible?"

"Well at the time I thought it was, but now I don't feel so bad about it."

"For heaven's sake," David said, "what is it?"

"One day while I was in gaol, I was working in the wash-house, doing my chores as usual, when one of the inmates attacked me. She had been after me for ages but I wouldn't take any notice of her. I tried to keep a low profile but it didn't work out that way. She had me in the end, so now I will tell you what happened. After baiting me for weeks, she had me down on the floor. Somehow she had a homemade knife or blade, caught hold of a handful of my hair and cut it off, together with a part of my scalp. That is why I don't wear my hair down.

The woman who did it was in solitary a few times on my account. The other times weren't too bad but this episode was more dangerous than the others were. She nearly killed me. I was very ill for a while, I thought it was going to be the end of me."

"Oh my darling," David said, "I can't bear to think of it. You will have to show it to me one of these days. I need to still keep my thoughts in anger for that monster that did this to you. I mean my sister's husband, if he hadn't attacked you in the first place, you wouldn't have been in gaol would you?"

"No" Nan said, "while I was in the sick ward in gaol I thought that I would like to be a nurse. That is why I went to work at the Infirmary scrubbing. I thought that if I was already there, it would be easier for them to accept me. It didn't work out like that though. Dr Morris, who I got to know while I worked in the sick ward in the gaol, tried his best but because I had been an inmate they just couldn't, so from then on, you know all about me. It was you who got me going onto the Tearooms. So as far as I am concerned, my fate was planned the minute I was born. I will have to put all the bad things behind me and just think of the good that has come from it all."

When Annie got up the following morning, everything seemed so bright. Annie couldn't make out why the sun was shining so early in the morning, but when she got to the window, she saw it had been snowing through the night. This was quite a surprise and Annie thought that it must have caught a few people off their guard, because the old folks have an idea when snow is on the way, with all their different signs.

Even Uncle, who has got his own theories, hadn't mentioned anything about snow. I suppose there has got to be a first time.

Her first stop was to call William. There were only a few more days before school was breaking up. He was thrilled to bits when he saw the thickness of the snow and would have gone out straight from his bed if his mother had let him. Typical boy, but Annie made him eat some hot oats, some toasted bread and he had hot milk. He protested nearly all through the breakfast but Annie wouldn't have any of it. "From now, until you want, you can play in the snow. You go to school, then you will be able to play with the snow again when you are in the playground, so does that make you happy? Oh! I forgot, you will have time to play with it this evening before it becomes dark. Right now?"

In the Arms of Merlin

William nodded, but he was straining at the leash.

It was very quiet all the morning so Annie thought that she would go upstairs to do a few little jobs that had been waiting for her to do for ages. She went into the wardrobe to look at her clothes. She had quite a few things hanging up now. Not a lot but far more than she had ever had. She realised that she would have to get some sort of container to take them over to Plas yr Arad before the wedding. Perhaps she could have some tea chests from the grocer's down the road.

She would have a word with David when he came tonight, unless he wouldn't be able to get through the snow. "We'll wait and see," Annie thought. By lunchtime she had done a few things that needed her attention. She had also put some meat on the hob to boil to make some cawl. Nothing like it on a day like this. If David did come into work and called tonight, he could have some too.

Annie thought for a minute, "I wonder if he has ever tasted cawl," she didn't think that the upper crust ate anything like that. She would find out tonight if he came.

Annie put her white apron on and made her way downstairs. There were three people having tea. She just walked past them, asked if everything was all right and passed a remark about the weather. She looked out of the window and the sun was shining and the snow was thawing.

"Thank goodness" Annie thought to herself but she didn't let on to anyone else.

By the time William came home from school, every bit of snow had gone. The temperature must have gone up during the day and saved the situation. As pretty as it was, Annie didn't want any snow at all until after the wedding, because it does make things harder and she needed some plain sailing for once in her life.

William was very disappointed when he arrived home, but the girls cheered him up by saying it would snow again in the next week or so. He was a little boy who took disappointments in his stride. His little life had been full of them, so thawing snow wasn't the end of the world, especially as he knew that it would snow again next week, because he believed anything the girls told him. He thought the world of them.

As they were locking the front door, Jack was standing on the doorstep waiting to come in. He was his usual cheery self, he didn't realise that he would be in town today until first thing. It was then that he received a note from David, to hire him and his transport, to move some timber. There wasn't enough time to let Auntie know for her to be able to come with him. "Doesn't matter," he said, "she can come up with me next time."

Annie would have liked to see Auntie May before the wedding, to see if she needed anything, or help to get something for the wedding. Perhaps if the weather kept as it was, David would let her use the carriage to go down to see her. School was breaking up at the end of the week, so perhaps William and she could go down for the day.

She went to get a pen and paper and wrote it down, for her to remember to ask David tonight. "Oh yes," she thought, "the containers for our clothes and what about the Christmas arrangements?" She must also get a list from William to see what he wanted from Santa Claus. Everything had all to be seen to and he time was flying by.

She let the girls get on with their work, she took Jack upstairs, the place smelled with the aroma of cawl.

Jack said, "what's cooking Annie, is it cawl?"

"Yes," Annie said, "how did you guess?"

"The smell still hangs around in my nose from the good old days when my mother used to make it. It never seems to go away, the same as the memory of my mother."

"God Bless her Jack" Annie said, "it is definitely time for you to find a wife."

Jack smiled at Annie and said "I know who I would like but I am afraid to ask her in case she won't like me."

Annie said "who is she? Do I know her?"

"I am not saying any more," Jack said, "but I hope to pluck up the courage to ask her one day."

Annie giggled and said "perhaps you can ask her at the wedding?"

Jack blushed just like a girl and was really embarrassed by Annie's comments.

"We'll see," he said, as he helped Annie to lay the table.

Annie went to call William, who had gone out the back to play with something or other. As she was coming upstairs, David was knocking on the front door.

It made a lovely change for Annie to have two guests for dinner. They all sat down to eat after Annie had explained about the cawl.

"Oh, it's all right, we get this at home. It is a first course with us. Our cook is an excellent cook too you know," he told Annie.

David was enjoying the soup but hadn't had the rest of the meal before. After you drank the liquor, with bread if you wanted it, you then ate the vegetables and the dumplings with the meat. That was your second course.

David had never had it like that before and he enjoyed it as well.

Annie cleared the plates then fetched out a large tin of steaming hot rice pudding. It smelled delicious. "You didn't guess that, did you Jack?"

"No," he said, "we didn't have many afters, just lucky to have the meal and we were happy."

Afterwards Annie thought, it was only since she had been at the Tivoli that she had had rice puddings. It was the same for William. He was eating many a thing that he had never eaten before, or even seen before, but things were going to be good from now on for Master William Owens.

Annie thought for a minute, "should she change his name to Jones after the wedding, for them all to be of the same name?" Another thing to put on the list.

When William had gone to bed they all sat around the fire and had a great time chatting. It was funny really. Jack knew the first part of Annie's life and David knew the second part of her life.

Jack retired to bed later. David just sat on the sofa. He had his arm around her shoulders cursing himself for thinking that he would frighten her if he went a little too far.

"Never mind," he thought, "there would be plenty of time very soon."

David got up and started to make his way to the door to get his coat, when Annie caught hold of his arm and kissed him in a way she had never kissed anyone before, not that she was experienced in that art, but she took David by surprise and it made him feel even worse.

He would have to go, or he wouldn't be responsible for himself.

David wasn't usually like this but he loved this girl with all his heart and he wanted her more than anything in this world.

Annie was still kissing him and making matters worse, until in the end Annie said, "David, you are making me say this and I feel terrible but I know that you want me and I certainly want you, so please don't think that I am a hussy, because I am not, but I can't wait for you to take me."

David couldn't believe his ears, "you don't know how long I have wanted this but was afraid to upset you, after y our experience."

"Oh darling! How could you compare that with the love we have for each other? I always try to put that at the back of my mind. You are talking about a different thing, that was lust. One good thing came out of it, that is the only consolation I have. So please darling, stay with me tonight and let us be one?"

David didn't have to be persuaded too much. He blew out the lamps, took her hand and by the time they reached the bedroom they were both shaking.

Everything was in pitch darkness. They didn't bother with any more lights. By the time they had reached the bed, they had taken most of each other's clothes off.

One or two last steps and they just fell on the bed. They started to laugh. Annie thought to herself, "this is how it should be." He was kissing her with such passion now that she didn't know what she was doing. She just couldn't get all her clothes off, so she stopped in her tracks.

David wondered what was the matter.

She said, "David, this is ridiculous, I am going to stand up to get undressed properly or it is going to spoil our first time together."

David thought to himself, "what a girl. I am so glad that I have found this woman to be my wife, she is a child in a woman's body."

Even though there wasn't any light, David could see her silhouette and she looked perfect to him.

Once Annie got settled, she went to lie next to David and her whole mind was in turmoil. She couldn't believe that making love was going to be like this. One minute she felt that she was on the ceiling looking down, the next minute she was inside him and looking through his eyes at herself.

They rolled all over the bed, every inch of it. She could hear him telling her over and over that he loved her.

Annie thought that it was the first time that she had ever told him that she loved him too.

They just lay next to each other. They were exhausted.

In the Arms of Merlin

Annie thought that they had only been in bed for a short while but when David looked at his watch, they had been there nearly four hours.

Annie couldn't believe it and kept saying about it.

David was quite amused and gave a little smile, kissed her and said "darling, time just flies by when you are enjoying yourself."

They both started laughing in each other's arms and hugged each other.

While they were lying there together in the darkness, David decided to make his way home. He didn't have to come into the office in the morning, but had quite a lot of work to do at home.

He got dressed, told her not to get up, gave her a long lingering kiss, he didn't want to leave her for one minute but thought better of it.

He said "so long" and went down the stairs and out through the front door.

CHAPTER 17 – GRANDMAMA

His horse was tethered in the stable in the Alehouse down the road. He had made arrangements with the Landlord to use the stable anytime he wanted. The yard was all open, so he didn't have to call anyone. That was a blessing, especially at this time in the morning.

David arrived at the yard of the Alehouse, got into the stable, untied the horse and walked him out to the yard. He jumped on and walked him carefully. It was freezing hard. He rose his collar and drew his coat around him tighter.

By the time he had started riding he was getting his heat and it was quite enjoyable now. David had always loved riding, it wasn't only as a mode of transport but to him it was a pleasure.

The first thing he was going to do after they got married was to get a horse for Nan and a pony for William. Thinking about it, he could start that plan of action tomorrow, or he should say today.

He arrived home twenty minutes later, things and people were starting to move in the household. He went into the hall and took the stairs two at a time, arrived in his bedroom, stripped off and just slid into bed. He thought "I am whacked but I will have a few hours."

As he lay there, his thoughts wandered to the night before and knew that he loved Nan with all his heart and was looking forward to the time when they would be together for always.

He dropped off to sleep with Nan in his thoughts and it seemed only a couple of minutes later that his mother was in the doorway calling him. She thought that he had overslept.

She apologised for disturbing him but didn't realise that he didn't have to go in this morning.

In the Arms of Merlin

David was glad in a way that she had called him, as there were quite a few things to be done before the wedding next week.

After he had eaten breakfast he asked Letty if she would like to come for a ride with him.

She said, "yes, I would love to," so they went to the stables and took off. As they were riding, he told Letty why he had asked her to come with him, "I am going to get a horse for Nan and as you are about the same height, I thought it would be surprise for her."

"Oh," Letty said, "she is going to be delighted, that's one of the things she has been looking forward to. It will be quite easy to choose a pony for William."

"Yes," David said, "we will ride cross county to Davies the Hafod, he breeds good horses." So off they cantered.

It was a bright and crisp morning and Letty was as good a horsewoman as David was a horseman. He enjoyed riding with her, he would have to have patience with Nan, he didn't think that she had ever ridden, so he would have to start from scratch with the both of them. David was looking forward to fun and games.

Today she was riding side-saddle and took every fence and hedge as good as David. He was delighted when he rode with Letty and hoped that Nan would be half as good as her.

They reached the farmyard, dismounted and Mr Davies appeared.

David hadn't spoken to him about buying any livestock, so the farmer had a little surprise to have David Jones coming to him to buy two horses. Well one horse and one pony. It didn't make any difference, it just meant money for Davies the Hafod. It took about two hours to choose, ride and pay for the deal. David was very pleased, so was Mr Davies.

They made arrangements to deliver the animals to Plas yr Arad in the morning around eleven o'clock. David thought he would have time to go to the saddlers to get a saddle and bridle for each of them.

School had broken up for the Christmas holidays. William would be home tomorrow, David thought he would go straight up to the Tivoli to see if they both could come over to Plas y Arad, to see what he had bought them.

David couldn't contain himself, he just wanted to see their faces when he brought the two animals out.

Nan's was a grey mare and William's was a little chestnut pony. The only thing was, he would have to hide the saddles and bridles somewhere on the way home, or better still, he would ask John to send them back to the Plas with one of the workers, then they would be saddled ready for action. That's a much better idea, David thought to himself.

David got up at the usual time next morning and had a good breakfast, chatted with his mother and Letty.

John had left earlier.

Letty was full of excitement, thinking about the look that would be on their faces. She even offered to ride to the saddlers herself, to get the saddles and bridles, bring them back and saddle them up by the time they got back. David thought that was the best idea yet, so that is what happened.

Annie was taken by surprise when David requested their presence at the Plas this very morning. It was rather busy in the Tearoom, so Annie compromised with David, if he waited until after lunch they could come.

William just wanted to go straight away, but Annie had to be sensible. David cooled his heels for another hour.

When the time came for them to leave, all were agog with speculation. They were trying to guess what he had for them. They had no idea, which made it better. David thought he wished that he could have done a 'Ben Hurr', but had to control himself.

They arrived eventually. Lady Elizabeth was waiting on the steps. She kissed Nan and then kissed William.

She ushered them into the drawing room, where there was a huge fire in the large grate. "Take your coats off," she said "and have a warm."

"No," David said, "don't take your coats off, I need you both outside."

Lady Elizabeth said, "oh come on then you two, we won't have any peace until you have gone outside."

David had been impossible since yesterday, gave a smile, rang for the butler and asked him to get his mother a coat.

They all made their way outside.

Letty had saddled the two animals and was holding the grey mare, while one of the grooms was holding William's pony.

As they turned the corner, the boy gave such a squeal, he even frightened David. He ran ahead of the others and by the time they got to where the animals were, the pony was already nuzzling William's head and face.

Nan was really shocked, she didn't have a clue but was delighted with David's presents.

William was over the moon, that's all he wanted to know was, when would he be able to ride him?

"Him!" said David, "haven't you got a name for him yet?"

William thought for a few seconds and said, "I know what I want to call my pony."

"Yes?" David said.

William turned to the pony, put his hands over her ears and said, "hello Meg." He turned back to David, "that all right?"

David said, "it couldn't be better, what about your mother's horse?"

William said, "I am to name hers too?"

"Yes, if you will," Nan said.

William thought for a minute. "Right Mama, what do you think of Silver?"

"Great," Annie said, "the name is perfect my darling."

William was really pleased with himself.

After Letty had given William a few lessons and Nan had held the mare's head, patted her and talked to her, they all went back to the house. It was absolutely freezing by the time they got back into the drawing room.

The butler and a maid were serving tea, William was far too excited to think of eating. Annie knew that he was suffering, sitting down having tea with a lot of grown-ups and his beautiful pony Meg was in the stables waiting for him to come and walk her around and help to groom her.

"Don't worry William, you have got all the time in the world to be with Meg. Perhaps Lady Elizabeth will allow you to come over tomorrow, if I can get someone to bring you here."

"Don't be silly Nan," she said, "why not let the child stay here for the night, he can be with Letty and the pony all afternoon and first thing in the morning."

Nan looked at William to see what his reaction was. She could see that he was delighted. A part of it was the fact that he loved Letty and she had to be with him, to start to teach him to ride his darling Meg.

Nan thanked Lady Elizabeth for having William to stay.

"It's no problem," she said, "it will be nice to have young children around the place again. You must think, it will only be a week and he will be living here the whole time. He might as well get used to it now.

It was the first time really that William realised that he would be living here so soon. Time to an eight year old doesn't impress them at all. This place would be his home forever.

He was delighted, he loved Letty to pieces. He also thought the world of David's Mama and John, but William's favourite was Blod the cook. If William would ask her, "can I have a ton of sweets?" she would give them to him without a second thought.

Ever since he could remember, had had always been friendly with cooks in general. He seemed to be drawn to them, whether it was they had homely figures or it was the thought of the food, he had never thought about it until now. Since thinking about it, he reckoned that Blod was the all-time favourite, she certainly could cook. She had given him things that he had never seen or heard of before and he hadn't turned his nose up at anything up to now. He certainly had an aristocrat's taste buds.

After tea was over, David took Nan home. The Tivoli was closed, so they made their way upstairs to the living quarters. Nan prepared a pot of tea with a tot of brandy in it.

They were frozen to the marrow after that journey home. It was lucky that William had stayed, he would be in the warmth of the Plas.

Little did Annie know that he had persuaded Lady Elizabeth to allow him to go back to the stable to see his precious Meg and there he stayed until Letty went to get him for them to eat dinner.

She took him upstairs to have a wash. He didn't have a change of clothes so they had to put up with stable smell. Nobody passed any comments.

William was very talkative at the table. Lady Elizabeth didn't have the heart to tell him that it wasn't done but there was plenty of time to each him the dos and don'ts of etiquette.

She had really got to know the little boy in the last few weeks and she had got very fond of him.

He always struggled to call her by her title and Elizabeth felt sorry for him at times, so this evening at the dinner table she looked at John and Letty, then at the boy and said "William, how would you like to call me Grandmamma?"

William couldn't believe what he had heard. "You mean that you are now my Grandmamma!"

"Yes" she said. "Next week your mother will be married to my son, so that makes you my grandson. Do you like that idea?"

William thought for a few minutes and said, "I am one of the luckiest boys in the world. It wasn't long ago that I was all alone and now I have got a mother, a father, a grandmamma and lots of uncles and aunts I have the most beautiful pony in the world and I am going to live in the country. I have never been so happy."

"I hope it always stays like that for you son" John said, "we will try to see to that for you."

They sat around the fire for a while. Letty was playing some board game or other with William. David was reading and Lady Elizabeth was having a little snooze. Everything in the garden was lovely.

It must have been nine o'clock. William was starting to yawn. Letty didn't think about the time. William was way over his bedtime.

John looked at the clock and said, "don't you think it's time you went to bed?"

William rubbed his eyes and had to give in, so Letty got up and said, "I'll take him Auntie."

"All right" they both said, they could see the delight in Letty's eyes.

He got up off the floor, went over to his Grandmother, kissed her and gave her a hug and thanked her for letting him be her grandson.

She was choked and said "get on with you boy" and ruffled his blond curls and nudged him over to John.

In the Arms of Merlin

He wasn't sure about John, was he to kiss him or just shake hands with him? John made up his mind for him and caught hold of him and gave a huge hug and a quick kiss on his forehead. David said to William, "that is not too sissy, all right?"

William smiled back at both of them, then he took Letty's hand and skipped off out to the hall and out of sight.

Lady Elizabeth was slightly overcome with the events of the evening. It had been very difficult for her to come to terms regarding Nan and her offspring, because they were both connected to her beloved daughter, Barbara. It was lucky that Nan and the child were loving and caring. No-one would have guessed what trauma they both had been through. It was hard to realise that William was that monster's son, he must have taken after his mother. She could not have picked a better girl for her only adorable son and she knew that they would be happy.

William was the grandson that she should have had when her daughter was married to Ernest; he had been quite nice when she met him. What happened, she didn't know. Whether it was because her daughter wasn't too strong and he couldn't cope with it, but on the other hand, he should have loved her more because she wasn't well, but everyone is not the same.

John brought her back from her reverie and said "what is it Auntie? Is there anything wrong?"

"No my dear, I am thinking what that child said and how lucky I am to have him around us and wouldn't George have loved to be his Grandpapa, but there we are, there is nothing we can do about that."

At six o'clock sharp, William was up and dressed. He went down to the kitchen to see his friend, she was delighted to see him and asked him what he wanted for breakfast.

He said "can I have bread and jam?"

In the Arms of Merlin

"Of course you can, my handsome boy," she said and off she went to get it for him and a big glass of milk, which had just been brought in from the dairy.

"Now this is what I call a breakfast. Mama makes me eat oats and I don't like them that much but I try not to upset Mama. I really struggle every morning. Do you think she would mind if I told her one day? I don't want to upset her."

"Now look here," Blod said, "if you want, I will tell your Mam for you. I don't think that she will hold it against you if you are not keen on hot oats" and she gave a hearty laugh and sat opposite William while he ate her homemade bread, butter and jam.

After had had two rounds of the stuff and finished his milk, he wiped his face with his napkin and thanked Blod very much. He asked to be excused, left the table and went to the cloakroom to get his coat and cap.

He ran through the kitchen door and around to the stables, to his beloved Meg and there he stayed until lunchtime.

They all knew where he was. As soon as lunch was over, he was out again, but Letty went with him to start him riding properly.

Letty was quite pleased with William's progress. He was a very alert child and listened to all that Letty had to tell him.

That was the main thing in learning to do anything.

At 6 o'clock, David came to get William to take him home. He didn't make a fuss but David could see that he was loath to leave his new found friend, Meg. That was certainly a partnership for life.

Grandmamma had told him at the lunch table, that she would take him to town one day this week for an extra Christmas present. He had to be dressed properly to ride his pony. William just couldn't wait but would have to.

On the way home, David told William that his mother would call at the Tivoli to take him shopping the following day.

"I can't wait to tell mam," he said, "she will be willing won't she?"

"Of course she will. I think she will be glad. She has lots of things to do before the wedding and they are very busy in the shop."

William was quiet during the rest of the journey.

They got home just as the girls were leaving to go to their homes. They all made a big fuss of the little boy and said that they had missed him. He lapped it all up.

He went upstairs and gave his mother a big hug and kissed her a couple of times.

"What is it?" she asked, "You have only been away for one day and night, didn't you enjoy yourself?"

"Yes, I enjoyed myself but I did miss you," then everything just poured out about the pony, the riding lessons and Grandmamma taking him shopping the following Monday to get his riding clothes.

Nan looked at David and said "I think someone is going to get a little spoilt."

David said, "I don't think that spoilt is the correct word in this situation. He is my mother's first grandchild and apart from that fact, he has to have clothes to ride his pony. Let my mother indulge, it doesn't harm anyone does it?"

Nan said "I didn't mean anything by it. I am pleased that your mother and William are going shopping. I haven't got time. It is so busy downstairs, that I really think that I will have to get another girl in to cope with everything. I am so glad that we aren't going away after the wedding. I don't think that I'd be able to get round to it."

"You would if you had to darling. I have told you before; you must not try to do everything yourself. You have got to delegate, just remember that."

In the Arms of Merlin

Nan sighed and said; "I will learn one day. What about food?"

"Don't worry about it. Go and get yourself ready. I will see to William. Just show me where everything is and we shall have a little treat. You will not cook tonight and after the wedding your cooking days are over and so are your running about carting trays of tea and cakes.

An hour later they were on their way to a little Inn just outside town. It was bitterly cold, so they huddled up on the seat of the trap.

David could see that things were getting on top of Nan. This was the only thing he thought that he could do to help the situation. David had no idea how to cook, so this was the next best thing.

They got to the Inn. David said "you two go inside while I tether the horse."

In they went. The bar room was empty, the Landlord was sitting in front of a roaring fire having a puff on his pipe. He was surprised to see a lovely young woman and a little boy walk through his door on such a cold night.

He got up immediately and ushered them to the fireside. "Good evening," he said, "how can I help you?"

Before Nan could answer, David arrived at the door, "oh Mr Jones" he said, "come on in, now I realise who I have got here. What can I do for you Sir?" the Landlord said.

David said "we are looking for some of your excellent food."

"Well," the landlord said, "you have come to the right place, I shall be back in a minute."

They were all standing in front of the fire, absolutely frozen.

David said "I think I made a big mistake in bringing you out this way in this weather."

"No you haven't darling" Nan said, "everything will be great now."

David looked at William, "are you all right son?"

William said, "yes Dada, isn't this great fun."

David relaxed a bit after they had both said their pieces.

The Landlord arrived back with his wife in tow. She had a chat with Nan. She recognised her from the Tivoli. She explained to Nan and David that there wasn't much call for anyone eating at this time of year, so they didn't light a fire in the room set aside for eating. As there wasn't anyone else in the bar they could have their food in front of the fire and they would have to take pot luck.

Nan said "whatever you give us will be fine won't it David?"

"Certainly," he said "it was a very mad idea in any case, so whatever you have got we will eat it with relish. I have tasted your food before." He then went up to the counter and ordered a ginger beer for William, a sherry for Nan and a glass of brandy for himself and asked the Landlord to have one himself. That was a start to a lovely evening.

Joe, the Landlord, in between chatting, was going back and forth to the kitchen. He put a pure white tablecloth on the table, placed the cutlery neatly and added the condiments. In half an hour, the Mrs came in with a tray laden with good looking and smelling food. She had cut ham off the bone, fried it with eggs and had boiled a few potatoes. It looked absolutely delicious. "Come on then folks," she said "before it gets cold."

The three of them scuttled along to the table and ate as if they hadn't eaten for days.

By the time the meal was eaten William was nearly asleep. The poor child was way past his bedtime and was extra tired because of his new relationship with his darling Meg. He had worked very hard, between the riding lessons, the grooming and the walking of the pony.

As soon as the meal was over David got up and went to pay for everything.

In the Arms of Merlin

"Thank you very much," he said, "it was a great meal, highly recommended. We shall come over again but on a warmer night and earlier. You don't want your clientele dropping off to sleep," as he tousled the little boy's hair.

William didn't moan, he just smiled at the two men.

So off they went. It was absolutely freezing now as they clip-clopped down the road back to town.

William was fast asleep by the time they arrived at the Tivoli. Nan opened the front door while David carried William straight upstairs and into his bed.

Nan said, "don't bother about his clothes, I'll just loosen them when I go to bed."

"All right," said David as he left the bedroom.

Nan just covered him with the bed clothes and came into the kitchen, where David was standing in front of the stove. It was the warmest place in the house.

Annie made a pot of tea and they both sat at the table.

"As much as I would love to stay tonight, I can't. You wouldn't believe how much work I have got to do tomorrow. I wasn't going to stay late tonight but you looked so tired that I had to help you somehow and taking you for the meal was the only thing I could do. Never mind," David said, "I really enjoyed myself. I hope you did too?"

Nan answered him with a kiss.

David drank his tea and said "I had better start making my way home or I will be here all night again. That is what I want but I have got to be sensible. In three days' time, we will have the rest of our lives together, won't we my darling?"

Nan nodded her head and gave him another kiss.

"No more kisses now," he said, "or I will never get home. Don't bother to come downstairs, I will lock the door and push the key back in through the keyhole. Go straight to bed and just dream of me and our life together."

In the Arms of Merlin

Annie went into William's room, loosened his clothes and gook his boots and jacket off. She thought that he would be all right like that. She gave him a kiss on his forehead, left the door ajar, undressed and went straight into bed.

She didn't dream of anything. As far as she knew she just slept the sleep of the just.

CHAPTER 18 – THE WEDDING

It was very busy all the morning. Annie sent Maggie down the Lane to see how they were getting on. They were just as busy. People were shopping now for Christmas. There was a Christmas Market selling poultry and nearly everything you needed for the festive season.

When Maggie came back with the news that the Lane was in the same predicament as they were at the Tivoli, there was nothing much that Annie could do. The only solution was to try and get someone in this week instead of waiting until after the wedding. Where was she going to get someone at such short notice?

As they were passing each other back and forth into the kitchen, they were talking about the situation when Rose chirped up and said, "I am sure my mother could come in for a couple of hours until Christmas."

Hannah said, "I didn't think, I'm sure my mother could come in too. It isn't as if it's all day. The children are old enough to be left for a while now."

"Do you want us to ask?" they asked Annie.

"Well if you think it will be all right," she said, "I am getting desperate. I know we will be closed for the wedding but there are two more days to think of. I don't think David will let me come in to help."

They all had a good laugh at this last remark.

Annie sent Rose to ask Hannah's mother and her own. She couldn't spare the two of them. In half an hour there were two more helpers in the Tivoli Tearooms. One extra in the kitchen and one clearing the tables and that made all the difference to them all.

Annie was very pleased, she didn't want to work her girls into the ground.

They had decided that all the clothes and everything else would go over to the Plas after the wedding. There would be plenty of time David reckoned. He had the entire East wing done out when he started going out with Nan. She knew nothing about it. She didn't go over there a lot, she was so busy. She was going to have a big surprise after the 21st. Letty and John were living through and through with David and his mother. Annie thought that they would be too, but obviously David didn't want it like that.

Annie was glad that she didn't have to worry about carting the clothes and all her little 'knick knacks' over to the Plas. She was leaving all the furniture for Esther and her father. They had decided that they would move into the Tivoli before Christmas. Esther's father wouldn't be very busy with his trade at Christmas, so he would take advantage of the situation and get his brother-in-law to help him to move. It all worked out because it was his brother-in-law who was renting the house from him, so they would help each other. Things were on the move.

Two more days.

Jane Davies called in the shop on the Thursday morning and said "I will come down on Saturday morning early to see to your hair and get you dressed. Is that all right?"

Annie didn't think about that and was surprised at Miss Davies' offer but was glad of any help. "What about you?" she asked Miss Davies.

"Oh," she said; I will be dressed ready for the wedding when I get here Saturday morning so don't you worry about me. What about the two girls, are they staying with you Friday night?"

"I haven't thought about that," Annie said.

"Well," Miss Davies said, "It's a good job I called this morning."

"I think it is," Annie said.

In the Arms of Merlin

When David called that night she gave him a message for Letty. She told Esther while they were passing each other, at one time or other.

The morning of the eve of the wedding arrived. Annie was at sixes and sevens, so Esther took it upon herself to tell Annie to go upstairs and do what she had to do and if she had done everything, "just put your feet up and relax."

Annie didn't know where to start, when the front door opened and there stood Auntie May.

Annie ran to her and hugged her and said, "my prayers have been answered."

They both shed a little tear, thinking that Annie's mam should have been with her on a day like this. It was wonderful that Auntie May had thought of coming.

It was a miracle. Annie needed someone to help her through this day. Apart from the different jobs, there was the emotional side of it as well.

Annie felt that now she could take on the world. Nothing would stand in her way, she thought to herself.

"Come on Auntie May," she said, "I'll make you a cup of tea when we get upstairs. All right?" Off they went.

The girls could see the difference in Annie already. They carried on with their jobs and chatted the whole time, it was lovely.

All of a sudden, Annie asked, "what made you come up today?"

"I don't know," she said, "but something was drawing me up here. I had to come. I don't know how I am going to go back?"

"Don't worry about that, " Annie said, "I'll ask Auntie if you can stay with her."

"Oh no," said Auntie May, "I haven't got my clothes for the wedding."

Annie thought for a minute. "Did you buy something special for the wedding?"

"No," Auntie said.

"Well don't worry, you shall go down to the Emporium and get yourself a new rig-out, from top to bottom. A gift from me. What do you think of that?"

Auntie May said, "I couldn't think of it."

"Well you have got to," Annie told her. There is no way any of us can take you home. By the way, how did you come up?"

Auntie May chuckled, "I came up with a farmer I know, with a sow and piglets behind us. It was so funny but beggars can't be choosers."

They had another little laugh.

Everything had been done and every room was sparkling. They were both content to sit down for a small snack.

They had a good wash and got dressed and made their way down the lane to ask Auntie if Auntie May could stay the night with them.

"There's no problem," Auntie said.

All of a sudden, Annie thought about Jack, "won't he be looking for you?"

"I thought of that," Auntie May said, "I put a note on my front door so he will know where I am."

They didn't bother to have tea in the Lane. They made their way to the Emporium to see about clothes for Auntie May. They got into the shop and were swept upstairs by the manager who knew a good sale when he saw one.

It took about an hour to get Auntie May fixed up. She looked lovely.

She was thrilled to bits. It was the first time that she had ever bought clothes in a shop. She either made them herself, or bought second hand ones in the market, so today was marvellous for her.

Annie was so please; things worked out better than she ever thought. She didn't know what sort of clothes auntie had and would have embarrassed her by telling her that her clothes were not fit for her to come to the wedding. Everything had worked out perfectly for everyone.

They trudged back to the Tivoli with their purchases. Things had cooled down in the Tearooms and the girls were getting themselves together to go to their homes.

Annie said, "thank you very much for letting me do my own thing today. I don't think I would have got round to do everything if it wasn't for you. Also my Aunt being here made everything more pleasant and enjoyable. Close family is what one needs at a time like this, so please girls don't go home for a minute. I want you to come upstairs."

They all looked at each other and wondered what Annie had in mind. Annie and her Aunt made their way upstairs, the girls followed.

Annie ushered them into the sitting room, thought how nice it looked with a glowing fire in the grate. Everything was gleaming. "Good old Auntie," she thought as she went to one of the cupboards. The girls were chattering as Annie put seven champagne glasses on a tray. She also got a plate with some sweet biscuits. The next job was to get a bottle of sparkling wine and take it all into her friends. They were all delighted. They had never had anything like this in their lives before and Annie was pleased that she had thought about it.

She opened the wine with great difficulty but succeeded in the end. The girls started giggling as soon as their lips touched the wine. "How lovely," Annie thought as she had her first sip and enjoyed every mouthful. It only took one glass each and the bottle was finished. Every one of the girls were giggling, so was Annie. She was even sorry that she had not bought another one but there you are, it might have been too much for them all and it would have spoilt everything. After a few laughs and more giggles, they all trooped downstairs. Annie gave them all a hug and a kiss and they left for their homes.

By the time she went back upstairs, Auntie May and Esther had washed the glasses and put them away. Everything was in its place and tidy.

Auntie May suggested that she go over to Auntie's house, so that she could have an early night as she felt a little tired.

They put their coats on and off they went into the darkness. It was very cold but it wasn't freezing – "thank goodness," Annie thought. They knocked the door and Uncle came to open it.

William just jumped all over Uncle. Annie protected but Uncle said, "leave the boy alone, he's excited. It isn't every day one gets to be chief guest at a wedding is it?"

William looked up to his mother and said, "am I Mama?"

Annie said "of course you are my darling. You are the most important person in my life and after tomorrow we will be a real family. We will be three and we will have to look after each other won't we?"

"Oh yes," William said, "I will be like all my friends in school. They all have Mamas and Papas."

They didn't stay long there, as Auntie May was busy cooking, so Annie made her farewells and off home they trundled. William skipped all the way. Once they got into the Tivoli, Annie saw to William. She had plenty of hot water in the boiler by the side of the fire, so she brought the big zinc pan out and gave William a bath. He was starting to get shy now, so Annie let him get on with the job himself.

She just popped in now and again to see that he was doing everything that he was supposed to do.

At one time when Annie popped in, he asked her if his neck was clean and Annie said, "if you have washed it, it must be clean."

He had finished washing himself and now was just playing with the sponge and the water. Annie left him to have a cup of tea that Esther had made.

They talked for a while about the following day. Annie said "I thought the 21st would never come."

"Well," Esther said, "it will be here in the morning. I just hope it will be fine."

"I hope so too," Annie said. Then William called to say that the water was cold and that he was freezing.

Annie jumped up and ran to the kitchen and there was William shivering and still sitting in the water. Annie gave a smile and said, "why ever didn't you get out William?"

"Oh no" he said, "I was afraid that Esther would come and see me."

Annie could hear Esther giggling the other side of the door, while she put a towel ready for William. She tried to hide a smile from him.

He was now sitting in his night-shirt couched right up next to Esther, so Annie went to make him a cup of cocoa that would make him relax and have a good night's sleep ready for the day in front of him tomorrow.

After the cocoa was drunk, Annie told Esther to go and have her bath and by the time she had finished, the water would be hot enough again for Annie. There wouldn't be enough time for the three of them to do the same in the morning.

By the time Annie had finished her bath and was dressed for bed it was 11.45pm. Esther was still sitting in front of the lovely fire, loathe leaving it and Annie felt the same so she suggested a small nightcap.

They both had a glass of sherry with the thought that it would make them sleep. They were both too excited to think of sleep but sensible Annie said, "Miss Davies will be here at 8 o'clock in the morning if I don't get to bed soon I will be

In the Arms of Merlin

still sleeping when she comes. We have got quite a lot of work to do, even if it's only drying my hair."

"All right, you win," Esther said, "my sense tells me that you are right, but the other part of me says stay up all night."

Off they both went to their respective beds.

It was a while before Annie dropped off. She said her prayers all the way through. Usually she dropped off in the middle of them but always woke up to end them.

The next thing she heard was William calling her, "come on Mama, it's a lovely morning, we are going to a wedding."

Annie opened her eyes and said to herself, "this is going to be the first day of the rest of my life and I have got two wonderful people to share it with me" and out of bed she jumped.

After calling Esther, the first thing she did was to get the stove drawing. It only took a few sticks to get it going again. It never went right out thank goodness, or they would have been freezing.

The fire was drawing well. Esther was laying the table and William was looking out onto the street below, watching the comings and goings of the tradesmen and the porters carrying things to the shops.

Everything was quit down below, in the Tivoli. It was closed and seemed funny that there was no nose at all coming from there. She supposed that was something that she had to get used to after the wedding.

Annie hoped that David would be willing for her to come in now and then.

Breakfast over, they cleared up the dishes. Everything was done and their first visitor arrived. It was Jack. Esther went to open the door for him and they both looked a bit red around the gills by the time they came upstairs. It was only then that Annie realised that it was Esther that Jack had fancied when he had told Annie that night that he was afraid that she would turn him down if he approached her.

Annie turned her head away, smiled and thought, "from now on you will have all the help you need to make this relationship start."

Next to arrive was Miss Davies. She started on Annie straightaway. She washed her hair and dried it; half with a towel and half with the fire. It came eventually and she started to put it up in suaves and waves, long pins and short pins.

"Now then" Miss Davies said, "that will never move."

"I hope not," Annie said.

Miss Davies was confident.

Esther had given William a wash and had started dressing him but William insisted that Jack take over. He knew that his mother couldn't help him at all.

Esther also had started to get dressed. She had no bother with her hair, it was naturally curly and just fell down over her shoulders. She was lucky.

By the time they were all dressed, Annie's aunts and uncle had arrived and didn't they look a picture?

Annie was really proud of them and was happy that she had been able to help Auntie May yesterday to find something for her to wear. She would never have got round everything if her Aunt hadn't come up, so that was Annie's way of paying her back.

A coach was coming to get Auntie May, Auntie Sal, Esther and Jack at 10.45 am and the other coach was coming at 10.55 am to get Uncle Will, William and Annie.

Jack was waiting in the doorway for the first coach and the four got into it and off they went.

Annie was now beginning to get nervous. There were thoughts running through her mind that had never occurred to her before. She knew deep down that she was being silly but nerves can do funny things to your imagination.

In the Arms of Merlin

She stood on the top of the landing, with William holding her hand. "You look lovely Mama," he said.

She thanks him and said "you look very smart yourself."

She could see that he was pleased with her comment. Uncle Will turned around and said, "my dear girl, you don't look lovely, you look absolutely beautiful. I didn't think anybody could look as good as you do. You wait until David sees you."

"I know, " Annie said, "he has only seen me dressed up properly about three times since we met."

"Well," Uncle said, "he's in for a treat today, isn't he William?"

"He certainly is," he answered.

As he was starting his way down the stairs, the coachman came to the door and said, "are you ready Madame?"

Annie said, "I'm as ready as I will ever be."

She walked down the stairs. As she came to the door she could see that there were a few women waiting on the pavement to see her going to the Church. Annie got into the coach and as she got inside, she could hear the remarks about her. Thank goodness they were kind ones and all saying about her beauty and her attire. The other two got into the coach, the coachman closed the door, got up onto his seat and off they went, slowly up towards the Church.

It was a beautiful morning, it could not have been better. The coach stopped outside the Lytch Gate and Annie could see loads of people outside the Church lining the way in.

Annie was really shaking now. She got inside the Church door where the vicar, Letty and Esther were waiting.

The vicar came up to Annie, took hold of her hand, squeezed it and said, "you look lovely my dear."

"Thank you," Annie said.

The two girls came up to her, then Letty kissed her and whispered another compliment in her ear.

From nowhere Miss Davies came and tidied her head-dress and veil and pulled her train right down to the floor.

The vicar looked at Annie and asked, "are you ready Annie?"

"Yes," she said.

The vicar made his way down the aisle and was waiting for Annie to walk towards David.

As she arrived at his side, he looked at her and was overcome when he saw how beautiful she looked. He knew that she was going to look lovely for him, but he didn't think she could ever look as she looked today. Everyone gasped as she stood by his side.

She could see the love in his eyes as he looked down at her, also the admiration. She felt quite proud.

The vicar interrupted her thoughts as he started the wedding service. Letty took her bouquet and William passed the rings to the vicar. He looked as proud as punch. Everyone had a smile for him.

The service was over and the vicar said, "I pronounce you man and wife."

The vicar shook both their hands and asked them to follow him to the vestry to sign the Register. The wedding party followed, so did the aunts and uncle, William, Lady Elizabeth and John. They signed the register, shook hands and had kisses from everyone there.

They walked down the aisle to some magnificent music, then went straight out to the carriage and off to the Plas for the reception, which was going to be held in the ballroom. It all looked magnificent. The tables were all laid to perfection. Lady Elizabeth had certainly done them proud.

Annie was glad that she didn't have to arrange this as well, it would have been impossible for her.

"Now Mrs David Jones," a voice at her side said. It was David. He caught hold of her and kissed her for at least a minute.

Annie tried to struggle but he wouldn't have any of it. Annie was still shy and was very embarrassed.

David said, "we have just got married. Don't you think people expect us to kiss?"

Annie wasn't convinced but she let him kiss her again in public once more and then it would be the last one.

"Poor Nan," David thought, "she is so shy, thank goodness that she is not shy with me when we are on our own."

They then stood at the entrance of the ballroom, waiting for the guests to come in. There was an orchestra playing and the atmosphere was marvellous.

David just wanted to take Nan in his arms and waltz her around forever, but they just had to stand there until all the guests arrived.

All the bridal party were waiting to greet the guests, also Lady Elizabeth and the two Aunts and Uncle Will. He didn't seem too pleased with the situation.

I don't suppose he had done anything like this ever. Poor old uncle.

There were over a hundred guests and after everyone sat down at their places, Nan and David sat at the top table.

Annie was so pleased with what Lady Elizabeth had done for them. Everything was perfect; the tables were immaculately decorated with flowers. As far as Annie could see, everyone was exactly the same, on the theme of a winter wedding.

The guests stood up when the Bride and Groom arrived at the table and sat down as soon as they sat down.

Letty was sitting next to David and William was sitting next to Annie. The butlers and the maids started coming around with the first course and that was how it went until the last course was served.

Annie thought there were nine courses in all. She had never eaten so much food at the same time before. She could see Uncle Will's face. It was a picture and so was Jack's. She was certainly going to have a laugh with them after it was all over.

The meal was finished. Next came the time to cut the cake. It was a five-tier cake, beautifully decorated with great skill. Whoever had made it was a perfectionist. It was so delicately don; it was as if the fairies had put the gossamer from their wings all over it.

It seemed a shame to cut it, but cut it they would have to do. The cake was cut and distributed to all the guests, with a glass of champagne, which was delicious.

Annie had tasted a few different ones by now but this was the very best taste she had tasted.

It was now time for the speeches – some were very good but some others were long winded. The best was yet to come. After everyone had had their say, David got up and spoke for five minutes. Not too long. His speech was superb, everyone gave him a great clap, even William. He was getting bored by now but David spoke about his mother and the love he had for her lifted the little boy a bit. He then thanked William for welcoming him to their little family. William was thrilled to bits.

With the meal over, the tables were being cleared. David asked the top table if he and his wife could be excused.

David took his new wife to see their new home. Annie didn't know anything about the new wing of the Plas, so off they went. She had no idea where he was taking her.

Eventually they arrived in the west wing. Annie couldn't believe her eyes. She said, "why didn't you tell me? You know darling, I was quite content to live with your

In the Arms of Merlin

mother and the others. It didn't matter to me, as long as we were together."

"Aren't you happy about our own place?"

"Of course I am but you have gone to all this trouble for us."

After she had got over the initial shock, he took her all around the west wing. It was absolutely fabulous. He also informed her that they had their own servants.

Annie protested, "we don't need servants."

"Now Nan, what have I been trying to tell you since I first met you? From now on, you are the mistress of the Plas, so you might as well get used to it."

He then opened a bottle of champagne which had been cooling in a wine cooler. The glasses were also on the tray. He had given orders to his butler before the wedding.

Annie took off her head-dress and veil and laid them on an armchair, with loving care.

She turned around. David was waiting by the table with two glasses in his hands and great love in his eyes. He walked towards her and offered her one of the glasses; she took it and put it to her lips.

David said; "I hope we will be as happy the rest of our lives as we are today."

They drank the wine, then they embraced and in a few minutes they were one.

They had started their married life.

When they came downstairs to the ballroom, they were all smiles. Annie had freshened herself up and just had her wedding gown on. She looked absolutely radiant as they danced together for the first time since they were man and wife.

One of David's friends had three children; two boys and a girl, so because of William, they were all invited to the wedding. William was very happy, he had two boys to play with and a girl to dance with if he wanted.

As they were dancing one time, David nudged Nan and said, "look over there." Letty was dancing with Jack, they really looked as if they were enjoying themselves.

"Oh," Nan said, "I thought that Jack liked Esther. Poor Esther."

"What do you mean, poor Esther? Look," David said, "she is over on the other side of the ballroom dancing with John."

Annie was amazed but it looked much better this way. They all had been accommodated.

"Oh you are nothing but an old matchmaker Nan," David said, "I bet you have been planning this from the beginning."

"Well," Nan said, "not the way it has turned out, this is much better than I could ever have done."

She was so pleased with the situation, she thought that they were pleased too.

The night wore on and about 11 o'clock, Nan had to take William to bed, he was shattered. He had had a very long day and had played hard during the reception. The other children had gone ages ago, so with William in his lovely new bedroom, Nan made her way downstairs, back to the dancing.

She hadn't had much of a chance to speak to her new mother-in-law, so she made her way over to her. Lady Elizabeth looked up as she saw Nan coming towards her. She got up and said, "this is the first time I have had a chance to tell you how beautiful you look today and the girls were lovely too. As a matter of fact, I think everything was perfect."

Nan put her arms around Lady Elizabeth and said, "most of it is down to you. Thank you Mama for all you have done and for accepting me into your family. I will do my very best to make your son happy."

In the Arms of Merlin

"I know that my dear," she replied, "he adores you and his new son. I know that everything is going to be alright for the three of you. What do you think of the west wing?"

"I can't believe that he had all that work done. I didn't know anything about it."

"He made up his mind about that when you first got engaged and now that I think about it, it was a good idea."

"I forgot to ask him who chose the furniture and the drapes?"

"Oh," she said, "it was between Letty, myself and Esther."

"Esther?" Nan said.

"Yes," Lady Elizabeth said, "John was picking her up every now and then for us to confer."

"Oh," Nan said, "so that is how things have worked out like they have."

She gave a chuckle and made her way back to David and onto another dance with the only man she had ever loved and would love until the day she died.

CHAPTER 19 – FIRST CHRISTMAS

They woke up the following morning to William jumping for joy. The snow had come back with a vengeance, there was quite a thickness. It must have started not long after the last guest had left.

Jack had gone home the same time as Esther and the aunts and uncle. He was staying at the Tivoli with Esther and Mr Evans. Auntie May was staying with Auntie and Uncle Will.

It seemed that Uncle Will was nearly sleeping, the wine had hit him early on in the evening. He wasn't really used to liquor at all, love him, Nan thought. He had been snoring nearly all night in one of the alcoves in the annexe of the ballroom.

Auntie Sal was ashamed of him. Lady Elizabeth saw the funny side of it and told her not to worry about him. He would be fine where he was and nobody would see him from the ballroom, so Auntie Sal didn't feel so bad about it then.

David's office was now officially closed until after Christmas, so there wasn't any problem about getting in through the snow. They all spent a leisurely day getting to know each other.

Nan couldn't get over the servant situation. She got up a few times to prepare a meal for them until David stopped her. She wondered how long would it take her to get used to this life and was hoping that David would be willing for her to go to the Tivoli a couple of days a week.

After lunch, Nan went upstairs to their bedroom to put her wedding dress away, but by then one of her maids had seen to that. Nan was a little disappointed but she would just have to get used to this life, or she was going to be miserable and she didn't want that. David only wanted the best for her, she understood his motives but had to get used to them.

In the Arms of Merlin

She went to the wardrobe, pulled out her dress and laid it on the bed, also the head-dress and veil. She caressed it with her fingers, it was so beautiful. She even thought quietly to herself that she looked lovely yesterday.

She hoped that the photographs would come out, there was so much fuss with the man who was taking the pictures, that everyone was worn out. It was the first picture that Nan had ever had taken and that in itself was a little thrill. There were so many pictures taken, I suppose in case some wouldn't come out, it seemed that the photography business was a very risky one, but surely would improve as the years went by.

It was still snowing heavily, there was quite a thickness on the ground. Nan hoped that it would not snow much more, or her family wouldn't be able to come for the Christmas festivities.

She knew that William would be really disappointed not to have auntie and Uncle with them for Christmas, "we will just have to keep our fingers crossed."

William had mixed feelings about it all. He wanted the snow but he also wanted the family to be with them.

As his mother told him, "you can't have it all your way.

The following morning the snow had stopped. The view from the terrace was breath-taking, you could see for miles and everything was covered with snow. The trees were like white skeletons, every individual branch was as if they had been painted with a fine white powder and the contrast between the blue sky and the snow on the ground was something that any artist would give their eye teeth for.

At eight o'clock they ate their dinner. It was a superb meal. Nan couldn't fault it and William ate everything that was put in front of him. Nan was so glad, because he wasn't like herself, used to the same food as the upper class were.

William had taken to it a little more than Nan. After the meal was over, Nan told William to ask to be excused, it was time to go to bed. He went all around the family, embraced them and gave them a kiss.

Last but not least, he got to David, went up close to him and whispered in his ear, "will you take me to bed Papa?"

David gave a broad smile and consented immediately.

Lady Elizabeth looked at Nan and so did Letty. As they were leaving the dining room, Lady Elizabeth sighed and said, "I have been waiting for this for a long time Nan, thank you very much for coming into our family and bringing that darling boy with you. It has taken a lot of the pain from my heart, after losing Barbara. You have given me something to live for once again and this Christmas should be like the ones we used to have when the children were small. I am really looking forward to it."

"So am I," said Nan, "this will be our first Christmas together, but it has an extra bonus, because I have David and a full family. I am so lucky. I have got to pinch myself sometimes to see if I am dreaming. I do hope nothing will go wrong, things don't usually work well for me."

"Don't you fret," Lady Elizabeth said, "David will look after you both and so will we."

Nan was very pleased with her mother-in-law's comments, the best thing was Nan knew that she meant every word.

David came down in about fifteen minutes. Nan asked him if he would like to help her pack some presents?

"Yes," he said, "where are they?"

"I have hidden them in a cupboard in our bedroom." She turned to Lady Elizabeth and Letty to see if they minded. They were quite happy to let the young couple go on their own to see the presents.

Apart from the fact that Nan did want to be alone with David, she needed to see to the presents as well. She had already packed David's present, so it didn't matter about him seeing anything.

He wondered about that and even asked her. He was like a child himself, but Nan assured him that he would see nothing belonging to him.

"Now this is what I call fun," David said.

He was very surprised at Nan's selection of gifts for the family. She must have done a lot of research to know what they all liked and needed.

David was so pleased that she had taken so much trouble and care to find out about them. Little did he know that it had been a nightmare for Nan, until she asked Letty to help her. Letty was marvellous, they even had fun going to do the shopping together, even if it was only a couple of hours at a time as Nan's time was limited, but everything had worked out perfectly.

All the packing done, they came downstairs to finish the evening off. There was a bottle of champagne newly opened in the wine cooler. They polished it off and rang for another one. By now they were all in a happy mood. Letty got up and started to play the piano. She played carols and they all sang. It was a delightful evening but had to end because it was after midnight when the singing ended.

Nan felt that she could have gone on all night, she had never experienced anything like this before and she loved every minute of it.

"Never mind," Lady Elizabeth said, "wait until Christmas night, then we have a party, as long as the snow keeps off."

David put his arm around Nan's shoulder, they said their goodnights and off they went to their part of the house, which was another thing that Nan liked.

By the time Nan got to bed, she was nearly asleep. She lay in David's arms, so warm and comfy and happy, she felt the security in his embrace. It was the best feeling she had ever had.

David started to kiss her. She just melted in his arms.

In the Arms of Merlin

It was a very bright morning when it arrived. They had breakfast in their own dining room.

Nan was informed that William had been up for hours. "What about his breakfast?" Nan asked.

"Cook has seen to that Ma'am" the maid said.

"Well you don't have to worry then," said David, "will you mind if I do some paperwork this morning darling?"

"No," Nan said. "I can help with decorating the Christmas tree, if nobody minds that is."

"I can't see anyone objecting to that my dear. I will see you as soon as I finish."

There was still no sign of John, he must have stayed in town the night before. Nan gave a smile and wondered where he had slept. She knew that Mr Evans would not have any jiggery pokery in his house.

She had forgotten to mention it to David the night before. Nan was glad that they had got together, they made a lovely couple and Nan had the feeling that Miss Davies would be very busy before long again, making wedding clothes for another wedding.

It's funny how things happen. Even Letty and Jack were going great guns. Nan didn't think that they would rush into a quick marriage. Jack was building up his business and that was very hard work, but thanks to David he was doing alright.

Everything revolved around Nan. It was all through her, that all these people had got together and everyone doing so well. Nan hoped it lasted.

By the time she got to the main drawing room, the decorating had started. Lady Elizabeth was supervising and Letty was flitting here and there.

William came in at one point but only stayed for a few minutes, just to see how things were getting on. "I will be back later, I am helping to groom Meg. Is that all right Mamma?"

"Yes darling," Nan said, "I am glad that you are helping with your pony. Watch the time for lunch," his mother said.

"It's all right," he said, "I shall have my lunch in the kitchen with cook, she is making something special for me. You don't mind do you Mamma? It will be all right won't it?"

"Of course it will be all right, you carry on. I shall give your apologies to the family. All right, now off you go," she said and patted him on the head as he passed.

There were two trees. One in the dining room and a twenty footer in the drawing room. There were four of the staff seeing to the tree, so Nan just looked on.

They finished the decorating then one of the maids asked if she could get Nan's gifts to put under the tree in the drawing room.

Nan was about to say that she wanted to keep their presents over in their quarters, under their tree, but changed her mind as she saw the happiness in Lady Elizabeth's face.

She told the girls to follow her and she would see to them.

As she was leaving the drawing room, she asked her mother in law if they could have a tree in their drawing room.

"Of course you can dear," she said. "I am surprised you haven't asked about one before now."

"Honestly, I didn't think about it until Mary asked if she could get the presents. If someone could put the tree up for me, William, David and I could decorate it ourselves, if you don't mind," she said, "it will be our first."

Lady Elizabeth gave instructions to the butler about the tree for Nan. By four o'clock, there was a tree standing in the drawing room of their apartment. It was a beauty.

Nan went to the kitchen door to try and call William.

"He'll never hear you from here ma'am," the butler said, so he put his boots on and went over to tell young William that his mother wanted him to decorate their tree.

It took him about half an hour to land up in their apartment. His face was still red after the cold, but soon settled down after a while.

Nan had asked for a tree but didn't realise that she wouldn't have anything to decorate it with. She felt quite stupid, not realising about the situation. She looked at the butler and the maid as if she had been hit on the head. When she told them about the problem, Fredrick, the Butler, gave a little smile and said, "don't worry ma'am, Daisy and I will find you something. We will be back shortly" and they were, with a very large box of decorations. They weren't new, but as far as Nan was concerned, they were beautiful.

She thanked them very much and said that she could manage now, so they took their leave.

William, who had gone to get David, arrived back with the news that Papa would be a few more minutes.

Nan decided to wait for David to come. While they waited, William sat next to Nan on the chaise longue. He really cuddled up to her and said, "are you happy Mamma?"

Nan was surprised at his question, "of course I am darling, aren't you happy?"

"Mamma, I have never been so happy. I didn't ever think that I would ever live like this and have a Mamma and a Papa and a whole new family. I am the most lucky boy in the world."

"I hope it will always be like this for you son." Nan held him tight and kissed him on his golden curls.

That was how they were when David walked into the room. He said, "what is going on here?"

"We were just having a cuddle Papa, while we were waiting for you."

"Well," David said, "I feel I need one as well" and there they were all three of them kissing and cuddling each other, until Nan said "that's enough, let us get on with our tree or Grandmamma will wonder where we have got to. Come along," she said exactly like a school Ma'am.

After they had finished the tree, they all stood to admire it. David said, "is this your first tree Nan?"

"Yes," she said. "What about you William?"

"I haven't even seen a tree so close before, leave alone decorate it."

"Well," David said, "I might as well tell you, it was my first time as well."

They all started laughing and by that time Grandmamma had arrived to inspect the tree. When she heard what they were laughing about, she joined in too, because she hadn't decorated a tree either. Well that was the last straw as far as Nan was concerned.

It didn't snow any more, it just was very cold. The snow was really hard and a little dangerous. It was a good job that nobody had to go out in it.

It was now Christmas Eve. By the time all the guests arrived, it was lunch time. There was Auntie Sal, Uncle Will, Esther, Mr Evans, Jack and Auntie May.

Auntie May hadn't gone home after the wedding, in case she couldn't come back. That was a good idea, her staying the extra few days.

Nan didn't think that Auntie May had ever stayed away from home ever before. Everyone was taken to their rooms and they all met in the dining room. They were quite a crowd, thirteen in all.

They all sat down and lunch was served. Nan could see that her family and friends were a little nervous, but they all managed perfectly well. Everyone seemed to relax, as the wine kept flowing.

Uncle Will would be asleep again before long, Auntie said "don't worry about it."

Lady Elizabeth said, "he can sleep it off this afternoon." Everybody laughed and they all seemed to relax and get on with the meal.

Uncle Will was in bed by three o'clock. It was the chuckle of the day. Auntie was very embarrassed about the situation. David had to have a word in her ear, not for her to worry. It was starting to spoil the holiday for Auntie.

Nan thought that David had convinced her that it didn't make any difference that he had to go to bed after every meal. "We will just have to water his wine down, that should do the trick" and that was what they did.

Uncle Will didn't know anything about it. He had his own bottle. Everyone was happy.

They didn't have Christmas dinner at lunch time, they usually had it in the evening, but because of William, they thought that a Christmas luncheon would be favoured.

The ladies adjourned to the drawing room after the meal was over. Uncle went to bed for a few hours and the men went to David's study and had a few glasses of the best port, which had been bought especially for the occasion.

Jack was lapping it up and told David, "I could get used to this."

"Well," David said, "it is in your own hands. It's up to you how hard you work. There will always be work for you, so think hard. I don't want to tell you your business, but if I were you, I would employ and get another rig and horses, so really think about it. You can go a long way, if as I said, you extend and work. It will all pay for itself before you look around."

Jack was very thoughtful all the afternoon, Nan didn't know anything about the conversation earlier. She could see that Jack had something on his mind, so she called him to one side and asked him.

In the Arms of Merlin

Jack was glad to speak to someone about what David had told him.

When Nan heard what he had to say she was relieved to hear it. She thought that something terrible had been said. "Oh my dear Jack," Nan said, "is that all, be sure if David has told you to extend your business you do it. He would not tell you to jeopardise anything belonging to you or yours."

The heavy cloud lifted from Jack. He was so relieved after speaking to Nan, he would go down to the bank the first thing after the Christmas Festivities were over and then he would show everyone what he was made of.

After the men had finished chatting and drinking their port, they came into the drawing room. William was getting a little bored with the few toys he had had from Santa Clause. He was in between ages. Toys were really too young for him. He had loads of books and board games, he had things for Meg. He had a beautiful pair of riding boots from Grandmamma which Mr Evans had made with loving hands. He thought of the young boy as his own grandson.

William was a very lucky boy. Everybody loved him because he had such lovely ways, considering that he had been brought up in an orphanage. It was lucky that he had turned out as he had. It could have been so different. Nan thanked God very often for the way the boy had turned out. He was getting on fine in school and had many friends, girls as well as boys.

Nan felt as if life was pretty good at the moment. She had found a man who truly loved her. She had no money worries and an adorable little boy. What more did she want? But even now, she would think about the bad old days and a shiver would go up her spine and it would un-nerve her for a while.

She couldn't think why she could be so morbid, with all the good things that were going on around her and her new

In the Arms of Merlin

and old family. Everyone had love in their hearts for her but the same old foreboding was still there.

She would lie at David's side in bed. He would be fast asleep and her mind would go backwards. Then she was lying there in torment for hours. It was now starting to tell on her.

One morning, David turned to her as he awoke. He could see that she had been crying. He had noticed it the last few weeks. She looked as if she had something on her mind.

David took her into his arms, kissed her tenderly, looked straight into her eyes and asked what was troubling her. David thought perhaps she was sorry that she had married him, or didn't like living out in the country. There were lots of possibilities and it frightened David as to which one it was. The time had come for things to be brought out into the open.

"Now then," he said, "what is the matter? I am very worried about you. Can you tell me, have I done anything to hurt you, have I said anything? Please darling tell me. I am thinking everything. Put me out of my misery."

In between her sobs, she told him that there was just something hanging over her. She didn't really know what it was, but the depression was there and that is it.

David said he was thankful that it was nothing to do with him, so he could help her. He sat up in bed and turned to Nan and said, "how about coming into town with me in the morning, for you to start back at the Tivoli. You are not bound to work all day, just long enough to get you back to my old Nan. Your life has changed so much and you can't cope with it, so what do you think of that idea?"

Nan couldn't believe her ears, she hadn't thought of it like that. Perhaps David was right. Her life had completely changed. I suppose it had been too much of a trauma for a very hard working girl to actually be doing nothing. The only thing she had to do was look after herself, even William didn't need her as much as he used to.

She sat up like a bolt, put her arms around David and said, "thank you darling, why didn't I confide in you sooner? I should have challenged you sooner but I thought it would pass. That is our first lesson in our married life, not to keep anything from each other in future."

Nan was the first up the following morning. By the time David and William came down, she had prepared breakfast and was back to her old self.

David looked at her and gave a sigh of relief.

After breakfast, they made their way into town. William to school, David to work and Nan to the Tivoli.

The girls couldn't believe their eyes when Nan walked in. "What's up?" Esther said.

"I am back, I won't be able to work full time, but I shall be here some time every day. I am going crazy at home all day with nothing to do, so here I am."

Esther and the girls were delighted. It showed they had all missed Nan, but they all envied her finishing work and living a life of leisure, but that was not for Nan.

She had a marvellous day, she was nearly dropping when David came to fetch her. She was tired but the sparkle was back and that pleased David very much.

William had a life home every day with a farmer, whose son was in his class. They took it in turns to do the journey every day.

"I sent word home to tell them that we would be eating with them tonight. I hope I have done the right thing?"

"How lovely of you," Nan said, "that was a good idea. I am surprised how tired I feel. I suppose it will be better tomorrow."

That is how things went for the next few months. It was so nice to be with the girls again, meet all the customers, have a chat with them, hear all the local gossip.

By the second week, Nan was back to normal and everything in the garden was lovely.

CHAPTER 20 – NEW ARRIVAL

Spring was certainly beginning to show. The snow had all gone and the little green leaves were starting to peep through the earth. The trees were changing from the gnarled branches to a softer look, with buds starting to break out. The temperature was rising and the days were starting to get longer, so spring was around the corner.

Nan's spirits were certainly starting to soar.

Lady Elizabeth had gone to London for a few weeks and Letty was very busy courting Jack, who by the way had listened to David's advice and had bought another rig and was on his way to having a very large business. He had employed another three men. Nan was so happy for him, apart from the fact that he was one of her best friends, he was such a dedicated worker and nothing would stand in his way, if he had a mind to it. She was happy that Letty and him were going to make a go of things together. It had surprised Nan when he went for Letty, she thought that Esther would have been more his type, but there you are, you never know do you?

Nan didn't think that Letty would have looked at him twice if he hadn't been a friend of hers and was going to end up as a big business man, so good things do come out of bad sometimes.

Nan got up at her usual time this particular morning. She called William and went down to the kitchen to start the breakfast.

Two of the maids were already there. When they saw Nan, they started towards the stove. Nan stopped them, "you can go and do something else girls," she said.

They just looked at each other and went to another part of the west wing to start something else. They had never had a mistress like this before, but they all liked her. She was still only a young woman, not much older than themselves. All the staff were very happy at the Plas, some girls that they knew had a terrible life, so these girls appreciated being treated like human beings. Even Lady Elizabeth was a good mistress.

Nan was standing at the stove, waiting for the eggs to boil. She had to watch them because William wouldn't eat them unless they were soft, so Nan had to time them to the second or he wouldn't eat them.

All of a sudden, she had to hold onto the bar on the front of the stove and thought "good grief what is going on?" She held on for a minute while everything was going round and round, she felt herself leaving go the rail and she felt herself just folding down to the floor. She couldn't do anything about it.

She didn't know how long she had been on the floor but one of the girls had come back for some cleaning stuff and seen her mistress on the floor, deathly white. She had such a fright that she just gave out a scream, that rattled through the whole west wing.

David couldn't understand what was going on. He made his way downstairs to where he thought the scream came from. By that time, Lily met him. She by now, was in a terrible state.

"What is the matter?" he said, "cool down."

"It's the mistress, she's in a heap on the kitchen floor."

David's heart nearly stopped beating. He ran into the kitchen and there she was, still lying quietly. He kneeled on the flagstone and put his hands under her head and told Lily to go to the stables and tell anybody to ride into town to get the doctor, but immediately.

David was scared, Nan's face was ashen. He tried to pat her hands, then he patted her face. All of a sudden, her eyes opened and she wondered what David was doing with his arms around her and that she was on the floor.

"What happened?" she asked.

"I don't know," David said, "you tell me. I have never been so scared in my life."

Nan started to move, she hadn't hurt herself when she fell. She wanted to get up from the floor, so David helped her and guided her over to one of the kitchen chairs.

By this time, the kitchen was full of staff and Nan was a bit embarrassed. She asked David to tell them that she was all right and for them to go back to their work, which David immediately did.

He fussed over her for the next few minutes, then he picked her up in his arms and carried her back upstairs.

Nan protested and said that she was fine and was going to make their breakfast, but David would have none of it.

As he was leaving the kitchen, he gave instructions for someone to make William's breakfast. He would have something after the doctor came.

Nan was shocked, "you haven't sent for the doctor?" she asked.

"What do you think?! I come downstairs and find you on the floor. You are damned right, I have sent for the doctor."

Nan couldn't protest any more, she still didn't feel all that good, but didn't show David.

It must have been three quarters of an hour before the doctor arrived.

Nan had now undressed and was right into bed. She must have dropped off and woke as the doctor walked into the bedroom.

David was still lying by her side. He got up and made his way towards the doctor to shake his hand in welcome.

The doctor looked at Nan and said, "what is the trouble my dear?"

In the Arms of Merlin

Nan blushed and said, "I don't know, I was cooking breakfast for William and my husband, when everything went black and I just slipped down to the floor."

"Right," the doctor said, "let's have a look at you. Do you want to stay David? If you don't, just go and get Letty for me, there's a good boy."

David went to get Letty. She was still in bed and hadn't heard any of the commotion, but as soon as she was told about Nan, she jumped out of bed and went straight over, to be with her.

Doctor Morris greeted her also in the same personal way that he did with David. They had all been brought up together.

David left the room. The Doctor started to examine Nan.

Nan was very embarrassed, she hadn't had much to do with doctors in her life and this sort of examination was totally alien to her.

Letty was a little red around the gills too.

Examination over, Doctor Morris said, "there is nothing to worry about Nan, so go and call David back in," he told Letty.

She obeyed and brought David back.

"Well," David said, "what is it Will?"

Will Morris started to smile and said, "I have great pleasure in telling you that you are going to be parents."

David's face was a picture, so was Nan's. That was the last thing she thought of. She couldn't believe it. Neither could David.

He got to the bed and took her into his arms and kissed her all over. Then the tears came. The three of them were crying on the bed.

Will Morris said, "what on earth are you crying for? You should be laughing, not crying."

David felt a bit of a fool and said, "I am crying with relief firstly and I am crying with joy also, so work that out."

Will could see how the situation was with David. He caught him by the hand and shook it vigorously.

David started to smile and so did the two girls.

"Right," David said, "that is the end of your cooking for anybody and the end of the Tivoli."

Nan looked up to the doctor for help. He realised what she wanted for him to say, so he compromised and said, "now listen to me, the both of you. Nan is having a baby, she's not ill. It is quite normal for someone to faint like she did this morning. You are a sensible girl, you have had one child, so you know all about it."

"But that was a different kettle of fish Will," David said, "Nan was in the wash-house when she was carrying William, until nearly the end of the pregnancy, so I am afraid you will have to guide her on this one. Knowing her, she will carry on all the time if she has her way. I know her by now, so Will, you tell her."

"All right," Will said, "I will see to things for you."

Letty went downstairs and left them on their own. By this time the fear had gone from David and the excitement was here now. He would never forget the look on Nan's face, when he got into the kitchen. He really thought that there was something radically wrong with her. The thought of it still gave him a shiver down his spine. He didn't think that he could live without his darling Nan.

He held her in his arms for ages, they didn't even talk. They just lay there oblivious of everything and everybody, until one of the maids knocked the door with a tray of tea, which Letty had ordered for them.

Nan stayed in bed until lunchtime, came straight onto the lunch table. David was waiting for her. He got up as she entered the room and made his way towards her. He kissed

In the Arms of Merlin

her gently and ushered her to her seat at the table, "I hope you don't mind darling, but I invited Letty to eat with us?"

"Of course I don't mind," Nan said, "it will be nice to have a chat with her. I don't get much time since going back to the Tivoli."

David rose his head as soon as the word Tivoli was mentioned and Nan said, "don't get yourself upset now David, I shall be sensible, don't you worry."

David didn't have to nag her again about the Tivoli.

Having this baby was very important to Nan. She knew how David must feel, so she wouldn't do anything to jeopardise this next stage of her life. News of the baby went around the family and their friends like wildfire.

Nan thought that David was the proudest man in the world, leave alone the town.

As soon as William came home from school that day, David took him into the drawing room where Nan was resting. She had her feet up and a small blanket over her legs because the weather was still a bit cold, even though there was a roaring fire in the huge grate.

He ran over to his mother, put his arms around her neck and asked her what was the matter, because she was lying down. The boy wasn't used to seeing his mother in that position.

Nan said, "there is no need to worry, Mama has just had a faint."

"What does that mean?" he asked his mother.

"It sometimes happens when ladies who are going to have babies feel the baby moving inside them for the first time and it makes them faint. There is no problem and it will never happen again. Will it Dada?"

"No," David said. It took a few minutes for the penny to drop with William, he was quiet for a few more seconds, then it dawned on him what was going on. He turned to

In the Arms of Merlin

David and jumped right up into his arms and hugged him and said, "I am going to have a brother to play with at last."

Nan was flabbergasted, to think that he had gone to David first and not to her. After the initial shock for him, he ran over to his mother, put his arms around her gently and said, "thank you Mama" and gave her a kiss, sat by her side and held her hand for a few minutes and fussed over her all the time.

That night in bed, Nan and David had a talk about the baby. Nan asked him if the new baby was going to make a difference to his love for William?

"How could you think such a thing?" he told Nan. "You know that I love William as much as life itself. He will always be my first son and you don't have anything to worry about on that score. I could never turn my back on that boy, it doesn't mean that I will love our other child any the less. Nan forget about things like that and we'll just look forward to our next son, or daughter, all right?" he asked her.

Nan was convinced that David meant what he said and the thought went out of her head forever more.

Lady Elizabeth came the following day and when she had settled down after her long journey, they both went to her in the main drawing room, to give her the good news.

She was delighted, "it will be lovely to have a young child about the house again."

William was growing up so quickly and he spent most of his time in the stables with Meg and the grooms. Letty was as bad as him. They both smelled of horse when they came into the house. There were times that Lady Elizabeth would send them packing down to the kitchen to have their food, if the smell proved to be too much.

They would both go running down to the kitchen, laughing and giggling to themselves. Those two were great pals.

One evening Nan was helping to dry William after a bath. He kept his mother outside the bathroom as much as he could, but she had to come in at one time to see if he was doing all right. She was drying his hair this night and they were talking about the events of the day and out from William's mouth came a statement that Nan had been waiting to hear for weeks. She didn't think she would have heard it from him."

"Where did you hear that?" she asked William.

William stopped in his tracks and didn't know what to say next.

"Don't worry darling," Nan told him. After all he was only a little boy and to keep a secret like that was hard.

He now looked as if he was going to cry and Nan said, "don't worry, I won't tell anyone what you have told me. Your secret is safe with me."

William looked a little relieved and made his mother promise that she wouldn't tell anyone. Before she would give her promise, she asked him, would he be willing to tell Dada?"

William thought for a minute and said, "all right, but he has got to promise as well."

After William had got into his night-shirt and dressing gown, they made their way to their drawing room.

David was reading a book. He looked up as they both entered the room and said, "my, don't you look clean?"

William ran over to him and jumped on his lap and his father just put his fingers through his damp curly hair.

"Dada," Nan said, "William has got a secret for you to hear, but you must promise not to tell anyone."

David looked at Nan, she smiled and said "all right William, tell your father what slipped out with you earlier on in the bathroom."

William looked his father in the eye and said, "Letty and Jack are getting married soon."

David couldn't get over it. "Is that right?" he asked Nan.

"I don't know," she said, "it is William who is Letty's confidante, not anyone else."

They both chuckled, "well that's all I can say William, she must think a lot of you to tell you such a secret and you haven't told a soul."

"Yes," William said, "but it slipped out tonight with Mama."

"When did you find out?" his father asked him.

"This morning," William said.

"My, my," David said, "that is a very long time to keep a secret. Don't worry son, I won't tell a soul."

It was two days later. They were all having dinner in the main dining room, when Letty made her announcement. Everybody took it as news so poor William didn't have to worry about his slip up.

This year was going to be a very busy year. The wedding would be the busiest.

Letty asked Nan to go with her to see Miss Davies about her bridal clothes.

"Certainly," Nan said, "I will have to have something for myself, I am beginning to show. Miss Davies will see to everything for us."

The following day, the three ladies went into town to see Miss Davies, gave her all the details as to what they wanted, then they all went down to the Emporium to choose their materials. The three of them were catered for immediately and they were all pleased with what they had.

Lady Elizabeth invited Miss Davies to stay at the Plas, if she wanted, to save her going home every night and coming back every morning and that was what Miss Davies did.

It was a much better arrangement than before, because after sewing all day, she was brought home to a very cold house, with no fire at all and going to bed was hard. Sometimes if she did light a fire, it got very late, then she had to go to bed and leave it, but it helped a little in the morning, as it wasn't so cold.

Lady Elizabeth said one of the grooms would bring her to her home anytime, for her to keep her house aired.

Miss Davies was delighted, and that is what happened.

CHAPTER 21 – ANOTHER WEDDING

There wasn't as much time to spare with this wedding as was with Nan's, so she had a chat with Miss Davies about William's clothes for the wedding.

She said that she would do it with pleasure, but would have to rush it, so in fairness Nan decided that it was time that William had his clothes from the same tailor as his father.

Miss Davies was pleased with Nan's decision. It would have been a rush for her but she wouldn't have refused Nan. She had been so good to her and since her wedding, nearly all the gentry of the town came to her to have their clothes made, so Miss Davies owed her living to Nan. Thank goodness things had been resolved and she had a good life now.

No-one had seen Letty's dress in the making, she was keeping it out of sight until it was finished.

The day arrived; Letty called Nan and Lady Elizabeth to come to the sewing room. They both arrived at the same time and as they walked in, Letty was standing in front of the long mirror in all her glory. She was absolutely stunning.

The dress was made of white satin, very tight at the bodice, with a full crinoline. She had a coronet of orange blossom and a long, flowing, pure white veil.

Lady Elizabeth couldn't get over it. "It's beautiful, you have succumbed yourself this time my dear," she told Miss Davies, who in turn was admiring the vision before them.

"Fine clothes do not make fine people," she told Lady Elizabeth. "I had a perfect mould to put my material on, that is my opinion. It was like Nan here, she also had a perfect figure for me to work on. That dress wouldn't look anything if I put it on anyone like me, so all the praise doesn't go to me, aren't I right?"

In the Arms of Merlin

Yes you are," said Lady Elizabeth, "but our part of it mattered the most."

Letty was wide eyed and a little tearful.

"Now, now my dear," Lady Elizabeth said; "no tears. Your wedding day should be one of the happiest days of your life, so please don't cry, or we will all be crying and that will never do. I know it is an emotional time for you and John. It would have been sol lovely for both your parents to be here with us, but that can never be, so you will have to make do with David and myself, not forgetting Nan and young William. We are your family and we will never let you down.

John and yourself have been like my own, ever since you were brought here after the tragedy of your parents and that is how it will be, until the day I die and then David will take over and he will see you and your new husband Jack right, so don't you worry about anything. All will be well."

Spring arrived and Nan felt a little happier. She didn't have that awful feeling of foreboding hanging over her now that she had confided in David. It was as if he had lifted it all away from her. It had certainly helped that she had gone back to the Tivoli, it was only a few days a week and before long she would have to finish there, as she didn't want anything to happen with her pregnancy. She was going to enjoy having this baby, having William was a nightmare. Apart from the fact that she was only fourteen, she didn't have any family and the way she had got pregnant used to haunt her every waking hour of the day.

It was on her mind, even after he was born. When she was in gaol, she thought of that vile man and what he had done to her. From this very moment, Nan thought to herself, those thoughts are not going to spoil things for this baby. From now on, her only thoughts were going to be lovely ones.

On the morning of the wedding, the sun was out of sight behind some dark clouds. Nan was disappointed with the weather. She told David that it was very cloudy, he said, "don't worry, Mr Griffiths, the old boy in the Lodge, told me exactly how the weather was going to be today, so please don't bother yourself about it. Once mid-day arrived, it's going to be fine, even hot."

Mr Griffiths had got a system of his own to find out about weather.

"I didn't have enough time to hear exactly how he does it, but when I get more time, I am going to listen to what he says. He has been right every time I have asked him."

"That's a good thing to know," Nan said, "does he tell everyone?"

"No," David said, "I think it is only me. I take time to talk to the old boy. He lives on his own and appreciates a chat. Not that I have got time to chat very much with anybody, but I seem to have taken over where my Papa left off. Papa was very fond of Mr Griffiths and I suppose he feels that he's talking to part of my father when he talks to me. I don't know," David said, "I might be wrong, but that is how I feel."

After breakfast they went down to the main dining room to see if everything was going to plan.

All was well. Letty was very nervous and Nan told her to come up to the west wing for a while, to have a chat to take her mind off the events which were to follow.

Nan couldn't believe that Letty was so nervous. She always thought of Letty as a tower of strength. Her own wedding was different I suppose, than helping someone else.

"There are so many things to go wrong aren't there?" she told Nan. "I can't believe all the things that I worried about."

"Letty you shouldn't have worried at all," Nan said, "what are we here for?"

In the Arms of Merlin

"Nan you had your own problems to think about and I didn't want to put on you both thinking about my problems. There wasn't all that to worry about, just silly things."

"Well all the more reason why you should have told David or me. From now on, no more keeping anything to yourself. It doesn't matter how big or small the problem, you must share it with us. Is there anything at the moment or are you worry free?"

Letty smiled, she could see the funny side of the situation.

The biggest worry was, would everybody come to the wedding and would Jack think that she looked lovely. She dare not tell Nan the sort of things that had her in such a state.

I suppose it didn't help that Lady Elizabeth had popped up to London for a few days to buy her hat for the wedding.

"Never mind Letty," Nan said, "it will all be over as soon as you turn around. I seemed to worry a lot more than I showed. I was coming into your family. I didn't know if I was going to be accepted or not. As you realise, I was from the other side of life. A little no one, who had the cheek to fall in love with the most eligible bachelor in the County. Also one of the wealthiest too.

So my dear Letty, you will be fine. I know Jack is an ordinary working lad, but he is a good worker and a lovely boy. David would not have taken him under his wing, as regards to the business and in a few hours you will be his wife and I know you will have a good life with him. So throw your cares and your worries over your shoulder and enjoy your wonderful day."

They didn't have a full lunch, they had a snack, as the wedding banquet was only a matter of hours away and they didn't want to spoil that. If it was anything like David and Nan's, they were in for another treat.

The cooks had excelled themselves and they would this time again.

In the Arms of Merlin

By two o'clock everyone was dressed except Letty. They were all in the drawing room in the main house.

Jack didn't have parents. He lost his mother just before he started the business with David. He only had a sister, who was married with one son. She was a very nice girl, and her husband was too. He wasn't at the wedding because he was in the army and couldn't get home in time.

Jack had brought them up yesterday to stay with Auntie and Uncle. He was also staying there with them. Auntie Sal had a house full, so she was in her element.

She had cut time down in the Lanes, because it was getting a little bit much for her. She still had her money coming in from the business, Nan had seen to that. She vowed that neither of them would be short of money again. It was her way of paying them back for what they did for her when she was in dire straight.

John, Mary's little son was as happy as Larry. Uncle Will had taken to him and they played all the time. He missed William/ Since Nan had moved, they only got together once a week now and that was only since Nan had gone back to the Tivoli. That was going to stop now that Nan was pregnant, so uncle made the most of little John.

We were all ready to be taken to the wedding; everyone had gone off in their respective carriage.

John, who was giving her away said, "I had better go upstairs to get Letty. "Off he went, is seemed only a few seconds that they were both standing on the landing, looking down at us.

It took my breath away to see her walking down the broad staircase on John's arm. She was a vision of loveliness. Nan had never seen such a beautiful bride and she was smiling like a bride should be.

Nan was glad that they had that little chat this morning. She thought that it had done the trick.

I suppose at the last minute, one does think awful things that can go wrong, but Nan could see that was all behind Letty now.

She was just looking forward to her new life with the man that she loved, with all her heart. As they got to the bottom of the staircase, Nan went up to Letty and kissed her and whispered in her ear, something that no-one heard, but Letty gave a beautiful smile as she listened. They all went up in turn to give her a kiss.

William was so excited he couldn't contain himself, until Nan had to be a bit firm with him, or he would have been in a state by the time he arrived at the Church.

David and his family went in the last carriage.

Lady Elizabeth had already gone with the maid of honour, who was Esther, who by the way also looked lovely. She had a crinoline, in sky blue, a little coronet of flowers and a posy of the same flowers. They all made a lovely sight.

When David and his family landed outside St Peter's Church there was a crowd of people there waiting.

Some from Nan's Tearooms, others mostly tenants. Everyone was chatting and looking in a wedding mood.

There were a few children running around the place, little boys mostly, waiting for the bridegroom to throw money at them after the wedding was over.

The service was over in no time. As they walked back down the aisle, Jack gave Nan a broad smile and a cheeky wink, which Nan reciprocated.

As they came out of the Church door, the sun was in full view. It was so nice. Everything looks different when the sun shines and it certainly shone for Letty and Jack.

They stayed outside the Church for about ten minutes, being kissed and congratulated by all their friends and families, before they all made their way back to the Plas for the banquet.

In the Arms of Merlin

By the time David and Nan got back, Letty and Jack were standing at the entrance of the ballroom receiving their guests. They made a lovely couple, both so good looking and of course they had excelled themselves today.

There was a long line in front of them, because they were the last to leave the Church. They had to pick the vicar up to save him riding over on his horse.

They had a good chat on the way. Even William was chatty with him. The vicar had started talking about horses. That was it for William, who ate, drank and slept horses.

She hoped that he would change one day because it could get a little boring sometimes. Nan supposed that young ladies would be the topic of conversation with him later on but Nan was sure that she would have to have a horse somewhere in the background for him to be at home with her. Poor thing, Nan thought.

It seemed to be hours later that the meal was over. Then the time came for the speeches. They all took their turn to speak. It had all been planned by John and Dr Morris, who Jack had asked to be his best man. Jack didn't have a friend really, no-one to be able to stand up and take control of a wedding, especially this one, with most of the gentry of the county, so seeing as he, Will, was a friend of the family as well, Jack asked him and he did very well.

David was called up and gave a great speech; then it was time for the groom to get up. He started to stand up, but was asked to sit down for a minute, as there was one more to speak.

Jack was shocked. As far as he was concerned, everyone had given their speeches. There was a murmur going around the ballroom, wondering what was going on.

All of a sudden there was a scraping sound by Nan's side and young William was getting up and making his way over to Letty and Jack. Nan couldn't believe her eyes, he looked to shy, making his way to the top table. He had something in his hand.

Nan couldn't make out what it was, or what he was going to say to them. She was getting really edgy by now.

William arrived by Letty and Jack. He shook jack's hand, kissed Letty and presented them with the thing that he had in his hand. He gave the most wonderful speech that Nan had ever heard from anyone, leave along an eight-year-old.

The tears were streaming down her cheeks. She got out her handkerchief and turned to David and could see that David was in tears too.

After he had finished his speech, he turned to the guests and bowed and walked back to his seat by Nan.

She didn't know what to tell him, so she just took him into her arms and they both cried together.

Letty knew that she was going to cry at some time in the day, but she didn't think it was going to be William who was going to make her cry.

No-one at all had any idea that he was going to do anything.

When had he written his speech, or where?

Nan supposed that it was down at the stables he had prepared it. Never mind where it was done, it was perfect.

Nan was so proud of him. That he had taken it upon himself to stand up and do what he did. The gift that he had given them was a horse shoe, which had been burnished like silver.

"The blacksmith must have helped him with that," David said.

Nan could see the pride in David's eyes as he talked to William. No wonder the little boy was excited outside the Church.

After all the speeches were over, Nan felt a little tired, so she asked to be excused and went to lie down.

David took her up but William stayed, as there were a few friends and relatives to play with, so he was happy.

Between, Nan was so full with the delicious food of the banquet – which it was – and she was getting so big, she undressed and went to lie on the bed.

David was a little worried. It wasn't like Nan to gib anything, especially a wedding, certainly not Letty's. He lay down by her side and questioned her how she was feeling.

Nan tried to explain to him that it was nothing. She was just too full and tired out. David wasn't satisfied, so he went downstairs to ask Will, their doctor.

It was better to be safe than sorry.

Everything had been cleared away by the time David got back to the banqueting hall. All was ready for the ball, the musicians were on the stage and Jack and Letty were being asked to start the dancing off.

David just caught Will, as he was going onto the dance floor. David whispered in his ear and he asked to be excused from the dance and said he wouldn't be long, so off they went back to Nan, who by now was fast asleep.

David was surprised to see that Nan was sleeping and was a little relieved, there couldn't be too much wrong.

He looked at Will and said, "by George, I don't believe this."

"Don't worry," Will said, "she is really exhausted, I will just check her over, then she can go back to sleep." Will shook Nan gently until she woke.

Even Nan was surprised that she had gone to sleep, she sat up slowly and wondered what Will was doing there.

David explained that he was worried, so he had fetched Will.

"No more umming and harring," Will said, "let me examine you," so amid protestation Nan let him give her the once over.

After a thorough examination, Will was satisfied that all was well with Nan. He said to her, "now go back to sleep and you David, come back downstairs with me to give this girl some peace."

David put a cover over Nan and kissed her tenderly and said, "I will come back in a while to see how you are. All right darling?"

"You fuss too much," Nan told him, gave him a lovely smile and went straight back to sleep.

David left her in peace.

By the time he got back downstairs, the ball was in full swing and in the middle of everybody, there was William dancing with Letty, as if he was a grown up. They looked so happy dancing together, you could see the adoration in William's eyes.

David hoped that Letty's marriage would not make any difference to their relationship, although David could see no problem, as Jack was a very nice boy and he also thought the world of William.

David made his way to where his mother was sitting. As he sat down beside her, she asked how Nan was and what was the trouble.

David explained that she was just exhausted and all was well.

Lady Elizabeth looked relieved after talking to David.

All of a sudden, William came from nowhere and jumped on David's lap and whispered in his ear. David was smiling as William moved over to his Grandmama and whispered in her ear too.

She didn't smile or laugh, she was speechless. No-one else was told anything about the whispers until the following morning, but Nan was told later in the evening.

What William had told David and his grandmother was, Letty had told him, that he was to be Godfather to Jack and Letty's first child. William was over the moon, the only thing was, he couldn't tell anyone about it and that was going to kill William. He just couldn't keep a secret for love nor money.

It was two hours later that Nan arrived back in the ballroom. She had put something looser on, had a good sleep and had rested her body, so she was ready for action.

Everyone fussed over her as she sat down and turned to David and said, "now ask me to dance," and off they went.

Even though Nan was rather big in her pregnancy, they were a handsome couple. They stood out in the crowd.

Nan had a dance with all their friends and danced nearly every dance through the course of the evening. She was enjoying herself and was glad that she had gone to change and had a rest.

Letty and Jack had sloped off earlier in the evening. They must have been tired and had better things to do.

Around two o'clock, the music stopped and people started to make their way home.

They all came to Lady Elizabeth to thanked her for the lovely day and the ballroom emptied in no time.

Lady Elizabeth asked David if they would like to come and have a hot toddy before retiring.

David was so tired and was just about to decline the invitation, when Nan chirped up with, "thank you, that will be great."

David followed the ladies, absolutely exhausted. They arrived in the drawing room. Lady Elizabeth rang for the butler and ordered three hot toddies. William had been put to bed earlier, so it was just the three of them.

"Thank you Nan," Lady Elizabeth told her daughter-in-law, she knew that David was ready for bed, but Nan had heard the urgency in Lady Elizabeth's voice.

They sat and talked for about an hour. In the end, David was asleep in the chair, his mother didn't mind, it was Nan she wanted to talk to in any case.

In the Arms of Merlin

She knew that Letty and Jack would stay with her until they bought a house of their own. She was dreading that time, when they would leave her. She still had John but he wasn't the company that Letty was.

She loved John dearly, but Letty seemed to be closer somehow. Perhaps because she was a girl. Boys don't seem to be as affectionate as girls, or perhaps she shouldn't say less affectionate, they don't shower their feelings as much.

Little did Lady Elizabeth know, but Jack had talked about this situation. Jack was quite content to stay at the Plas for the time being, but perhaps later on they could build on the land. They would then be on their own, but close to Lady Elizabeth.

Nan tried to reassure her mother-in-law that she was sure that they wouldn't be leaving for a while. She seemed pleased to hear that and seemed more content after speaking to Nan.

She was so glad that David had found such a girl as Nan. She was a treasure and to think how she had been brought up and the life she had led.

It was wonderful how she had turned out; from a gaol bird, a skivvy, a businesswoman to the Lady of the Manor and a very nice girl too.

Lady Elizabeth counted her blessings every morning when she woke up and hoped it would always be the same for her family.

At long last, Nan could see that her mother-in-law was ready to go to bed. They both got up and Nan woke David. He was in a deep sleep and Nan had quite a job to wake him.

Eventually he got up, gave his mother a kiss goodnight, put his arm around Nan and they made their way to the west wing. They got to bed eventually and slept right through until William came into their bedroom and woke them up.

They took their time. David was the first to bathe, then the maids came up with more water for Nan and William.

Usually he would have been gone downstairs like a shot but Nan wouldn't let him go today. He tried to get away without washing even, but failed today.

Nan had to smile at William, he hated washing and if he could get away with it he would.

Nan let him go into the tub first so that he could go out to see his own darling Meg.

Once he had been seen to, Nan had her turn in the tub. She took her time, as it was quite a treat to do that. She was usually rushing to get William to school, but today she had only to think of herself.

David came upstairs to see how long she was going to be. She told him to carry on and have his breakfast, but he wouldn't have any of it.

He said it wasn't often they could eat their breakfast together and at leisure. So that's what happened.

After breakfast they both went out for a walk, they even went to the stables and guess who was there? Yes Letty, but Jack was with her this morning. It was funny really to see them together on the morning after their wedding. You would have thought that horses would be the last thing on their minds. But there you are, it takes allsorts to make a world.

CHAPTER 22 – VISITING AUNTIE

All the relatives who had come to the wedding were invited to luncheon, so it was a full house. John and Esther were looking very much in love and Nan couldn't help thinking how long would it be before they had another wedding on their hands. Nan hoped that it would be after her baby would be born.

After a couple of hours chatting at the lunch table, Jack and Letty took Auntie May back home. Jack wanted to take the pony and trap but Lady Elizabeth insisted on a carriage. The pony and trap was all right for Letty and Jack but not for Auntie May.

Nan was glad about those arrangements. Auntie May would never get up to a trap. She wouldn't have moaned mind, but it would have been a mammoth job for Letty and Jack.

After fond farewells they left. By this time everyone had gone. Lady Elizabeth made her way slowly through the hall.

Nan said, "how about coming over to us for the afternoon? Goodness knows how long those two will be before coming back."

Lady Elizabeth stopped and said "thank you very much, that will be lovely."

There was a definite change in her footsteps. It looked as if she had perked up a bit after having the invitation from Nan.

Later that night in bed, David told Nan that she was the most perfect woman that he had ever known. She had such tact and consideration for everybody. David couldn't get over how she could deal with people, considering her upbringing. It must have been while she was in the business that she had picked up such diplomacy.

In the Arms of Merlin

David could see that his mother was dragging her feet as they walked back to the drawing room until Nan asked her to come over to them for tea, then the spring was back in her step. She must be feeling that this was going to be the start of the loneliness, with all the children leaving home, but as Nan told David, she didn't think that Letty and Jack would be moving out for a while, because Jack was just starting in business. Nan knew how proud he was and she didn't think that he would be willing to let Lady Elizabeth buy their house for them.

David said his mother had thought of giving them a house as a wedding present, but held back at the last minute, realising that she would be sending them away from her, so she waited until after the wedding.

Nan was seven months pregnant now and was much bigger on this baby than she was on William. It must be the different lifestyle she thought to herself. She had to work very hard when she was carrying William. It didn't make any difference in the workhouse if you were pregnant or not, more than likely they worked them harder to punish them for being wicked girls.

Nan shivered when she thought of those bad old days and thanked God that she had come from there. She had often thought of ending her life when she was in gaol, as nearly every day was a day from Hell. She would never forget it but on the other side of the scale, she had made two good friends from the hell-hole.

Nan tried not to think of the terrible place, but sometimes her thoughts would nearly always land up in the gaol.

David was always asking her, "what is the matter now?"

She never told him, nor did she ever tell him what she had gone through there, just that incident with Lil and her hair. She had to tell him about that, because he wanted her to leave her hair down and she couldn't. He had a terrible shock then, thank goodness he didn't know any more.

Letty and Jack were settling down to married life. Jack was working very hard and would be home late at night, but as David said, it would be like that for a while until he levelled out and then things would get better.

Letty didn't moan about Jack at all, she also realised how businessmen had to work. She knew how David and John, her brothers, had been a few years ago, but their working hard was down to no-one at home waiting for them. Things were different for the two of them now and their business was well established, but Jack was getting there.

It was a weekend that David had to go to Bristol on business. He offered Nan and William to come with him but Nan declined. She had an idea of her own. She thought that William and her would take a ride to see Auntie May.

She told David about it and asked him if he thought it was a good idea?

Seeing that she didn't want to go with him, he thought it was a great idea and made arrangements for a coach to take them down and fetch them back the following day so they would have a nice long stay with her Aunt.

William was so excited, he wouldn't go to sleep the night before they went. Nan had to go cross with him and tell him that if he didn't go to sleep she would leave him behind. That stopped his nonsense immediately and off to sleep he went.

They all had to get up early in the morning, David to make an early start as well, because he had to meet a Sea Captain before the ship sailed on the tide, so after fond farewells, they all set off at the same time.

William was so excited, he hadn't been down to Auntie's for a long time. He loved it down there, there was a boy living next door to Auntie and they played together for ages the last time, so William was looking forward to seeing his friend again.

It only took about an hour to get to Auntie May's. It wasn't all that far, it took longer to go by coach and pair than riding on horseback, but the latter was out of the question at the moment – later perhaps, but not now.

When they arrived on the doorstep, Auntie May nearly had a fit. She had no idea that they were coming, she was so pleased to see them. She would think about the food later, she thought, but after the hugs and the kissing and the coachman had gone, Nan pulled out a very large bag and it was absolutely full of food.

Auntie May's mouth just dropped nearly to her boots; "you should have never done this," she told Nan, "I would have gone down to the shop later, to see about the food."

"Never mind now, Auntie." Nan said, "let's sit down and have a cup of tea."

William had gone off like a shot as soon as he landed on the doorstep of Auntie's house. They wouldn't have to worry about him until his tummy would start calling out to him, so they sat in peace.

Auntie always had bara brith and welsh cakes in the house, no matter what time of the month or the year, she made those even if she was ill. She had to make those cakes in case someone would visit her.

They ate the bara brith. Nan had three slices and she also had three welsh cakes with farm butter on them. She hoped that they wouldn't be too rich for her. She immediately put that thought out of her mind and ate another two. By now she couldn't move.

Auntie was laughing at Nan. She had to go and lie down on the sofa in the front room. Auntie put a coat over her legs, closed the door and let her sleep.

While Nan was sleeping, Auntie went to look in the huge bag of food that Nan had brought down with her, because there was no use looking in her pantry, there was nothing there. Life had got very hard for Auntie these last few months, but she wouldn't tell anyone, she was a proud woman and had looked after herself since her husband had died years ago. She had never asked for a penny from anyone and she certainly wasn't going to start now.

In the bag she found a large ham that had already been boiled. There were potatoes, leeks, onions, peas, kidney beans and broad beans. There was an absolute feast in the bag.

Auntie was nearly in tears as she brought the stuff out from the bag. Two hours had gone by and Auntie had a delicious dinner going, the smell was wafting through the little cottage.

Auntie hadn't cooked a meal like this for a good few years. She cleaned the potatoes and the other vegetables, made a sauce and remembered that she had some parsley in her little garden. Everything was now in full swing.

The door from the front room opened and out came Nan. "Auntie," she said, "why did you let me sleep like that? I should be out here helping you. I didn't come down to make work for you."

"Now look here my girl," she said, "it has been a pleasure to cook this meal. I don't get much of a chance to have a whole ham in my pantry and all those fresh vegetables. It has been a real treat for me, so you enjoy yourself eating it, as much as I have enjoyed cooking it."

Nan went over to her Auntie and put her arms around her, they stood together in an embrace. "I do miss you Auntie," Nan said, "I can't seem to get down as much as I would like to these days. David and I have thought and talked about the situation a few times. I think that if you would like, you could come to live with us, or if you would rather keep your independence, David could get you somewhere near us. What do you think of that?" Nan asked.

In the Arms of Merlin

Auntie was flabbergasted with Nan's suggestion. She couldn't believe hear ears. She was on half dishing the dinner out. She had to sit down and there she was with a big ladle in her hand and her apron in her other hand, drying the tears from her eyes.

Nan couldn't understand why she was crying and went over to her, put her arms around her and said, "don't worry Auntie, I can be too forceful sometimes. If you don't want to move from here, you have only got to say."

Auntie put the ladle down on the table and used her two hands now to wipe her eyes. Her whole body was shaking with sobs.

Nan was starting to get upset and said, "Auntie don't worry, I will never mention it again. You can stay here till the end of your days."

By now Nan was crying and she wished that she could cut her tongue out. She had certainly spoilt everything for Auntie and herself. Why had she been so foolish to approach Auntie with the suggestion? She certainly would have to change her ways and not jump so quickly into something that would come into her head.

By this time William was playing outside, could smell the dinner and had come in through the back door. The first thing he saw was his mother and his Great aunt in each other's arms, both in tears.

He stopped in his tracks and said, "what is the matter Mama, has someone died?"

"No, no, my darling, there has just been a misunderstanding between Auntie May and me."

By now, Auntie May had stopped crying. Her eyes were all swollen and his Mama didn't look much better.

After Auntie had got her breath back, she looked at Nan and said, "you certainly came down here to an answer to my prayers. I wasn't actually asking the Lord for you to come here today with all this food, but I was praying for him to give me some help. I wasn't asking for a lot, just enough for me to live on and there you were on my doorstep. Nan, the Lord certainly answered me this time."

Nan was shocked when Auntie was telling her how she was living hand to mouth, with just enough food to keep her going after he husband had died. They had a little money put away for a rainy day. It wasn't much but Auntie had lived frugally and it had lasted until a few months ago.

Nan was so taken aback by what Auntie had said, she didn't realise that there was a difficulty at all.

"Oh Auntie," Nan said, "why didn't you tell me? I am so wrapped in my own little world that I didn't even think about you being short of money. When we got married, I took you to buy your clothes for the wedding. I didn't think that you didn't have any money of your own. I just wanted to give you a treat. I wished that you would have told me."

"Nan," Auntie said, "I could have never have told you, I was just keeping my head above water. I went to the big house up the road and asked if there was something that I could do. The cook, who I knew, took pity on me and said I could come in a few days a week to do some washing and that is how I have survived. Things were gradually getting worse. In another month I would have had to go to the workhouse."

"But Auntie, I would have found out by then, wouldn't I?"

"Listen Nan fach," she said, "you have got your own life to lead and I didn't' expect you to visit me ever again. We live in different worlds, you have come on in your life, I would never think of living off you."

"Auntie, where would I have been if it wasn't for you? I would have no-one left in this world, so don't tell me any more. By this time tomorrow, we will be on our way to your new home and we will keep you like the lady you are. I don't want to hear another word."

In the Arms of Merlin

By now, the dinner was starting to catch, so after calling William again, because he skedaddled out when he saw the two women crying.

Auntie carved the ham and Nan put out the vegetables. They sat down for their lunch all smiles, especially William because he loved Auntie May dearly.

After they finished washing the dishes and the saucepans, everything was put away in its place. They sat down and had a good talk.

After their long discussion Nan said, "all we can do today is pack everything, then we can come back down to get the furniture and you are out of here. Just go next door and tell Mrs Evans that you are coming back with us for a few days, then by then, David will have found somewhere for you to live. The next move will be your furniture coming up to your new home Auntie, you know that you're welcome to stay in our house, you wouldn't have to lift a finger to do anything, but I know that won't be your cup of tea. Am I right?"

"Well yes," Auntie replied. "Oh Nan, how ever can I thank you?"

"There's no need, you have thanked me once and that is sufficient, so let us go and do some packing."

There wasn't a load of stuff there to pack, so they all sat down and had another lovely meal that Auntie had put together. She was good at that.

They all went to be about nine o'clock, because they were all done in and they wanted to get up fairly early in the morning to finish off what hadn't been done.

They ate a hearty breakfast and after clearing everything away, Auntie asked about the food that was over. "Do you want me to pack it away and bring it home?"

"Good gracious no," Nan said, "how much is left over?"

"Quite a lot," Auntie said.

"Well take it into Mrs Evans next door, but if you know of someone else, take it to them."

"Are you sure?" Auntie said.

"No more to be said, take it now."

Poor Mrs Evans was lost for words when she saw the whole load of food that Auntie had taken in next door. Nan could hear the kids screeching for joy when they saw the food. I don't suppose they had seen so much food at the same time.

Auntie said so long to Mrs Evans and the children and came back in tears. "I am going to miss them."

"They are going to miss you too," Nan said, "never mind, we will come down again. It is not that far and if push came to shove, I could drive, but that will be after the baby is born. Now how does that sound Auntie?"

"It all sounds great to me my dear."

It was about eleven o'clock that the coachman knocked the tiny front door. He had a bit of a shock to see that he had an extra passenger in his coach but didn't mention it. It wasn't his place to do so. He just carried on putting a few bags under the carriage, helped his mistress and her aunt into the carriage and was about to pick young William up, when William suddenly asked his Mama if he could ride on top with the coachman.

Nan said, "all right, but don't you ummbug George, or you will have to come into the carriage straight away.

George smiled and said, "it is all right Ma'am, he will be fine up with me.

George was one of William's friends in the stables; the little boy got on well with all the staff at the Plas. He mingled with all classes in life. He could talk with the servants, also he would converse with any Lord or Lady that came to the Plas and there were many of them, friends of Grandmama and Dada too.

In the Arms of Merlin

They drove for an hour and the sway of the carriage was starting to make Nan feel a little sick, so by the time they drove up the drive to the Plas, Nan was very glad to get out and have some fresh air.

The carriage was stopped just at the bottom of the stone steps that led up to the balustrade in the front of the house.

George got William down first, then he helped Auntie, then Nan. Nan was going to say something to William, but he was off like a shot.

"Don't worry Ma'am," George said, "I will give him a message when I get back to the stables."

"Thank you George," Nan said, "just tell him that I want him to be in the house at one o'clock promptly for luncheon. We have a guest."

"I will tell him Ma'am, George said and smiled, as they moved off up the steps.

The two ladies got up the steps and entered into the hall. There was nobody around, so they made their way to the west wing to David and Nan's home.

Poor auntie, as she was walking along the corridor towards the living quarters she told Nan, "I don't think I could live in a place like this."

"Of course you could, you would get used to it. I had to and I have been in places that you would never think of being in, so don't you worry, you will get used to things around here before long."

Nan settled her Aunt in her bedroom and left her to empty her carpet bag and put the few possessions away out of sight, in case anyone came in.

She had just finished putting her things in the drawers, when there was a knock on the door. She was startled for a few seconds and thought that she had better say, "come in."

As she did, a young girl came into the bedroom and put a tray with a silver service down on a table with some delicate bone china cups.

In the Arms of Merlin

Auntie looked at the young girl and said "thank you." She curtsied and off she went.

Auntie sat down on one of the comfortable armchairs in her room. By that time Nan had arrived. She sat down and started to pour the tea, it went down like nectar and they both had second cups but that didn't taste as good as the first one. It never does though does it?!Nan thought it would be better for Auntie to have a cup of tea in her room today, she must have been physically and mentally exhausted.

How long had things been going bad for her? I don't suppose she would ever know, but never mind she was here now and we will look after her from now on.

When David came home from his long trip to Bristol, he was dog tired. H kissed Nan, gave her a hug, welcomed Auntie and asked to be excused. He had to go and lie down. He was so tired. He asked Nan, "you don't mind do you darling?"

"Don't be silly," Nan said, "off you go, we will see you at dinner. Don't you worry, Auntie and I have got lots to talk about."

As David was going upstairs to their bedroom, he wondered why Auntie May was here. She didn't come very often. He didn't mind, he was fond of the little lady. I suppose Nan will put me in the picture when I see her later. Then all his thoughts were about just taking all his clothes off and jumping into bed and to oblivion.

It was six hours later before David woke. He opened his eyes and realised that he was in his own bed, gave a big stretch and just lolled for a few minutes more.

He got up eventually, bathed, got himself dressed and made his way downstairs.

Nan turned to David, put her arms out towards him and asked him if he felt better after his sleep? "I was just going to come up to see how you were getting on, dinner won't be too long."

"I am ravenous," David said, "I haven't eaten since I had breakfast and that was at five o'clock this morning."

"Good gracious," Auntie May said, "you must have been tired to be able to sleep through hunger."

David helped Nan up from her chair, it was getting hard for her to get up on her own these days.

Echoes of the dinner gong were still echoing as they sat down to eat. David had never felt so hungry, he went through his first course like a hot knife through butter. Even William commented on the speed that his Dada was eating.

"You will be ill Dada," William said, as David was going through the second course. He started to slow down now, his digestive juices were beginning to get satisfied.

He was more relaxed by now and started to converse with Auntie May. Before he asked her about her visit, Nan chirped in with what was going on. David was a little puzzled with what Nan had said, he couldn't quite understand what she was talking about, so instead of going in blind, he changed the conversation, no doubt Nan would enlighten him when they were on their own.

They got through the meal eventually and then adjourned to the drawing room. James the butler brought a large brandy on a tray for David and his usual cigar. He had already asked the ladies if they minded him smoking they both told him to go ahead. David was glad because he didn't want to go to his study on his own, he wanted to be near Nan, he had really missed her these last few days. He wouldn't have to go away again for quite a while, certainly not before the baby was due.

On their way to bed, they looked in to see William. He was fast asleep, his blonde hair all over the pillow.

"I know I shouldn't say this," Nan said, "but isn't he a handsome boy."

"He certainly is," David said, "and a credit to you Nan. When I think what you have been through, I love you all the more and I couldn't love William any more if he was my own son."

Nan was very touched with what David had said.

David went on to their room and Nan knocked Auntie May's door. She had just got into bed and had her back to Nan.

"Are you sleeping Auntie?" Nan whispered.

Auntie lifted up her arm, not able to answer Nan, she was gently sobbing.

Nan was so surprised, that she ran towards the bed and sat on the side and gently rubbed her Aunt's shoulder and said, "don't cry Auntie dear, everything will be all right. David will see you right, so don't worry any more. You will soon make friends and you will never have to worry about money again."

"Oh Nan," Auntie said, "you are a dear girl, I know it was the worst day of your life when you arrived the day of the fire, but that was the best day in my life. Through that terrible disaster, I was given a good daughter like you, so whatever happens in the future, I will always be grateful to you and David."

"We will have a talk in the morning", she told her Aunt, "so no more crying and off to sleep. Goodnight and God bless you." Nan left the room.

By the time she got into their bedroom, David was in bed. She thought that he may have gone to sleep, but no he was wide awake. Nan could see a long night in front of her, once she got into bed!

David put his arms around her and kept kissing her. He kissed her eyes, her nose, her forehead, her cheeks, her hair, her mouth, her ears, until she had to tell him; "David slow down."

He answered, "I am sorry darling, I just can't keep my lips off you."

In the Arms of Merlin

Nan smiled, she had never heard David say that before, she didn't want him to think that she didn't want him to kiss her, she loved David's way of showing his love for her, so she humoured him for another ten minutes, then broached the subject of Auntie May.

David looked serious when Nan told him about their visit while he was away. David couldn't believe that things were so bad with the poor dear. "How ever didn't she tell you sooner?"

"It was just luck that we went to visit when we did. Goodness knows what would have happened, there wasn't anybody to ask for help where she lived. She would have had to go into the workhouse."

"Well she will be all right from now on," David said, "She can live here as long as she wants."

"But no David," Nan said, I think that she would like to have a little place of her own. Do you know of somewhere near us for her? She is a very independent lady you know.

"All right," David said, "I will look around in the morning.

Nan felt happy now that David had taken over the job of seeing to Auntie May.

CHAPTER 23 – IT'S A GIRL!

They both woke up about the same time. The sun was streaming into the bedroom.

"It looks as if it is going to be a hot day." David said as he threw the clothes off his body.

Nan did the same. They lay there together, just enjoying each other's company.

David made the first move to get up. He kissed Nan as he got out of bed and told her to stay for a while.

Nan wasn't in the mood to stay upstairs on her own.

By the time she got downstairs, Auntie was already at the breakfast table and was being looked after by Mary. Nan could see that auntie was a little ill at east, but was coping all right.

They all ate a hearty breakfast and chatted through the meal.

David was back to his old self once again. He had got over his tiredness and was raring to go. Looking forward to a good day's work.

As he left the ladies, he kissed Nan on the cheek and said, "I'll see to that business as soon as I can today. All right?"

Nan nodded and said, "will be see you at lunch?"

"I don't think so," he said, "I might be eating out today. See you later then darling," and off he went.

It got hotter as the morning went on. Nan had made Auntie happy by giving her some socks to darn.

While auntie was happily occupied with the darning, Nan went up to her bedroom to sort some of the baby clothes out. She had bought everything new. She didn't have anything after William, poor baby, he had very different clothes to what this baby was going to have. Never mind,

William is no worse off with the bad start he had in his little life.

Everything was in the drawers, ready for the arrival of the next member of the family. She had even put the things ready for the midwife for the actual birth.

Mrs Thomas had been a midwife in this district for about twenty-two years and had a very good reputation and that made Nan very happy. She was more scared about having this baby than she was of having William. She couldn't remember who delivered William, but she didn't do a very good job. Nan had a terrible time on that confinement.

Nan's attitude was entirely different this time, she was so ignorant of the facts of life and so young. Probably that was the reason for everything that went wrong, so Nan read all about childbirth and now knew what to expect and knew what were the best things to do to help herself, so if all this preparation worked, things should be so much better.

David came home around five thirty, he was healthily tired.

Nan left him for a while, then she made her way up to their room. He had bathed and changed and was lying on the bed. He wasn't sleeping, so Nan went to lay by his side.

She asked him what sort of a day he had had.

"Not bad. By the way, "he said, "I have been enquiring about a cottage for your Auntie May. There will be one coming free in a few weeks. She really does want to live on her own doesn't she? There is no problem with her living here with us, is there?"

"No," Nan said, "she's so independent. That is how she would like it, if it is at all possible."

"Well, that is how it will be, if she changes her mind, she can always come back here to live."

"Oh thank you David, how I was ever able to find a man like you I'll never know."

In the Arms of Merlin

David smiled and said, "it's the other way about you know."

They both hugged each other and their laughter could be heard all over the wing.

It was three weeks later that the house came empty.

Nan took the pony and trap and they both went over to see the cottage. It was a tied cottage. The family who had been living there had moved out of the area to where the wife's parents lived. One of them was ailing and needed looking after, so the husband was lucky enough to have a job as well.

As soon as Nan opened the door into the little hall, Auntie loved the place. She was delighted with it and put her arms around Nan, thanked her profusely.

"I don't know what I would have done without you" she told Nan.

"It was the same for me all those years ago, when I was in trouble, so it works both ways. Now no more about it. All right?"

The subject was closed. Auntie went to look at the rooms. "We will do this and we will do that."

Nan's head was spinning by the time Auntie had decided what she wasn't going to do to the little house.

Nan would have a word with Jack about getting the furniture from her old house. Nan would pay him as if he was working for David so that he wouldn't lose out, but David could see to that.

They must have been there for a couple of hours.

In the end they made their way back to the Plas.

Auntie was delighted and told everybody about her new home. She eventually went to the kitchen to tell cook and as she was leaving, she told her quietly, "you can come and visit me on your days off."

Cook smiled and said, "that will be lovely but don't tell the Mistress."

In the Arms of Merlin

"No, no," Auntie said, "we won't tell anyone."

One of the parlour maids went over with Auntie to clean the house ready for the furniture. They were at it all day.

Auntie came back home to the Plas, she was whacked and went upstairs to have a wash and change. She didn't come down when the dinner gong sounded, so Nan sent one of the maids upstairs to see where she was. She came back down saying that her Aunt was fast asleep on the bed.

"We'll leave her for a while I think," Nan said, "perhaps you will keep her food until later, then we can see how she is then."

"Yes Ma'am," the little maid said.

David and Nan had dinner on their own, which made a change. William had already eaten in the kitchen with cook. Nan had given her permission, he had eaten earlier and gone out again on his pony.

Auntie was firmly established in her new little home in a few days. It was as if she had lived there for ever. Auntie was so pleased how everything had turned out but insisted that she came up to the Plas and did all the mending and anything else that needed doing.

Nan gave in eventually, knowing that it would upset Auntie May if she couldn't help in her own way.

They were now two weeks into August.

Nan got up in the morning and felt a bit yucky, she didn't complain but as the morning went by, she started having niggly little pains in her back. She didn't think much about them and carried on with what she was doing.

By lunchtime, it was so hot that she had to sponge herself down. By the time she had finished, her waters had broken.

Nan managed to ring the bell. One of the maids came, saw her plight and ran for Cook. She came in, puffing and blowing, with her cheeks like two rosy apples.

In the Arms of Merlin

Nan had got to a chair by the time the cook had arrived. Cook panicked a bit, but Nan showed her self-control and Cook eased up and took control of the situation.

She gave orders to the maid to tell one of the grooms to ride into town, firstly to tell the Midwife and tell her to come as soon as possible, then to get the Master and Auntie May, all in that order. She was off like a shot.

Cook asked her mistress if she was able to walk?

"Yes, yes," Nan said, "I am fine, I am not moving because I don't want to make more mess than is needed."

"Don't you worry about the mess," Cook said, "that will all be seen to."

She took her apron off and put in around Nan. They took their time and made their way over to the bed. Nan felt that she was in competent hands with Cook and let her help her to get undressed, then cleaned her up and made her comfortable on top of the bed, put several towels under her, then put a light sheet gently over her.

As the minutes were ticking way, the contractions were starting. Nan could not believe that they had started to quickly after the waters had gone.

With William, she didn't go into labour for hours, but they say that not one birth is like any other.

Nan had been on the bed for fifteen minutes and by now the contractions were coming fast and heavy. She thought that she was losing control but Cook brought her back to reality and she was coping again.

Cook was looking nervously at the clock and thought that someone should have been walking in by now but there was no sign of anyone.

Nan gave such a howl and told Cook that she thought that the baby was coming.

"Right" Cook thought, "I have delivered several calves and puppies, so now's the time to shine. She rang the bell and told the maid to fetch hot water and all the paraphernalia of childbirth. The little maid was hysterical bringing the things into the bedroom and seeing her made Cook all the stronger.

By now Nan was in the middle of it, there was no turning back. The last time Cook looked she could see the baby's head crowning, the contractions were getting closer and closer and more severe, it was no joke now, Nan thought. Now she had started pushing, she couldn't stop herself, with this last push she gave a low growl and the baby's head was out.

"Oh! Well done Ma'am," Cook said, "it won't be long now. Wait a little minute if you can to get your strength back," but before she had finished saying that, Nan was giving another push and the loudest growl Cook had ever heard and the baby was there on the bed. "It's a girl, it's a girl," Cook said; and they were both crying.

In the middle of it all the doctor walked in. Cook hadn't told the groom to get him out but David had called him in case, so from then on Dr Morris took over. Poor Cook, she was shaking as much as Nan. She sat up by Nan's head and held her hand while the doctor got on with the rest of the delivery.

Everybody had arrived at the same time.

After the cord had been cut, the baby had been put in a sheet and given up to Nan, while they got on with the rest of the jobs.

She was a beautiful little girl with jet black hair and a screwed up little face. All crinkly and yelling her heart out. By now, David had come, so there they were; Nan, Cook, David and the baby, all crying.

The birth had been very fast and a bit traumatic for Nan but Dr Morris said she would be fine. The afterbirth came away easily and everything was over in one hour.

Will Morris' work was done now, so the Midwife took over.

In the Arms of Merlin

Will said to David, after congratulating Nan and giving her a big kiss. "Come old boy, let us leave Nan to the ladies."

Before he went, he caught hold of Cook's hand and said, "well done. Your Mistress was very lucky that you were with her."

David didn't know about the situation until then and as they were going downstairs, Will put him in the picture.

He said, "I shall speak to Cook later."

Another half an hour and Nan and the baby were presentable. Everything was in order. Cook had made her way back down to the kitchen and was sat down with a large brandy in front of her that James had got for her. The Master and the Doctor were having one in the drawing room. James and Cook were having one in the kitchen.

Cook was still shaking and was quite white around the gills. They were both laughing now but it was no laughing matter. In the middle of those contractions, Cook didn't think that she would like to go through that again in a hurry.

Never mind. All's well that ends well.

Will Morris went after at least three large brandies.

David went upstairs quietly, in case Nan was sleeping. He knocked the door gently and made his way in. Nan was lying back on the pillow, her face was so pale, she looked like a Dresden doll.

David was taken aback with the look on Nan's face. He asked the Midwife if everything was all right.

She said, "yes, everything is fine."

He made his way over to Nan, took her into his arms and said, "thank you darling, for making me the proudest man in the world."

Nan could see that he was pleased but said, "it is not the son you wanted."

David said, "it is not the end of the world that we didn't have a son, instead we have got a darling little girl, who will look like you one day. Let us just get on with brining up this little beauty. "What are we going to call her?" David asked.

"The choice is yours," Nan said.

"Are you sure?" David said.

"Yes," Nan said.

"Right," David told Nan, "what about three names, Barbara Margaret Elizabeth Jones. How's that?"

"Lovely," Nan said, "But which name shall we call her?"

David looked at her and said, "I think we will call her Margaret."

"Great," Nan said and the names went through the household like wild fire.

Nan had been resting for a few hours before she had any visitors. Lady Elizabeth we the first, then Letty came. There was no sign of William, but they knew that he wouldn't show himself until it was dinner time, he was going to have a surprise when he got home.

It was nearly five o'clock by the time William got home. His usual way into the house was through the kitchen. Nobody said a word to him about the events of the day but they told him that his mother wanted to see him, immediately in her bedroom.

"Bedroom!" William said.

"Yes," Cook said, "she's getting dressed for dinner."

"All right," William said, and off he went.

They were all smiling as he left the kitchen. He took the stairs two at a time. "I'm home Mama, what is it you want? I am just going to have a little wash, then I will be with you."

Nan couldn't understand. She thought that he would be dashing to see her and the baby. She didn't know that he didn't know.

It must have been ten minutes before he knocked his mother's door, peeped in and made his way over to the bed. That puzzled him for a start, Cook said that she was getting dressed for dinner. "Funny things, these grown-ups are, aren't they?" he said to himself.

As he reached the bed, he heard something different. He stopped and looked to his left and there was a baby's crib. "Funny" he thought, "was there a noise coming from that?"

He looked so bewildered that his mother said, "William, you have got a baby sister."

He couldn't believe it. He was so shocked. "Why didn't anyone tell me in the kitchen?" he said.

"I suppose they wanted to surprise you."

He ran the rest of the way to the bed and put his arms around his mother. By now they were both crying.

Nan said, "come on now William, go over to see your little sister."

He went over and was delighted with what he saw.

"She's lovely Mama, can I nurse her?"

"Yes, you will be able to nurse her but not yet, she is only a few hours old. You understand don't you my darling?"

"Yes of course I understand but I just want to hug her and love her."

"William," Nan said, "You have the rest of your life to love, hug and hold her. She is ours now and all those things are what we are supposed to do to our children, sisters and brothers."

William looked up and said, "am I having a brother as well then?"

"I don't mean it literally." Nan said, "I mean that is what life is all about."

William didn't really understand but he showed his mother that he did. He stayed upstairs until his father arrived in the bedroom, then after a bit more excitement between David, William and the baby, the male side of the Jones family went down to dinner and left the females upstairs in the bedroom.

David and William were all smiles as they made their way to the dining room. As soon as they sat down, the meal was being served. Nan's food was sent up to her bedroom.

By now the Nanny had arrived and had taken over the baby.

After the two boys had finished the meal, David sent word to the kitchen, to Cook, telling her to go up to her Mistress' bedroom, in about half an hour.

William was quite puzzled about that. That hadn't happened before, but as he thought earlier, these grown-ups are very odd beings.

As soon as William arrived in the bedroom, he asked where the baby was.

"Nanny has got her now," Nan said.

"Where?" William asked.

"In her quarters," his mother said.

William found out where that was and promptly went looking for the missing baby.

David went to lie on the bed by the side of Nan. All of a sudden, William came back into the bedroom looking very depleted.

"Whatever is the matter?" Nan said.

"That horrible woman will not let me see my own sister. What am I going to do? Send her away Dada." William said.

David sat up and called William to his side and said, "from now on Nanny is in charge of your little sister, so that your Mama can get well again, so are you going to listen to Nanny? She will tell you when you can go in to see the baby. Do you understand what it is all about?"

"All right," he said, "I will listen so that Mama will get better quicker."

It took a few days for William to comply with Nanny's wishes. When William realised that there was no way that he could get over the Nanny. He took another path He used to go into the nursery not even asking to see little Margaret. He would just stand talking to Nanny and asking her questions and generally being nice to her.

She was quite surprised, seeing she had stopped him in no uncertain manner.

As the days went by, they were just sizing each other up. As the time was going on, they got to be very good friends.

Nan got up on the tenth day just to the chair, the following day she started to walk around a little. She felt very weak and knew that she couldn't overdo things, so she just let the world go by.

She eventually got back to her old self and was downstairs doing things just like before, so William for one, was happy as he had always hated to see his Mama ill.

He thought that if she was ill she would die and leave him alone again. He didn't ever tell anyone about his fear, but he would be able to tell little Margaret when she got older.

Little Margaret was now getting on for four months. She was smiling and saying stories and noticing everything.

William liked to go to see her as soon as he came home from school every day. By now, Nanny and William were firm friends. She used to let him in to see Margaret any time he wanted. *It was good to have friends in high places.* William thought.

CHAPTER 24 – CHRISTMAS

All the house had been decorated for the Christmas festivities. There were garlands of holly and evergreen, hanging everywhere. There were kissing bushes in all the rooms. They were so pretty; and in the drawing room, there was a huge Christmas tree – it must have been thirty feet – with all china and coloured glass baubles all over it and on the top there was a golden angel, looking down at everybody.

Nan said it was their guardian angel, looking over them all.

A few friends and all the family came for Christmas Day. William was in his element. He had more toys and presents than he had had last year. He didn't know what to play with next. His Grandmama told him to put some of the presents away, not to have everything the same time and that is what he did.

After dinner Nanny brought Margaret down for a little while, so that everybody could spoil her too. She only stayed an hour, then Nanny took her up for her to have a nap.

It had been the best Christmas that William had ever had and he thought that everyone else had enjoyed themselves too. The last thing that they were going to play was charades. William had never played it before, he loved it and was quite good at it too. Mama promised to play it again sometime for him. He was thrilled.

By eight o'clock William was in bed exhausted. He went to sleep, thinking of the wonderful day he had. His last thoughts as he fell asleep were, *"how lucky I am."*

William got up in the morning and straight after his breakfast he was off to the stable to see Meg but today there were more fish to fry. He stayed indoors to play with all his toys. As soon as breakfast was over, he ate about six sugar mice. With all that sugar, he was brimming with energy. There was no holding him back.

After lunch was over, William decided to go down to the stable to his beloved Meg. His mother called after him and told him to put a coat on as it was freezing hard.

He obeyed immediately, put his gloves, scarf and cap on. He had decided to take Meg for a ride. He would tell Mama now, in case she was wondering where he was.

"Don't go too far away," Nan told him, "ask one of the stable boys to go with you." This is what he did.

He saddled Meg up with the help of Joe, one of the boys. He was about eighteen years old, a local boy, who had been working with them for a few years and a very nice boy he was too.

William was delighted. He could roam further away from home if he had one of the stable boys with him. Off they rode, the two of them. Joe rode bareback, that was one of the things William wanted to do before he was much older but there was plenty of time for that, William thought, so off they went down the drive, through the very large ornate gates at the entrance of the Plas. They turned left, then away to go.

It was a very fine afternoon, but very cold. There was still some snow on the ground but nothing to worry about.

Nan had watched the two riding out and thought to herself, what a good horseman William was going to make. He rode as if he had been born in the saddle.

He must have inherited that from his father. Nan gave a shiver as she thought about that man and tried to put him out of her mind but the thoughts persisted. She couldn't get him out of her mind, until Nanny brought Margaret down for a little while, then her thoughts were only for the baby.

David nursed her for quite a while, you could see that he was besotted with her. Nan didn't have the heart to tell David to put her down in her crib, he didn't have many days where he could be with her all the time. She was really spoiled that afternoon. "Never mind" Nan thought, "it was nice that she was going to be spoiled by her Dada, poor William didn't have any of that."

Nan looked at the clock and wondered where William was, "I suppose he is still in the stables, messing about down there."

"I will take a walk down," David said, "it's far too cold for you to go down," he told Nan.

Nan wasn't sorry, it was very cold and draughty in the stables, so off David went.

Joe and William had been riding for about half an hour when Joe pulled his horse up and made a suggestion to William that they turn around and make their way home.

The stable lad realised that they had come a might too far. It wasn't very familiar surroundings and the light was starting to fade. He said to William, "come on then, let's see who goes the fastest."

William accepted the challenge and off they raced. They were weaving in and out of the trees, when a branch flew back and hit Joe in the face and knocked him off his horse. The horse must have had a fright, because he then bolted and there was no way that he would stop.

William realised that there was something wrong, pulled up his pony and turned around and went back to where Joe was lying on the ground.

William was so frightened when he jumped off Meg. He could see that Joe's face had been cut with the branch and he was bleeding. William then took his handkerchief from his pocket and held it on the biggest cut on Joe's forehead, William was very frightened to see the blood coming from Joe's head.

By now, William realised that Joe was asleep and he couldn't make out why he was sleeping. He didn't realise that he was concussed.

In the Arms of Merlin

It was a very cold afternoon when they started out on their ride, but it was getting worse. William took the handkerchief from Joe's forehead to see how the cut was now and the bleeding had stopped. William was very relieved to see that, but now he wasn't sure what he should do. Joe looked very white and was laying quite still. He had fallen in a good place, right under the tree, there was a bit of shelter where he lay.

It was getting dark by now and William didn't have a clue where they were. They had never come up this way before. He could have got on Meg, but didn't know which way to go, so he thought the best thing to do was to stay with Joe until help came.

He got Meg to stand on one side of Joe and he lay on the other side of him. He put his arms around the boy, to try to keep him warm and there they stayed.

William kept talking to Joe in case he would wake. He must have dropped off to sleep, when all of a sudden an old man came into sight.

William was a little scared, he looked different to the men William had seen. He had long white hair and wore a long dark robe. William sat up and said, "good evening Sir, can you help us? My friend has been knocked from his horse by a branch and he has just gone to sleep. I don't know where we are. We haven't ever ridden this way before."

"Well," the old man said, "I can't take you home but I can make your friend comfortable and see that you are warm and dry."

"Oh thank you Sir," William said.

The old man picked Joe up in his arms and told William to follow him. William took Meg's reins and walked behind the old man. Suddenly they came to a clearing and to the left there was a large cave.

They all walked into the entrance of the cave. At the back of it there was a large fire. William was so relieved to

In the Arms of Merlin

see the fire, he didn't think that Meg and himself would be able to keep Joe warm all night.

The old man put Joe on some bracken at the side of the fire. William tethered Meg to a piece of rock that was jutting out from the wall. The man then told William to lay on the other side of Joe, where there was another bed of bracken.

"It was as if he was expecting us" William thought.

There was a large cauldron hanging over the fire and the man went further into the cave and came out with a bowl. He went to the cauldron, ladled some liquid out into the bowl and offered it to William.

William took it gladly and drank it over the side of the bowl. It was the best broth he had ever tasted. It was a pity that Joe was sleeping, because he was missing out.

William was now feeling warm all over and started asking the man more questions.

"I will answer your questions after I have put a herbal poultice on your friend's head."

William stopped and let the man get on with his job.

He came back with the pad for Joe's forehead and asked William if he wanted more broth?

"Yes please," he answered and commented that he had never tasted such good broth.

"That is made from a very old recipe," he said.

"I wish you would give the recipe to our cook."

The old man smiled. As he turned away, William thought, what a lovely face this man has.

Meg was having some water.

Joe looked quite comfortable. The fire was roaring and the old man told William, "why don't you have a lie down and rest, then you will be fresh by the time your people come to get you."

William tried once again to ask questions.

The old man just said, "now go to sleep my boy so that you will be awake when they find you."

In the Arms of Merlin

William put his head down on his arm, thanked their rescuer and said, "I don't even know your name."

"You don't have to worry about that my boy," he said, "you just go to sleep."

William fell into a deep sleep.

By now, Nan was going frantic. She had got word from David that he had got several of his workers to come back to the Plas to start from where the boys had started from.

He went down to the stables. Nobody knew which way they had gone.

"It must have been a different way," David said, "they would have been seen. The only thing we have to do is wait until dawn, there is no way we can search in the dark."

They fixed a brazier in one of the stables; there was plenty of straw for the men to lay on. They all had a hot drink, some bread and cheese.

It would have been better if David had told them to come over in the morning, but he panicked and called them out. The men didn't mind, they were nice and warm and they would be able to make an early start.

David put Nan to bed and asked Letty to stay with her. His mind was now working extra overtime. By the time dawn arrived, he had even buried William.

Cook came down to the kitchen about four thirty, to get some food going for the men before they left. Everybody had got up early.

David went upstairs to see how Nan was. It was a good job that little Margaret was there. She helped Nanny look after her and that occupied her for a while.

As soon as it was light they all set off. Some on horseback and some on foot. There must have been twenty men, David and John.

David's face was a picture, it had tragedy written all over it.

John spoke to him as they were riding along and said, "try not to worry, we'll find them soon."

David told John to take half the men and he would take the other half.

John said, "I think I will go up to the woods on Merlin's Hill."

David decided to take their usual path and off they went.

It was very cold, it had been freezing all night. The ground was very hard and slippery.

They got to the top of the hill, then into the woods. They made very slow progress, but David didn't daunt, the men were stretched right across the wood. David couldn't see the end man. It then started snowing, the going got really tricky.

They were deep into the wood now and starting to make their way out, when David heard a shout from the end of the row of men.

They all stopped and made for the end man. He said, "there is a cave here, we should go into it."

"Right," David said. They dismounted and made their way into the cave. It was pitch dark. One of the men lit a lantern, so they walked deeper into the cave, when suddenly they came across the little group.

William woke up and shouted, "they have found us Joe."

Meg started neighing. William stood up and Joe opened his eyes.

William rant to his Papa and David put his two arms around him and didn't ever want to let him go again. "Whatever happened?" he asked the boys.

By now William was telling the whole story, about the branch, the blood and Joe going to sleep. Then he told them about the old man and how he carried Joe into the cave, put us to lie around the fire, gave him hot broth and put a remedy of herbs on Joe's head.

David was puzzled. "Fire," he said, "there has been no fire in this cave at all."

William was going frantic now, Joe couldn't help him out because he was unconscious. He then told them about the old man with his long white hair and his long dark robes.

"Are you sure you didn't have a knock on the head as well?" David asked his son.

"No Papa, honestly he was here and if it wasn't for him we would have frozen. The accident happened a good way from here and I couldn't carry Joe, he would be too heavy for me. I asked the man what his name was but he didn't answer me. But he was here Dada honestly."

David looked at the men, who were mumbling to each other. "He's back once again then," they said.

With the description the boy gave, it looked as if Merlin had come back to help the boys, they would have perished if they had stayed where they were.

Everyone was stunned. The little lads must be something special for Merlin to come and help them.

One of the men put a blanket around Joe. They heaved him up on the horse's back, he got on behind him. David did the same to William, put him on his horse and got on behind him.

One of the men led Meg back down the path and they all made their way back to the Plas, to Nan, Lady Elizabeth, Letty and all the servants.

The servants gave a big cheer when they came into sight.

Nan ran to the hall and was out on the front steps and down them in two minutes. She dragged William from the horse, put her arms around him and just wept with joy.

David thanked all the men and said that there would be something extra in their pay at the end of the week. They all doffed their caps to their Master.

David then told them to go into the kitchen to have something hot to eat and drink. Everyone dispersed.

One of the stable lads was sent to look for John and the other men, to say that the boys had been found.

Nan took William upstairs, gave instructions to the maids to bring hot water up from the kitchen for William to have a bath, so that he wouldn't catch a cold. She also told cook to see that Joe was brought upstairs for him to have a hot soak too.

Cook couldn't hear of it, she said, "we will see to him downstairs Ma'am."

Nan didn't want to argue, so she left it to cook.

William wasn't even that cold. Nan thought that he would have been frozen and gold him so.

The story about the old man came out. Nan was astounded and listened intently to William's story.

She left him in the tub for a few minutes and went to repeat the story to David.

David said, "there wasn't any evidence of a fire at all in the cave. William said he even had broth and the old man put a pad of herbs on Joe's forehead. We didn't find anything like that, so we don't know what to think."

By this time, William had dried himself and was in his night-shirt. He wanted to talk some more but his mother told him to get into bed and he could talk later on when he had rested.

William was adamant that he was not tired. He said he had slept all night in front of a lovely fire.

"Never mind, you just go into your bed and rest, we will talk later."

CHAPTER 25 – ABDUCTION

Nan was so relieved to see that the two boys were safely home, she didn't dwell too much on William's story until later on while they were all having dinner together that she realised about the facts. Lady Elizabeth, Letty and John had been invited to dinner as a celebration, so they had high jinks that night.

After dinner, the two men went into David's study to have a smoke and a brandy. They talked seriously about what William had told them, it was quite weird, but as the village people said, not impossible. He had been seen around the hill before but only a few times.

It only took a few hours for the news to get around the village, then around town. By the end of the week it was around the county and came to the ears of a certain Squire, who was in an Ale-house in the next town.

He was quite interested in the story but was more interested when he found out whose son he was supposedly meant to be. By the time he got home, he had put two and two together and made five. He was an evil man and hadn't changed any since he had raped that little maid. He had followed her progress since coming back from America and was just biding his time, because that boy was his son and heir.

Why should that upstart David Jones have him when he was his son?

He had never remarried after Barbara had died. He just wanted to have a good time but things had got too hot for him in America, so he had to come home to Wales and to the Big House.

He had only been home a month when this story broke out. He had thought about that child for years and realised that it had been a mistake to throw him into the orphanage.

In the Arms of Merlin

He should have let Barbara bring him up as she had wanted to, but it was too late now to think about that. He would claim this boy for his own and the sooner the better.

A few weeks had gone by since the near tragedy. William was gradually getting back to normal, doing the usual things that eleven-year-olds do.

William had stopped talking about the old man with the long hair and beard, but in bed at night he would just lay there, close his eyes and the face of the man would come straight to him, he would be with him until he went to sleep. He kept that secret to himself, he didn't even tell his pal Joe from the stables.

The two boys had not been riding since the last escapade. Nan wasn't too sorry. She would never forget that episode ever and neither would David. He hadn't told his thoughts to Nan at all about those terrible few hours, he would keep them to himself, as there was no point in upsetting her all over again, as she had gone through enough in her young life.

David tried to put it all behind him, even William had stopped talking about it. Little did he know what was in William's mind's eye as he fell asleep every night. Spring was now in the air, the green was starting to come back on the trees, everything was looking fresh, the air was getting warmer and everything was coming alive again. The sheep had started dropping their lambs and it was quite an interesting time for an eleven-year-old. He would follow one of the shepherds all day if he wasn't at school. In the end, Ned the shepherd, would let him go with him on his trips up the hills to see how the lambing was getting on and when he came home there were some very big stories to tell.

David was delighted to see that the boy was interested in the farm, as he had been as a boy himself.

In the Arms of Merlin

Nan was a little apprehensive about him going all that way up into the hills but David said, "he's quite safe with Ned, he won't let anything happen to him, so don't vex now."

Nan thought no more about it.

It was now the middle of March. The lambing was getting a bit too much for Ned, so a young boy was taken on to help him. He was a boy from Pembrokeshire, that came up to Carmarthen to look for work.

He told David's Estate Agent that his father had died and his mother had been thrown out of the tied cottage. He had come to look for work. His poor mother had gone to the workhouse, so Mr Shingleton had given him this job on the strength of his story.

William took to him straight away and when he was off from school, he went up the hills with Tom. They had a great time. Tom was about twenty years of age, quite a good looking boy, very fair and as neat as a pin. He didn't actually look like a farm hand at all but he knew what he was about as regards sheep.

Spring turned into summer and the holidays arrived. William was delighted, not that he didn't like going to school because he loved every minute of it. He was a very bright boy and there wasn't any part of learning that he couldn't do, but holidays were great.

Nan didn't see much of him any day, unless she told him that they were going to visit Auntie or someone else, then he was around close to the house, so that he could hear his Mama calling him.

His mother had told him that after breakfast he must come in to have a bath and get changed, they were going into town to get him measured for a new suit. The boy was growing tall and his last suit was getting too tight and short in the leg for him, so Nan thought that they would do that today.

In the Arms of Merlin

She went upstairs to see how Little Margaret was getting on. She had been bathed, fed and dressed and was lying in her cradle quite contented.

Nan went back downstairs to get things going for the short journey into town, also told Cook that there would be no-one in for lunch but sorted dinner out for the evening. There would be no guests tonight, it would just be David, herself and William, just as Nan liked it. She was still a shy girl deep down and still felt a little threatened by the upper class. She told no one about her inner feelings, not even David knew how she felt. She was so haunted by her past but she tried hard for it not to show.

By the time William was bathed and dressed, it was eleven o'clock.

Nan and William went out to the front steps to meet the carriage.

The driver got down and walked around to open the door for them. Nan got in first and William was helped in. They both sat in silence for a little while; William got a little fidgety and moved from one side of the carriage to the other, until Nan quietly reprimanded him.

They got out of the carriage outside the Tailors. Nan then gave instructions to the coachman to come back to collect them in two hours' time. She wanted to call in the Tivoli to see everyone and to have lunch. It would be a nice treat for herself and William. He still loved to see the girls and enjoyed letting them tease him.

All the measuring behind him, William was happy. Nan chose the style and the material.

William took his mother's hand as they left the shop and off to the Tivoli they went.

It was very busy there, so nan went upstairs out of the way for a while. One of the girls told Nan that she would come and get her when a table came available. It must have been fifteen minutes before someone came to call them.

In the Arms of Merlin

By now William had lost his appetite and found a horse's.

Nan was quite ashamed with what William ate. Letty reckoned that he wouldn't need anything until the next day.

"You are very much mistaken," Nan said, "he will be sat at the dinner table just as the dinner gong is rung."

"It is no wonder that he is growing so fast," Letty commented; "he will be as tall as me before long." That was true, because he was nearly up to Letty's chin now.

After a long chat with Letty and the other girls, the coachman appeared in the doorway, so Nan and William made their way outside to the carriage, got in and away they went.

As soon as William got home, he ran upstairs and got changed, told his mother where he would be, then off to go to the stables for the rest of the day.

He was happy now. He helped quite a lot for a boy of his age, he could see what needed to be done and he would do it. He didn't need telling twice, he was very quick, it wasn't really a chore for him, horses were his life.

During the course of the afternoon, William had given them all the details of his morning in town and it was to be repeated next week again, for his first fitting. "What a bore," he told everybody, and they all gave a smile.

It was time for the last fitting. William had to be picked up from school. Nan didn't go with him that day, little Margaret wasn't well, she had whooping cough and had it pretty bad. Nan felt that it wasn't fair on Nanny if she left her for too long, she had very bad coughing and choking bouts, so she thought that she should be with her.

She sent a message to the stables to send Jimmy to town so that William had company on the way home.

William and Jimmy were very close, he seemed to be different to the usual boy that worked at the stables. Nan couldn't put a finger on anything, but there was something about this boy that she couldn't fathom. He seemed as if he was from a higher class than the usual lad. Nan had been watching him since he had arrived there; he was an expert horseman, as if he had been taught from an early age, just like William. These youngsters could ride after a fashion. It was only cart-horses the usual boys rod, but this boy could handle anything. It bothered Nan a little but she didn't tell David or anyone.

It was four o'clock, the carriage was standing outside the school gates. The coachman sent Jimmy in to fetch Master William and here he came like a whirlwind.

They both jumped into the carriage and off they went to the Tailor's shop. William went into the shop on his own. He had his last fitting, the Tailor gave him a note for him to give to his mother with the next instructions.

William was delighted that this was to be the last time for all this messing about and thanks Mr Evans, the Tailor.

On his way out to the carriage, he asked the coachman if they could go to the Tivoli. The coachman said "no", as he had no instructions to do so.

William was a little disappointed but he knew that there was no point in arguing, the coachman had been too long in his job to disobey his master or mistress, so they made their way out of the town towards home and that was that.

Jimmy sat in the carriage with William; the coachman could hear them playing about. Master William was very fond of the boy and he thought that the boy was fond of him too. Jimmy was a different kettle of fish, he wasn't like any of the other boys in the stables, he was a very good worker, very polite and what's more he was very well spoken. He was a bit of a mystery but Will, the coachman had other things on his mind today. His son, who had a crippling disease and wasn't very well, he seemed to be getting worse every day. They couldn't call the doctor because they couldn't afford to pay him. Jane his wife, had begged Will only this morning to

In the Arms of Merlin

have a word with the master to see if he could help them in any way, but Will wasn't willing. He was getting desperate now; the boy was definitely getting worse.

Will was deep in thought about the situation at home, when two horsemen came out from behind the trees. Will was so startled he pulled the horse up so abruptly that the horse reared up on his hind legs. He could hear commotion in the carriage with the boys, they were shouting, they must have had a fright.

The man nearest to the horse book hold of his bridle and held him down because he wanted to rear up again, but this man had him under control.

Will was still in shock when the second man said, "get down here."

Will was just about to protest, when a whip came out from nowhere and wound around his neck. The rider tugged on the whip and Will was on the ground.

As he landed on the hard earth, he heard the whip, then he felt it. He was still in shock, things like this didn't happen around here.

Who were these men, what did they want?

It wasn't very long before Will found out. The second man moved up to the carriage door, opened it and shouted to the boys, "get out here, the both of you."

Will tried to turn around to see what was going on but the whip came down again. This time it caught him right across the face, he couldn't see, his eye was full of blood. He couldn't move very much as his shoulder hurt. He must have fallen right on it.

Once more, Will struggled to get up but the whip came down again.

By this time the two boys were out of the carriage. The second man picked William up and threw him in front of him on the horse's neck. The one holding the horse's head went over, took Jimmy and sat him behind him.

In the Arms of Merlin

William was kicking and screaming, it was as much as the rider could do to keep him on the horse.

Will could see that William wasn't going to give up without a struggle.

Will was in so much pain he could feel himself leaving everything behind, but the last thought in his mind was that Jimmy wasn't struggling much. He was just sat behind the first rider.

By now, Will had lost consciousness and didn't see them ride off.

An hour must have gone by before will was found. A farmer was on his way home from the town with some pigs in the back of his gambo, when he came across the situation. He pulled his horse up, tethered him, then went to see what was going on. He knew it was the carriage belonging to the Plas, he also knew that Will Evans was the usual coachman.

He turned Will over and was shocked to see the state of his face. He had a lash from one corner to the other. He was bleeding profusely. He really didn't know what to do.

Eventually he decided to put his coat under Will's head and covered him with a sack from the back of the gambo and made his way to the village, as fast as his cart horse would go. His first stop was at the Ale House. He took a look inside to see who was there. There were quite a few men there. He told them his story.

The Landlord said, "I'll take my cart, it is all ready out the back, I was just about to go into town. He gave instructions for one of the men to go up to the Plas to tell them about the accident. Nobody had any idea about the boys.

There was pandemonium at the Plas when the man gave the news. The first thing the head coachman asked was about William.

The man said there was nothing said about the boy, only Will being unconscious on the road home to the village.

In the Arms of Merlin

As it happened, John was home. He ran up to the house to tell Nan where he was going and rode off to see what had happened. By the time he had arrived at the scene of the accident, the men had carried Will to the cart and lay him gently down. He was still unconscious; they got some more sacking and covered him completely.

John decided that he should be taken back to town, to the Infirmary. John didn't wait for the cart, there were enough men to help get him into the Infirmary, so he rode hell for leather to David's office.

David couldn't believe the look that was on his face. "John," David said; "what the hell is the matter with you man?"

John couldn't tell him what was the matter because he didn't know, but he shivered when he thought what might have happened.

David said, "sit down before you fall down," he then got up, went to the cupboard and poured a brandy for him. "Now," David said, "from the beginning."

John told him the story, as much as he knew of it.

David was speechless and eventually he asked, "do you think that William has been kidnapped?"

John put his head down and said in a very quiet voice, "it looks like it David."

David said, "but who and why?"

"We will just have to wait to see. I think you should go to see the constable."

David was out of his mind by now. He dashed out of the office, jumped on his horse and rode over to the constable's house.

He repeated the story to the constable.

He hummed and ha'hd and said, "I think you had better wait to see what happens next. Perhaps the boys had wandered off to get some help, so shall we wait?"

In the Arms of Merlin

By now David had lost patience with the man. He certainly had been chosen for his brawn and not his brains.

David just swept out of the house and made his way to the Infirmary.

By the time he got there, Will was conscious but was in a sorry state. Even though he was in terrible pain, he tried to sit up to speak to his master and kept apologising to him for letting the boys be taken.

"Tell me," David said, "who were they? What did they look like? Were they thugs or were they thieves? Were they rough or what?"

"No," Will said, "as far as I could tell, they were gentry. Well dressed and well spoken, especially the one who took the whip to me."

"I'm very sorry," David said to Will, "that this has happened to you but I will look after you and your family, so you don't have to worry. You must have tried your best to help them or you wouldn't be in the state that you are in. I am going home now, but I shall be back later and I will bring your wife to see you."

"That won't be possible," Will told his master, "she won't be able to leave our son, who is very ill."

"Will," David said, "this is the first I have heard of this. Why wasn't I told?"

Will dropped his head and everything seemed to come on top of him and the tears flowed.

David patted him on his good shoulder and said, "don't fret now, we will see to things for you."

John and David rode back to the Plas as fast as they could. "Nan must be in a state by now," David told John. "What am I going to tell her? That brainless constable is useless, what are we going to do? After listening to what will said, it must be a kidnap. Why did they take Jimmy too? I don't understand it at all."

In the Arms of Merlin

They got into the house. Nan was waiting for them. She was as white as a sheet and her eyes were like saucers. "What has happened?" she asked them.

They couldn't tell her anything really, they didn't have a clue.

David asked John if he would call at Will's home to see what was going on there. "Find out about the child and if he is alright to be left with someone, take Will's wife in to see her husband. Ask him if he can remember anything else that happened. Tell him to think deeply, anything, however small he thinks it is. I will have to stay here with Nan, in case anyone turns up with some news."

It was getting dark and there was still no sign of William or Jimmy.

It was hard work trying to pacify Nan. David had decided to send for the doctor, she would never get through the night if he didn't. God knows what he could do for her, perhaps he could give her a sedative or something. She had passed the baby over completely to Nanny and that was not a good sign.

Dr Morris arrived, he was shocked when he saw Nan. He couldn't make out what the problem was, he hadn't heard anything about the abduction. He had been with a very difficult confinement all through the day.

After a word with David, he realised how she had got into the state that she was in.

They managed to get her up to their bedroom and onto the bed. Will, Dr Morris, decided to give her something orally. He made out a draught for her; it was much later when she gave in to drink it. As she was dozing off, she called David to the bedside, drew him right down, so that his ear was by the side of her mouth and with great difficulty, because the drug was taking effect, she whispered just two words. As she uttered them, David went cold. He hadn't given that monster a second thought. It was now he realised, that Nan had it in her thoughts for a while.

He rose abruptly from Nan and said out loud, "you fool David, why didn't you think of this sooner?" Why hadn't Nan said something sooner?

Will Morris' ears pricked up as he hard David say that man's name. He moved towards David but before he could get to him, he was off down the staircase three steps at a time.

Will checked that Nan was alright and ran downstairs after David. He called to Letty, who was in the drawing room with all the others, told her to keep an eye on Nan and also told them where they were going. His last instructions were for someone to call the constable and tell him where they were going to.

By now David has jumped on his horse and was on his way. Will had travelled to the Plas in his little trap. He knew that that wouldn't be any good now. He ran to the stables and shouted for someone to saddle a horse for him.

They heard the urgency in his voice, so it was done in double quick time. Nobody knew what was going on until John came out to the stables, asking one of the lads to go into town with a letter for the constable.

By now, Will was riding as fast as he could but he didn't catch sight of David. It was quite a ride to the Squire's house, about thirty minutes Will thought. He eased off the horse because if he hadn't he would burn him out and he would never catch David up.

It was starting to get dark, Will had to slow down. In any case there was no sign of David. He rode on regardless and before long the Big House came into sight.

Will's heart missed a beat. He hoped that David hadn't done anything foolish.

At last he arrived at the very large ornate gates. The horse was lathering and slowing right down. There wasn't any sign of anyone as he drew up to the front of the house.

In the Arms of Merlin

There were no lights in the front but he could see lights at the back. He dismounted, tethered his horse on some railings and started walking around to the back. There was no sign of David.

Will walked towards the lights, which by now, he realised, were the stable outhouses. He could hear raised voices and came into view of a group of workers talking to David.

Will realised that David was out of control. He got up to him, took his arm and tried to reason with him, but to no avail.

The head coachman came over to the two men and said to Will; "I am very sorry Sir, as I have tried to explain, the Squire is not in residence and he hasn't been for about six months. You are welcome to look around the house if you want, I know my Master wouldn't approve but I can see that there is something radically wrong."

By now, David had cooled down a bit but was now lost for words.

Will took over, he asked where the Squire was.

The man said, "London," he also told Will that they got at least a month's notice before the Master came home because he usually brought loads of friends with him and everything had to be perfect when they arrived.

By now David was back to his sensible old self. He asked the man who was in charge.

The coachman said, "I am, together with the housekeeper, but she has gone away for a few days. There is only skeleton staff here for a month."

"How long have you been employed here?" David asked the man.

"About two years Sir," he said.

"Oh," David said, "that accounts for it then, you wouldn't remember would you? My sister was married to that monster of a man that is your master and as sure as I know that day comes after night, I know that he has abducted my son and one of my stable boys, Jimmy."

The man looked at David, wondering what he was talking about, so David stepped back a few steps and started to explain to the man.

After David had finished giving all the details, he leaned against the wall. He felt quite weak, his knees were like jelly and his head was spinning. It was getting more obvious by the minute what had happened to William and it was frightening the life out of David

He sat squarely on the wall to gather himself together. There were two things going around in David's mind.

The first thing was that Sir Ernest wanted to get rid of the boy because he could be a threat to him and the other thing was that he wanted William to be his son and heir.

Perhaps the man was mellowing. David didn't know what to think and his mind was in turmoil.

By now the head coachman was asking questions to David.

One thing he was bothered about was the boy he called Jimmy. David wondered about that too.

Why did he abduct him as well as William? He wasn't important. Why didn't they leave him, like they left the coachman and why didn't he get a beating?

There were hundreds of questions to be answered but who was going to answer them?

John and David left the Big House and made their way back home. It was very late by the time they got home.

Nan was fast asleep, the draught had done its work but what about when she woke up in the morning? David really didn't know how he was going to cope with her. He let sleep get hold of him and knew that he would be able to cope with Nan.

David and Nan were woken up the same time by a maid, who had brought them a tray of tea.

In the Arms of Merlin

Letty had given her orders, it was getting quite late. She knew that they were exhausted but she also knew that they wanted to start searching once again.

By the time they were both awake, the first thought Nan had was about her son. She started to cry, mumble, then it went to sobbing.

David put his arms around her and tried to comfort her, things were getting worse. David thought that he was handling this the wrong way. He decided to take another approach, sat Nan up, took her by the shoulders and gently shook her until she stopped.

It must have been quite a shock for David to shake her like this; David had never done anything like this before. By now, Nan had stopped sobbing. David was so glad, he hated doing this to his beloved. It really was the best thing that he could have done, Nan was shocked into sensibility.

It was such a relief for David to see that Nan was behaving more like the old Nan. He couldn't blame her really, it must have been a terrible shock for her to know that Ernest Langley was back in the county. It was almost certain that he had abducted their son. The only consolation David had was that he didn't think he would harm him because he wanted an heir to take over after his days.

It seemed that Ernest Langley had a Ward, his name was James. He had brought him back from London. He was the son of a distant cousin, but the Squire wasn't too fond of him. More than likely that is why he must have decided on taking William. This was only a thought that was running around David's head. He didn't show anything to Nan, but he thought that he might tell John in confidence and they would go from there.

David and Nan went downstairs together to have breakfast, not that either of them ate anything. Nan just played with the food on her plate, not uttering a sound.

David had eaten as much as he could. He excused himself and as he was giving Nan a kiss and words of comfort, Lady Elizabeth came into the room.

David had left word the night before for her to come and keep Nan company while he went out again to look for William. "That was good timing Mother," he said, "I was just going to send one of the servants to tell you that I was about to leave."

"Where will you look again?" His mother asked.

He gave her a long pleading look, so she didn't enquire any further, for which David was very grateful.

He went straight down to the stables, his horse was all ready to go. When John arrived, they went outside to discuss what was going on in David's mind. John was of the same opinion as David. He was going to suggest it to David today.

After their talk, they decided to search further afield. There were four other men on horseback and six men on foot, so they could cover quite an area.

CHAPTER 26 – A TERRIBLE BEATING

It was very cold and William was shivering, partly because he was freezing and partly because he was frightened. He couldn't understand what was going on. Jimmy was sitting at the table not saying a word to him. The tall man who had whipped Jim the coachman was laying down on a sort of sofa, sleeping.

William tried to talk to Jimmy but he wouldn't answer him, poor little boy, he couldn't understand it. Jimmy was a good friend of his. He tried once again to question Jimmy, but he just shouted at him and told him to be quiet.

By now the tall man had woken up and asked what was going on.

William was sobbing quietly into the crook of his arm. The tall man got up, touched William's head and said in a gentle voice, "don't worry my boy, all will be well soon."

Jimmy got up from the table looking very angry and said, "you have never spoken to me like that."

The Squire was taken aback with the young man's nerve to talk to him like that. He just ignored his comment and kept looking at the handsome boy sitting in the chair. He had never had a feeling like this before. He was looking at his own flesh and blood. He could see himself when he was young, sitting in that old dilapidated chair and it gave him a real thrill.

He told the boy, "you must be patient for a few more hours, then I will take you from here and you shall live like a prince."

Jimmy was now really mad but didn't say another word to his uncle. He thought better of it, because he had been on the wrong side of that whip himself, through doing something, or saying something, that didn't please his uncle.

By now the Squire was standing by the door, his hat on his head and as he opened the door he told Jimmy, "look after the boy or you will be sorry."

Jimmy just scowled at his uncle's back.

"Did you hear me?" he asked Jimmy.

A grunt passed his lips.

"I will be back in a few hours, see that you give the boy some food and don't forget – no nonsense," and off he went.

By now William had realised that he was in an old farm-worker's house. It must have been empty for a long time because there were loads of cobwebs and dust everywhere. He didn't have any idea where he was. It couldn't be anywhere near the Plas, or he would have recognised it.

He tried once again to get something out of Jimmy but he just had some more growls from him.

"Don't call me Jimmy, my name is James and I am the ward of the Squire, so shut up and leave me alone."

William said, "why did you work for my father and why did you pretend to be my friend?"

"It was all part of the charade, so do not ask any more questions because I am not going to answer you anymore."

William was really hurt by now, he felt like crying his eyes out, but he was determined to stick it out and told himself, *just sit tight and look and listen, something or someone will turn up and take me back to my home and my family.*

It was dark by the time the Squire got back. He had brought a few quilts with him, some bread and cheese. William didn't have a clue where he was getting them from. It must have been quite a way, because he took a long time to get back.

William didn't have any idea where they were, the only thing he knew was that they were near the river. Everything felt cold and damp and it was very misty night and morning.

In the Arms of Merlin

Thinking about the river, William thought about his home. Every morning when he got out of bed, he would look out of the bedroom window; the first thing he would see was the river. It was a part of his day. The Plas was up on a hill overlooking the river Towy. The land either side belonged to his father for a good few acres. William wasn't into acres but he knew that his father owned a lot of land, so that told him that he was no way near to the Plas. That thought daunted him a bit.

He had ridden and walked nearly everywhere on his father's estate and if he could get outside the little cottage, he might know where he was, but that was not to be, for a while anyway.

William felt a shiver going down his spine as the cold got to him. The Squire noticed this and made his way over to the boy and said, "what is the matter son?"

William looked up, he just couldn't hold back anymore, he had come to the end of his tether and the tears just flowed out.

The Squire was taken aback. He had never had anything to do with children, leave alone a son. He got up from his chair, went over to William and put his arm around his shoulder and tried to console him.

William struggled away from him.

This appeared to upset the Squire, he started to show his feelings by raising his voice, but realised in time and managed to control the terrible temper that he had and just told the boy, "don't worry, we will be away from here before long."

He gave William some bread and cheese and gave him another quilt to put around his shoulders. He spoke very abruptly to Jimmy and went out through the door.

After William had eaten the bread and cheese, he seemed to warm up a little and didn't feel so frightened. He pulled the quilt around his body tighter and lay on the sofa.

In the Arms of Merlin

He thought there was no point in asking Jimmy any more questions, he would only get cross with him again and William didn't want that. He had to have one ally in the enemy camp. Little did he know that Jimmy was more of an enemy than anybody.

Eventually, he got to sleep. When he woke up he could hear the rain hitting the roof and he could see it running down the wall at the end of the room. He opened his eyes but didn't move. He wanted to see how the land lie. He squinted over to where Jimmy was lying to see if he was awake. He couldn't quite see. He had to move a little. By this time Jimmy was awake. He must have been a very light sleeper.

William closed his eyes once again and lay quietly until Jimmy went back to sleep. He waited about ten minutes, then pulled the quilt away from his body, sat up, put his feet on the floor, kept an eye on Jimmy and started to get up. He was now in a position to look through the window. He couldn't see much, the windows were dirty and full of cobwebs. He was daunted now, he decided to sit down.

By this time, Jimmy was wide awake and started moaning straight away. He was on about the Squire tucked in a nice warm bed, while he lay on a hard settle, freezing cold, looking after a brat that meant nothing to him.

William couldn't get over how Jimmy hated him so much and told him so. "What is the matter?" he asked. "We used to be good friends when you worked for my father. What has changed? You seem to be a different person."

Jimmy turned to William and said, "you see, I am a different person, so be quiet. I don't want to hear your whining voice for a few hours."

You won't, thought William, *I will not talk to you again*. He lie back on the sofa, pulled the quilt over his head and turned his back on James, as he called himself, and decided to ignore him. Perhaps that would do the trick.

In the Arms of Merlin

It was a terrible day for William, his spirits were so low and his imagination was playing havoc with him. The things that were going through his mind were nobody's business. Where was his father? When was he and the men coming to fetch him like they had done before? The little boy put his hands together, out of sight under the quilt, and started saying a little prayer that his mother had taught him when he was younger. After he had finished saying the prayer, he added a little extra and said, "please God, will you send my father to get me? Amen." Then the tears started to flow once again.

He must have cried himself to sleep and slept for a few hours.

James was getting a bit worried that William was so quiet. He got up from the settle, caught hold of the quilt and flung it back and shouted down to William, "get up, it's too boring here just talking to myself, come one, keep awake and talk to me."

Poor William didn't know what had hit him. He had been ain a deep sleep and to be wakened up like that was awful. William was quite irritated by Jimmy's nasty ways and told him so.

That made Jimmy worse. He caught William by the scruff of his neck and threw him on the floor, shouted and told him, "stay there, until I tell you to move."

William now realised that he had gone too far with Jimmy. He knew that he wouldn't say anything untoward to him again, he didn't know that Jimmy had such a nasty streak in him, but he certainly knew now. From now on, William was going to be careful with everything he said and did.

There was no way that William knew what time it was but it seemed a very long time ago that he had woken up suddenly, the door opened and in walked the Squire.

"What's been going on here?" he asked, "what are you doing on the floor?"

William didn't answer, he didn't even look up at the Squire, who bent down, cupped his hand under William's chin, lifted it up and said, "what is the matter boy?" He could see that the boy had been crying, "has James hurt you in any way? If he has you must tell," he said, looking deeply into his eyes.

William shivered and said, "no Sir, he hasn't touched me."

The Squire looked at James, "you keep it like that too," he said.

Since the run up to the abduction and the actual snatch, the Squire's attitude towards James had changed. He just couldn't be bothered with him, the bond that had been there between them before he found out about William, had gone. It was only a tiny thing, just the thought that he was related to him and would take over his estate and his title, but now that had all gone out through the window.

James didn't realise it but he must have got an inclination of the situation.

William was now sitting back on the sofa with the quilt over him once again. He didn't know how much longer he would have been able to sit on the floor, it was just earth and it was starting to feel very cold. He was cold enough as it was.

The Squire caught hold of James' shoulder, guided him towards the door, he opened the door and they both went outside. As the door closed behind them, William made his way towards the door and tried to listen, but he could not hear anything because they were both whispering.

William scarpered back to the sofa before they came back in, none the wiser.

A few minutes went by before they came back into the cottage. They talked for a few minutes more, then the Squire left once again. There was a large calico bag on the table, Jimmy started to empty it.

William could see there was bread, cheese, a piece of ham and some ale. Neither William nor Jimmy had had a hot drink since they had been in the cottage, that was more than likely why they both felt so cold and miserable.

The Squire had pointed out that they couldn't light a fire, because the smoke would be seen and everyone knew that the cottage had been empty for years.

Jimmy growled at William to come and get something to eat.

The boy got up and made his way towards the table, quite looking forward to the change of diet. These last few days reminded him of the days when he was in the orphanage. Even though the memory of that place was fading, he still remembered the worst things and this stay in the cottage had brought memories flooding back to William.

They both ate their food in silence, Jimmy even offered some ale to William. The boy was surprised and thought perhaps Jimmy was going to be friends with him again, but he thought wrong. After the food was eaten, Will

William tried to talk to Jimmy but he didn't answer him, he just looked at the boy with hate in his eyes.

William thought to himself, *you had better be quiet he is going to do something nasty to you*. He went back to the sofa, curled up under the quilt and immediately dropped off to sleep once again.

It was getting dark when he woke. Jimmy was fast asleep on the settle. William didn't move; he just lay there, his mind working overtime. He was wondering what his mother was doing, he also wondered where his father was and all his workers. The only thing he could think of was that he must be very far away from his home, or he would have been found by now.

He then started to wonder what the Squire had told Jimmy outside, but he knew that Jimmy wouldn't tell him anything. The only thing he could do was to hold on as long as he could.

It was really dark now; Jimmy had lit the candles and was passing food over to William. "Eat all this food now," he told William; "it is the last meal you will have here."

William looked up and asked; "where are we going?"

"Ask me no questions and I will tell you no lies."

William didn't listen, he asked, "where is the Squire? When is he coming back?"

"He is not coming back," said Jimmy, "I have got to take you somewhere myself, that is all you need to know."

Thank goodness, William thought, to get away from this horrible, cold, dank place. Nowhere could be as bad as this.

It must have been very late when Jimmy woke William up. He said, "get up now, we are off."

"Where are we going?" William asked.

"You'll see before long."

"Can I put the quilt over my shoulders?"

"It's up to you," he told the boy, "it will only get in your way, but that is up to you."

William decided to keep the quilt over his head and shoulders, he didn't know how long they were going to be out in the cold night air.

Before they left the cottage, Jimmy cleared everything off the table and put it in the calico bag, threw it over his shoulder, opened the door and pushed William from behind and said "get going."

William was about to ask, *where are we going*? when Jimmy said, "don't ask where we are going, you will soon know.

There was no point in wasting his energy talking, so William said to himself, *be quiet*.

They walked for a while; it was very hard to walk in the dark. William stumbled a few times, cut one of his hands one time; then one of his knees. He cried openly now. Jimmy didn't help him at all, just growled at him and gave him another shove.

William was getting tired by now. They had been walking for a long time. Gradually the moon came out from behind the clouds. It had stopped raining and William could see a little way in front of him.

Before long they came out of the woods, that helped a bit. They were in fields now. It was very boggy under foot and William could feel himself going deeper into the ground as he walked along.

He suddenly realised that they were getting near the river, actually they were making straight for it. William could see it shining in the distance; perhaps they would follow the river until they got their bearings. William didn't know what was going on, he just carried on walking.

They got to the river bank before long. Jimmy told him to walk a little further down the field until they came to a part in the river that they could cross, "it is not deep and it will save us going all the way round."

William, wasn't very happy with this idea, but couldn't do anything about it. It was a good job that the moon was out or they would have been in real trouble.

They came to the place at last. Jimmy said, "here it is, slide down the bank and wait for me."

"I'm afraid," William said.

"There is no need for you to be," Jimmy said, "I know this place well and I have crossed it many a time."

That helped William a little. He was absolutely shaking by now, between the cold and the fear.

Jimmy arrived by his side and said, "right, start wading in, I will follow you."

What could William do but do as Jimmy told him? The water started to creep into his boots, then up to his knees. The coldness of the water seemed to alert his brain, he thought he was in charge of the situation. The water was up to his waist by now; he stopped, turned to see where Jimmy was. He hadn't entered the water yet.

William shouted to him, "come on, why are you still on the bank?"

"It's all right", Jimmy said, "I am just getting rid of the bag of food, we won't need it again. Go on, I am in the water."

The last thing William saw was Jimmy up to his knees in the water, he thought to himself, *it's going to be all right, he is following me.*

The next thing William knew, he was over his head in water, he felt as if he was going down and down, he could feel this heavy thing around his neck and it was swirling about his body. *It's the quilt*, he thought to himself. *I have got to get rid of it.*

He had picked up a big nail off the cottage floor and stuck it into the quilt to keep it tidy around his body. It had been a very good idea at the time, he thought, but now it is going to kill me. He dragged the nail out from the quilt with great difficulty.

The water had made the quilt swell up; the nail was sticking to it. William felt as if an hour had gone by, by the time he got the nail out and the quilt just floated away from him.

He just kept sinking down into this big dip' he couldn't believe that he wasn't struggling. He was just cool and calm, he felt that he had gone down into the river hundreds of feet, but even William, as a young boy knew that that was impossible.

The only thing that William could think of was that he had drowned, but how was he talking to himself and able to see where he was.

Everything had lightened around him by now. He was still going down. Poor William, he didn't know what was

In the Arms of Merlin

happening. He wasn't hurting anywhere, he felt nice and relaxed. Next he felt nice and warm, warm enough to go to sleep he thought, and with that, he drifted off into a deep sleep.

Jimmy by now had got back on the river bank, he was shaking all over but the deed was done, he had got rid of the boy at last. Now to explain to his uncle how it all had happened. He had a plan worked out from the first day but had to bide his time.

His story was that William had waited until he had gone to sleep, hit him over the head with a piece of wood, taken the key from him, opened the door and ran off. By the time James had come round after the blow to his head, William had long gone.

James tried to follow his tracks but had lost them completely. He came out of the woods and walked up to the river along the bank for a few miles, then came across the quilt, which was floating in the water.

Jimmy thought it was a good idea that William had asked to keep the quilt over his shoulders, now Jimmy could say that he had gone into the river. He wouldn't have been able to say that without the sight of the quilt. Good boy William, this evidence is going to be good for me.

He didn't know how his uncle was going to take this news, but he had to face him and give him the bad news.

By the time he got to the Big House, dawn was breaking. He was frozen to the marrow and looked a terrible sight. He went around to the back of the house, there were lights everywhere.

The staff had to get up very early to get things done before the master got up. James opened the kitchen door and made straight for the fireplace. There was a very large old range there; the heat was bouncing out of it. Cook was standing in front of it doing something or other. Jimmy just gave her a push to one side and ordered hot water to be taken up to his room. The poor woman didn't know what to think, she just shouted, "whatever has happened to you Sir?"

"Nothing to do with you, keep your mouth shut and just see to the water." He had already taken his boots off, threw them into the corner and went upstairs to his room. He stripped off and put a night shirt on.

The maids came in with the bath and the hot water. He dismissed them, immediately took off his night shirt and stepped into the bath and wallowed in the hot water. He stayed in the bath until the water had got cold, rubbed himself down and put a clean night shirt and a dressing gown on, then made his way to his uncle's bedroom to face the music.

The Squire was shocked to see James in the first place. After he had stuttered and stammered the entire story, he went off his head. The servants could hear the noise from the kitchen, they couldn't make out what was happening.

By now the Squire was out of bed and thrashing James with his riding crop. James was in a heap on the floor, screaming in agony, there was no stopping the man. "Why did you have a bath before telling me? You stupid man, how long have you been home? Perhaps we could have saved him. I'll kill you," he shouted.

James thought that his time had come but he was saved by two of the servants coming in to see what was going on. The Squire stopped the whipping and the shouting, he didn't want them to know about the abduction, his name wasn't even linked with it at all.

The two men servants just stood looking at James, who was by now whimpering on the floor.

"Take him away," he told them, "out of my sight."

The two men rushed forward, picked the unfortunate man up, he winced with agony. The men tried not to hurt him more than they could. They carried him into his room further down the landing and lay him on the bed. There was blood coming from every cut on his body.

In the Arms of Merlin

One of the servants left the room and went to get the housekeeper; she would tend to his wounds. By the time she came to the bedroom, James was a whimpering mess on the bed. She was quite shocked to see the young man in this state, she didn't have much time for him usually but when she saw him she felt some compassion for him. Nobody deserved to be thrashed like this. She wondered what had made the master do this. She didn't support they would ever find out. She took the night shirt off and covered his naked body with a sheet. He was in no state to worry about anything, he was more or less unconscious. She got on with cleaning and dressing his wounds.

After she had put some balm on all the cuts, she ripped up a sheet and wrapped him in it, covered him over with a warm woollen blanket, so that he was more comfortable.

Mrs Whithers; the housekeeper, didn't have much time for James usually but today she felt so sorry for him. He must have been in agony, some of the whip lashes were quite deep, she hoped that they would heal, she had done her best for him. The would just have to wait and see.

Nobody saw a peep of the Master all day, only James the butler, who took his meals up to his room.

The kitchen could see by the trays that he was eating hardly anything. Something terrible must have happened to get him in such a temper. No-one had any idea what was wrong. "It will all come out one of these days," James said.

Things just went on as usual in the Big House. Just before lunch, Mrs Whithers took a small bowl of gruel, which she had made during the morning, up to James' room. She opened the door quietly, made her way over to the bed, put the tray on the bedside table, listened for a few seconds, made her way over to the window and drew the heavy curtains to let some light into the dark room.

She went back to the bed and had a shock when she saw James' face. He looked terrible, both his eyes were closed with the swelling, his cuts looked quite clean at the moment. She lowered her head towards James' ear and whispered, "how do you feel Sir?"

James tried to open his eyes and move but just let out a long groan. The poor man, he must have been in agony.

"Try not to move," Mrs Whithers told him. She knew that he wouldn't be able to lift his head up, she said, "wait a moment, I will be back now."

She went back down to the kitchen to get the feeding cup that they used to feed Lady Barbara when she was very ill and dying. Mrs Whithers remembered putting it in the back of the china cupboard after Lady Barbara had passed away, she could go straight to it. After finding it, she ran back upstairs straight to James' room, she poured the gruel into the feeding cup and put the china pipe into the man's mouth.

He turned his head away and started protesting, but Mrs Whithers put her hand on the side of his face that hadn't been cut and spoke to him quite firmly.

He realised that she was trying to help him, so he gave up the struggling and tried to swallow the liquid. James was glad that Mrs Whithers had been firm with him, he felt a little better after swallowing the gruel, his mouth felt cleaner.

"That's a good lad," Mrs Whithers said, "I will now go back and get you something to drink, I won't be long." Off she went downstairs; cook knew where she had gone with the gruel and put a large pitcher of cold water ready for her by the time she got back to the kitchen.

Mrs Whithers was glad that cook knew what she was doing, it made things much easier for her. She just couldn't leave that boy to rot upstairs, no matter what he had done. She was going to change her mind about things later, but that is another story.

All the kitchen staff took it in turns to see to James but Mrs Whithers was the only one to tend to his wounds. She did a very good job of it. James would be very badly scarred

In the Arms of Merlin

for life after he had got over the trauma and wrath of his uncle.

CHAPTER 27 – MERLIN TO THE RESCUE

After the fourth day and night of the abduction, Nan was in a terrible state. She just took to her bed, she didn't want to anything to do with anybody, not even the baby. They even had to get a wet nurse in to feed little Margaret. Nan was beside herself. Dr Morris couldn't do anything with her, he just gave draughts to make her sleep, but as he told David; "I can't keep her sedated all the time, I will have to stop before long, she might even die if I don't stop it soon."

David was very worried about Nan, he honestly thought that she was losing her mind. David would lie by the side of her, hold her in his arms and gently sob into her hair. Nan wasn't aware of anything that was going on around her. David thought that that was the best thing for her, until Will told him different.

Will was a very good friend to them, but in his capacity as a Doctor, he had to inform David what could go wrong, if he gave many more draughts to Nan.

After a long deliberation, David told Will to stop the sleeping draughts the following day.

It was 6 o'clock when Nan started stirring. Her personal maid came into the bedroom. David awoke as soon as he heard the door opening, he rose himself up on the pillow and turned towards Nan, she was beginning to wake. Good, thought David.

He dismissed the maid, got out of bed, put on his robe, saw that Nan hadn't woken properly so he went to his dressing room and had a quick wash. He had nearly finished dressing when he heard Nan calling. He rushed back into the bedroom, Nan was sitting up. That was a first, she hadn't moved before, just lay and cried.

David got to her bedside and took her hand and put it to his mouth. He took her in his arms and held her tightly.

She kept repeating "Oh David, oh David, what are we doing to do?"

David was completely taken by surprise by the way she had woken up this morning. It was as if she had heard what Will had told him the night before. David had been quite worried as to how Nan would react when the sedation was stopped. He hoped that his worries were over and he said a little prayer under his breath.

"The first thing that you are going to do is to get bathed, then you and I are going to eat breakfast together, then you are going to see the baby."

She tried to protest, but David was very firm with her. She got out of bed and nearly fell, she was so weak, she hadn't eaten food for four days.

David caught hold of her and helped her into the dressing room. He put her to sit on a small chaise and told her to stay there until he got help.

She nodded, David left the room, rang the bell and waited for the maid to come back.

When she arrived, he gave instructions to see that her mistress was bathed and dressed by her. "I will be back in a while, then we will have breakfast together in our room." As he was leaving the room he called to Nan; "I won't be long." Off he went to look for John. He found him eventually and they had a long talk on what they were going to do that day.

John was quite taken aback at what David had told him and on the other hand was pleased to hear that Nan was more herself today.

David said, "I must be off, as I have promised to have breakfast with her in our room. That is a start isn't it?"

John was so pleased, because he had loved Nan as a lover a few years ago, but now as a sister. Letty now was the love of his life.

Breakfast was on the table. Nan was waiting for him, he sat down and they both started eating. Nan was finding it hard to swallow her food. It seemed to go so far and then stick in her throat. She didn't show David, she just picked up her cup and tried to drink some tea. She got through the breakfast quite well.

David was very pleased with her and told her so. After they had finished eating, he said, "you know what I want you to do now?"

She nodded and rose, gave her hand to him and they both made their way to the nursery. The first sight of the baby and Nan was all right. David could have wept with joy at the sight of the two of them together. It had been hard on him to think that Nan was rejecting their little daughter. He knew that she couldn't help being like that, she was bereft with grief and worry.

In between going in and out of sleep, induced by the drugs that Will was giving her; *the Squire* would pop up in her nightmares. Now that she was fully awake, the thought of him was in her mind all the time. She nearly told David about her thoughts, little did she know that David had the same thoughts.

Little Margaret snuggled up to her, Nan's body seemed to quiver as she held the baby, she drew the little mite closer to her breast and just nursed her for a long while. The nurse was watching in the background, keeping an eye on the situation. She could see that Nan was back to normal, the loving and doting mother that she was.

During the days that William had been missing, the wet nurse had to feed the baby because Nan was right out of things.

The baby started to cry. Nan looked up and asked the nurse; "do you think that I can feed her now, or are those drugs still in my system?"

The nurse hesitated and said, "perhaps you had better give it a rest today, when Dr Morris comes over, you can ask him?"

In the Arms of Merlin

Nan was quite happy with what the nurse had told her.

There were about fifteen men gathered out in the cobbled yard in front of the stables. David gave them instructions on which way they should go, then after that he didn't know which way he was going to go. Some were on horseback, some were walking. David took half of them and John took the other half. They agreed to come back before darkness fell.

William was still under the water; he didn't feel cold or even wet. He just felt nice. He kept looking around and could see different things as he descended further. He was now convinced that he had died and gone to heaven, but no-one had even suggested that heaven was in water, so he had to think about that again.

From nowhere a tall figure appears. He came up to him and took his hand and led him over to the left. The man had long white hair and a long beard. He didn't seem to be wet at all. William looked closer at the man and realised that he was the one who had saved him before.

By now William was walking on firm ground. They seemed to change direction quite often. The water was still swirling around William, but didn't seem to be near the man. They had been walking for a while, when William realised that they were out of the water and were on dry shale.

William was breathing air into his lungs again. He could feel himself getting weaker and started to go down. The old man saw what was happening, swept him up into his arms and carried him the rest of the way.

William had lost consciousness by now and lay limp in the arms of Merlin.

He didn't know how long he had been asleep but was feeling very good, better than he had felt in ages.

He sat upright and looked around. He was in another cave similar to the one they had been before. There was a great big fire burning in the centre of the cave, the smoke was going nowhere. There was plenty of it but it didn't affect William in any way. He was really puzzled, he looked closer and could see some sort of vessel on the side of the fire.

Oh, William thought, that is where the nice smell is coming from. There was a movement from the entrance of the cave, the tall man came into view. "You are awake then, my boy?"

"Yes Sir," William said, "where am I?"

"You are in one of my homes," the man said.

William's deep blue eyes opened wider as he spoke, "you have helped me before, haven't you?"

The man nodded and made his way over to the side of the fire that the gruel was on, put some into a basin of some sort and handed it to the boy.

The questions stopped, the child was really hungry. He put the bowl to his lips and drank deeply. It was a taste that he had never tasted before. He made short work of the gruel and passed the bowl back to the man, who in turn asked him if he wanted more.

William accepted immediately and drank the second bowl with as much gusto as he did the first one.

By now William was feeling really good and was ready for more questions but Merlin was in complete command of the situation and questions were unanswered without William realising what was happening.

"I have to leave you for a while," Merlin said, "I have something to do in the woods. You will be fine here on your own, won't you?" he asked.

William nodded.

"If I was you I would try and have some rest, you have a long journey in front of you either today or tomorrow, so take my advice."

By now William really did feel like sleeping. He put his head back down on the soft leaves, looked up to the man and said, "thank you once again Sir." He immediately drifted into a deep sleep.

David and his men had been roaming around for hours. They had just come through very boggy land. David didn't even know whose land it was even, he didn't think that he had been there before either. The men were willing to go on further, the marshy ground was now giving way to rocky ground and the going was getting tough.

David had to dismount, so did a few of the other riders who were on horseback. They carried on climbing for another hour then David shouted, "let's have a spell men." He went to the pannier on the back of the horse, took out some bread, cheese and water. The water was very cold but it was better than nothing, it pushed the food down.

Everyone was talking at the same time and it got on David's nerves. He didn't like to say anything, because the men had been good enough to come along with him. He got up quietly from the rock that he had been sitting on and made his way to higher ground. When he got to the top, he looked around to see if he could see anything at all, but there was nothing.

He then turned his head and happened to look upwards, moved his head slowly and saw a few buzzards circling around a crag higher up the hill. He hadn't noticed them before. *Where did they come from? There must be a dead animal or something else there*, he thought, *poor thing whatever it was*.

He started to look in another direction when it suddenly hit him, could it be William? Dead or even dying? He went cold, turned on his heel, shouted to the men and told them to follow him, not knowing what was there, it could be his son.

It seemed ages before he got to the crag on the side of the hill. He looked back, the men were following. It was quite high by the time he reached the top.

In the Arms of Merlin

The birds had gone, he looked around, there was nothing to be seen, not even a dead rabbit. David couldn't make it out. He just flopped on a rock, put his head in his hands and tried not to cry.

One of the farmers came up to him, put his hand on his shoulder and squeezed it hard, which gave David that little extra control to stop the tears flowing.

He lifted his head, shook it several times and just stood there not knowing what to do next.

Suddenly, one of the workers called to his master. He had been thrashing at the grass around where they had been sitting, "come here Sir, quickly, there is some sort of entrance here."

David just flew to where the man was standing, so did all the others. They all beat the grass down until they found a large entrance to possibly a cave.

By now David's heart was beating like a drum, it was beating so loud that he couldn't hear. He carried on regardless, got to the entrance, lifted his hand up to the men and cautiously walked into the cave. He had gone in a few yards, then called the men to follow him.

They now came to a fork in the tunnel. David thought, *which way*, half of us go to the left and the other half to the right.

David took the left tunnel. Before they went any further, he told one of the men to follow the men in the other tunnel, "tell them to make marks on the tunnel walls in case they get lost." David knew that some of the tunnels went on for miles.

He found a piece of rock, tried to mark the wall, which it did, then waited for the man to come back from the other tunnel. Then off they all went.

Every now and then he put a mark on the wall. They seemed to walk for miles, they must have been an hour into the tunnel and nothing in sight. David was starting to daunt, he thought, we will carry on for a while, there must be something, the tunnel must be going somewhere.

On they walked. The torch that David had thrown together was now beginning to wane, it was coming down to the end. What could they do now?

David felt responsible for pushing the men into the cave without thinking about a second light. David thought that they had better turn back, he might be putting the lives of the men in danger. He shouted, "we are turning back men."

The men stopped, the torch was nearly out. In the silence, they could hear men talking, the tunnel lit up as if by a miracle, the other men had come out from their tunnel. Both tunnels had met in an opening that formed into a small cave, there was nothing in it, only some bones of some animals.

They decided to turn back, made a few more torches, then followed the others into the other tunnel.

Lucky for David's crew that they met up with the other men, they were able to gain information about the other tunnel, save time by not going back on themselves and decided to go forward again.

They must have gone on for another hour. The men were starting to grumble a bit, David didn't blame them, this tunnel was never ending. David stopped the party and said, "we will go on for a little way again, then we will turn back."

There was a lot of mumbling. After a while one of them spoke up and told David, "we have decided, we have come this far, there must be something at the end of this tunnel, so we will go on."

On they went. David was very relieved, he had a feeling that something was going to happen, he only hoped that it would be something good at the end of the tunnel.

As they walked along, they still kept marking the walls. It started to get lighter. David's heart started to bump again, it was nearly as light as day now. They had walked into a very large cave. It was well lit but David couldn't see where the light was coming from. His eyes swept the whole cave. He could see a huge fire burning in the corner of the cave and behind the fire there was a heap of leaves and ferns or something.

David then saw something that he had missed the first time he saw the fire. In the middle of the leaves and things he saw a little blonde head. A lump came to David's throat, he actually couldn't breathe. He moved forward towards the fire. Suddenly, a little boy shot up from the leaves.

David couldn't believe his eyes, it was William. He couldn't help it, he just gave out a huge howl and ran to the boy. He swept him up into his arms and was crying and laughing at the same time.

William was crying too and clung to David.

David, not wanting to let him go, clung to him too.

It was a sight that John and the men would never forget.

David put William to stand up. The little boy's legs just buckled under him. David swiftly took him up in his arms once again and they started to make their way back through the tunnel. It seemed to take less time to get out than they took to get in. They seemed to arrive outside much quicker.

David put William on his horse, jumped on behind him and he could feel William shivering, no, he was actually shaking. It must have been delayed reaction.

David took his coat off and put it around the boy, but he still shook.

David asked John if he would go on ahead, to tell them that they had found William and to get things prepared for him, like a hot bath, plenty of woolly blankets and some hot gruel and for them to tell Will Morris to come to check him over.

David thought that that would be enough to get on with. He also told John to tell Nan to keep calm.

It was an odd sight to see those men walking all bedraggled and full of mud. As they were walking along the countryside, David told them how much he was indebted to them all, he wouldn't have found William without them. He also told them that he would see them all right when he got home. They all let out a big cheer and marched on in silence.

In the Arms of Merlin

CHAPTER 28 – JAMES

It was 4.30am when Mrs Whithers walked along the corridor. She had got up earlier that morning to see to Mr James, he wasn't very well the night before. She was in a bit of quandary, there was one wound on the boy's back that she didn't like. When she had dressed it in the morning, it looked as if it was turning septic. She had done her very best to look after him and see to his wounds. She had given him clean dressings every night and morning, she even felt very sorry for the boy. She didn't know what had happened, but she knew that it was the Master who had done this to him. The man was a maniac; no-one in his right mind would have beaten anyone like this.

She walked into the room, rose her lamp up high over the boy's bed. He was on fire and delirious, he kept calling for his mother. Mrs Whithers was quite shocked to see that he had deteriorated since she was with him the night before. She went to the washing stand, poured some cold water into the basin, wet the flannel, squeezed it dry, then went back and wiped the boy's brow. She spoke softly to him and tried to smooth his hair, but decided that she was wasting time here.

She went to the servants' quarters to wake one of the stable boys, told him to get up quickly and get the Doctor urgently.

By this time, James, the Butler, had risen and was about to make his way downstairs but met Mrs Whithers who was making her way to his room to ask him for some help. James followed her immediately and got such a shock when he saw Master James. He thought that he was over the worst now, so he hadn't called to see him in the last few days.

Mrs Whithers told him that she had sent for the doctor. James agreed that she had done the right thing. Their conversation turned to the master. Once they mentioned his name, James tried to get out of the bed, but slumped to the floor. They managed between them to get him back on the bed.

James turned him over, for Mrs Whithers to tend to the wounds on his back. Mrs Whithers gasped with the deterioration in the wounds from yesterday.

"This is where the trouble lies," James said, "there are two, or even three, gone septic. This is what is making him delirious, you did right to send for the doctor earlier."

They didn't touch Master James' wounds, they just left him in peace. They covered him up with more blankets. James went down to the kitchen to get two jars filled with boiling water but the shivering didn't stop. They both knew that it wasn't the cold that was doing that to him. James had seen a few men die of blood poisoning in his lifetime and knew that this was the case here.

Mrs Whithers went over to the window, drew the heavy curtains back. It was getting light. It was raining hard with a bit of sleet in it. She didn't envy the young stable lad's ride into the town to get the doctor. They took one last look at the man on the bed and made their way downstairs to work out what their next move was going to be.

As James said, "we cannot do anything until the doctor arrives. We will go from there. If the doctor tell us what I am thinking, we will have to get a message to the Master." Once the decision was made, James had his own work to get on with but Mrs Whithers went back to the man's bedroom.

As she waited for the doctor's arrival, James was very restless. Mrs Whithers tried to keep him as comfortable as she could. She tried to wipe him down as best she could, she had to be very gentle, he was groaning in pain when she touched his wounds. He was shouting now, his voice was quite strong and could be heard all over the house.

James sent one of the footmen up to give Mrs Whithers a hand; he had sent a bright one to help her. He wasn't any help at all, so Mrs Whithers sent him away and told him to go to the stables and get tommy. He would be of more help to her she thought. Tommy arrived and things got easier for Mrs Whithers.

It was an hour and a half later that the doctor arrived. The young stable boy hadn't arrived back yet.

The Doctor came upstairs and walked into the bedroom, pulled the clothes off James, examined the slits on his chest, turned him over, looked at James and Mrs Whithers in turn and said, "what the hell has been going on here?"

"We don't know Sir," James said, "but Mrs Whithers has been tending to him for days."

He went hysterical when Mrs Whithers mentioned the Master.

"By the way," the doctor asked, "where is he?"

"We don't know Sir, only that he went to London but we think that he has been back and forth a few times last week."

"More than likely he has, to do this job on his nephew. What a man." The doctor said; "never liked him."

The two servants didn't open their mouths but looked at each other.

After looking through his bag, the doctor pulled out some ointment, gave it to Mrs Whithers and told her to put clean dressings on him straight away. "The ointment isn't going to be much good to him, but it will soothe him for a little while."

"James," he said, "here is some laudanum for you to give him every two hours."

"Yes Sir," James said, "what do you think we should do about the Master?"

"Send for him. I don't like the look of this man."

Mrs Whithers and Tommy spent all day with James, he kept rambling on about something but they couldn't make out what he was saying.

In the Arms of Merlin

Tommy thought he was talking about a little boy but Mrs Whithers said, "there aren't any boys around here that he could have known," so they left it at that.

It was afternoon by the time the doctor had left and Mrs Whithers could see the deterioration in James' condition. The young man was burning up with fever. Mrs Whithers could see that the boy was sinking fast. She hoped that the Master would arrive before long.

Before the doctor left the bedroom, he spoke to James and told him to send for him when the Master came home. The doctor had said, "I have got to get to the bottom of this."

James thought that he had better stay with Mrs Whithers until the Master came. He made arrangements for his jobs to be taken over by someone else. It took two of them to keep James under control; he was as high as a kite after the laudanum and his fever, the poor boy. The both felt so sorry for him.

James had sent Mrs Whithers below stairs to have a break and something to eat, he said that he would go later on. He sat by the bed just looking at the young man, feeling deeply sorry for him. He didn't think that he was going to survive.

After a while, he seemed to quieten down, as if the drug was doing its job.

James was starting to snooze when James started to talk. Every word was as plain as day. He was on about the two of them in the woodman's cottage, down alongside the river.

James asked him "who was with you?"

"William of course, who do you think?"

"Oh yes," James said; "but who is William?"

"That little bastard, my uncle fathered from that maid Annie." I have put up with my uncle's tempers and tantrums for years and done everything that he has asked me to do. I was supposed to be his heir but then things changed, as soon as he found out where the boy was.

All he thought about was getting him back and bringing him up as his son. I went along with the abduction of the boy; looked after him for a week in the cottage. I was sorry that I had to do what I did to the boy, I was getting quite fond of him, but I could never let him live, my uncle would have thrown me out. I wouldn't have had anything; he was going to give everything to William, after all the things I had endured. I couldn't let that happen, so I took the boy down to the river, told him it was shallow and made him walk into the deepest part. That was the last I saw of him.

I had put a quilt around his shoulders to keep the rain off him. He walked into the river trusting me. As he went down he turned around to see me and that look in his little eyes will haunt me for ever. After about five minutes the quilt sank to the bottom of the river.

I scrambled back up the river bank and I sat in the mud for hours crying. I was so sorry that I had done such a terrible thing to the little boy.

I will never forget that look he gave me as he was going down the muddy water. He looked right into my eyes as if he was feeling sorry for me, poor little boy.

I did it all for money, what am I going to do now? I can never live with a thing like that, so please God, let me die."

He started getting agitated again. James rang the bell, he needed help because James' strength had come back to him again. After struggling for a few minutes, he seemed to get weaker and that is how he was for the next few hours.

James could hear a commotion in the main hall. He went to the landing and had a quick peek to see what was going on.

There was the Master, in all his glory. He was in a violent temper.

The servants were doing their usual chores.

In the Arms of Merlin

No-one knew that the Master was coming home.

By the time one of the footmen came up to the hall, he was spitting blood. He *coffed* the man about his ears. The footman was terrified and scuttled away from the hall.

He then stormed upstairs, straight into his nephew's room and asked; "what the hell is going on? Why are you two sitting here with my nephew?"

James tried to explain to him that the man was very ill, but he didn't take any notice of him and went straight over to the bed, pulled the covers back and had the shock of his life.

He caught hold of James by the shoulders and shook him until his teeth rattled, but got no response from his nephew. He looked at James and asked, "what the hell is the matter with him?"

James told him how they had found him in his bed, all bleeding and delirious, so they had to send for the doctor.

He nearly blew his top when James said that.

He said, "you had no right to call anybody without my permission."

"But Sir, he was very ill, what else could we do? We are waiting for the doctor to call any minute." James lied.

He then stormed out of the bedroom and went to his own room and locked the door.

"Thank God," James said. He turned to Mrs Whithers and said quietly, "go to the stables and get one of the lads to get the doctor, for goodness sake don't let the Master catch you or we will all be in for it. Mrs Whithers went on her way.

An hour or so had gone by, by the time the doctor arrived. He wasn't very happy with what he saw. The boy had certainly deteriorated. He turned to James and enquired when the Master was expected back from London.

James was loath to tell the man but he had to, even though he knew what the Master would be like really. James had gone past worrying. Even he knew that the young man was slipping gently away from them.

James made his way to the Master's quarters. He gently tapped the door, didn't get any response, so he quietly started to open the door when the door was ripped from his hands.

The Master stood there shouting and bawling. James pulled himself up to his full height. He felt all his pride come back into his body, he actually stood up to this ogre of a man and told him in no uncertain manner what the doctor had told him.

James was shocked at himself. He didn't think he had it in him but he had had enough.

There was a shocked look on the Master's face, he was really taken aback by James' attitude.

After James had finished talking, the man just pushed passed him, mumbled something, then was on his way to his nephew's room. He just barged in and was shouting the odds.

The doctor turned around and lashed him with his tongue. He had never like this man and now was the chance for him to show it. He really went to town on him, he held nothing back. He told him that the boy was dying and also he said that he was informing the constable, because the boy had been whipped, causing him to die. "Someone has got to pay for this crime."

The Master just turned around on his heel, said nothing, which really infuriated the doctor more. He followed him over to his room, but he just slammed the bedroom door in his face.

The doctor put his fist up to the door and just hammered it for a few seconds but got no response.

He now knew that his next job was to call with the constable and give him all the details as he knew them.

James and Mrs Whithers sat with the boy until he drew his last breath. James looked at Mrs Whithers who by now was openly crying. She wasn't too fond of the boy when he was well, but he was only what his uncle had made of him.

In the Arms of Merlin

James held the woman for a few minutes trying to comfort her. She realised that she was in James' arms and wiggled out from them, pulled herself together, while James went to the dressing table to get a mirror. He put it in front of the boy's mouth and there was nothing.

He turned around to Mrs Withers, shook his head, then he drew the sheet up and covered the face of the dead youth.

He felt drained and he just sat down on the chair by the bedside, put his head into his hands and just sat still with the tears running down his cheeks. He didn't think that Mrs Whithers could see that he was crying as he thought that she was further away from the bed than he was. He was quite shocked when he felt her hand caressing the back of his head. He managed to wipe his face without her seeing him.

He stood up, turned around and found himself looking straight into Mrs Whithers' eyes. He had never seen her in this light before, the funniest feeling came over him, he couldn't make it out. He put it down to stress and tiredness.

The two of them had put themselves out for this young man, they had their own work to do, as well as looking after him, so really the boy was very lucky to have them both looking after him. The uncle couldn't have cared less about him.

By now James had pulled himself together and made his way to the Master's bedroom. He gave one good blow to the door, didn't have any response and just said in a loud voice that young Master James had just passed away and what was he supposed to do?

There was no reply, so James walked away from the door and thought to himself, he will come to me now. Little did James know that the Master was packing a valise and would be on his way back to London.

When they got back downstairs to the kitchen, questions were thrown at them by everyone. They just told them that Master James had died and he told one of the scullery maids to go to the stables to get one of the lads to ride back to the doctor's to say what had happened.

James looked at Cook who by now was in tears and said, "we will see what happens now."

James thought the Master was still in his room. He took the doctor up for him to speak with him. The door was half open. The doctor just barged in shouting on top of his voice until he realised that the large bedroom was empty. The bird had flown.

James couldn't believe it, he couldn't have used his carriage, they would have known in the kitchen. He must have saddled his own horse and ridden off to goodness knows where.

CHAPTER 29 – THE SQUIRE

Nearly everything was back to normal at the Plas. William was back in the stables. Nan's stomach would still turn over when she thought about the whole incident but David was still seething, his insides were churning all the time. Even when he was in bed with Nan holding her in his arms, he could see that man's face in front of him.

He tried not to show anyone how he felt and thought that nobody noticed, but John had. They were very close and one day at the office, John asked him about it.

David let it all come out. John had an idea that it was still bugging him, but he didn't think that it affected him that much. It was just keeping the kettle boiling, it was in his craw about his sister, Barbara. It was through him that she had died but this had really sent him over the edge. David was such a sensible man usually, but sensibility had gone out of the window. David was scared, he didn't know where it was taking him. Every morning when he got out of bed, his thoughts would turn to that man and the thoughts were getting worse.

He had decided to have a word with Will Morris, partly as a doctor but mostly as a friend.

After breakfast, he sent a message to the stables to get his horse saddled up. He told Nan that he had some business in town, he didn't want to worry her unduly.

Off he went. He landed up in the doctor's house just as the last patient was leaving. Will was surprised to see him but pleased on the other hand. He took a quick glance at him and could see that things were not right.

"Come in David," Will said and they both walked into the lounge, sat down and started to talk at the same time. They both had to smile; Will said, "you first."

David let it all spill out. Will wasn't sure how to advise him and if he had, he didn't think that he would listen to him. He did his best, but his advice fell on stony ground.

By what Will could gather, David wanted to look for the Squire and thrash him within an inch of his life. will really felt the same as David but could not advise him to do that to the Squire.

By now Will knew that whatever he advised him, he wouldn't do it. He had made his mind up what had to be done and that was that.

The two men rose up from their chairs and gave each other a brotherly embrace. They both left the room at the same time and the parting shot from Will was "don't forget, I am here if you want me."

"I know," David said and walked towards his horse, mounted him and didn't even look back at Will.

Will sprinted up the stairs two at a time. He got to his bedroom, as he wanted to change. He had now decided what he was going to do. First of all, he would go over to the other doctor in the town, another old friend and ask him to take any emergencies that might come up in the next few hours, then he was going to join David in his search for the Squire. He also thought that being there with him might control the situation.

Finally he got hold of Doctor Davies and explained the situation to him. He was all for David going after the Squire. "If I could, I would come with you, but as you see, I am up to my eyes in work. I have got yours as well now but don't you worry, I'll manage, so off you go and keep an eye on David."

It was 11 o'clock by the time David got back to the Plas. Everything was under control. He went down to the stables, got all his men together and put his plan to them and said that he wouldn't be offended if anyone wanted to drop out. He wouldn't think any the less of them. "I am going into the house now, I will be back in about fifteen minutes, so you have got enough time to make your minds up."

He turned his back on the men and strode down to the house and looked for Nan. He didn't tell her what was going on, he didn't want to worry her, he just said that some cattle were missing and he would need a few men to help him and that he would be back as soon as he could.

He took her by the shoulders and kissed her deeply, not even knowing if he would ever see her again. His mind was made up that that man had got to be punished and stopped from doing anything like this again, even if David had to kill him. It had to be done.

All the men that were available were there waiting for him. There were twelve altogether. They were all mounted ready. They couldn't walk like they did when they went to look for William because they were going further afield.

David's Estate Agent rode up front with him and asked what he had in mind?

"We have got to go into town," David said, "I shall call with the constable to see if he has got any more news about his whereabouts. There is no point in going to the Big House; he won't be near there. There a few places where we can try, but I am not going to rest until I find him."

In the Arms of Merlin

Harry Shingleton, his Estate Agent, was a very worried man as they rode into town. He would stick by his boss until the bitter end, it was time that that monster was brought to justice, or brought down.

David didn't have any joy with the constable at all. He enquired about where he was going with all his men on horseback?

David was ready with an answer, "missing horses at the far end of the estate."

The constable took the answer with a nod and a grunt, he knew different, but let him go on his way.

They rode for hours and had been to three places, but no-one had seen him.

They came to a clearing in the woods, dismounted and started to eat the food that had been prepared for them in the kitchen. They washed the food down with ale, it felt so good now. They re-mounted and got on their way once again.

By the time Will Morris had arrived at the Plas, David and his men had long gone. He was shocked and disappointed that he had missed them. He didn't think that they would have got going so soon, but by now, he realised that David was more desperate than he thought, so all the more reason for him to find him as soon as he could.

He rode into town and made his way to the office, hoping that John would be there and that he would be able to ride with him. He was there and was able to leave someone in charge, for him to go with Will.

As they were riding off, John was telling Will how he had been worried about David's state of mind.

They rode for miles and didn't utter a word.

It must have been around the same time that David and John thought about the cottage down by the river, where they had kept William prisoner after they abducted him.

John wasn't sure about its whereabouts but had a good idea. It was only a thought. It was the last place to look, it was so obvious that he wouldn't stay there. The Squire was a sly and devious fellow, as John said, "there was no harm in taking a look."

It took another two hours to get to the cottage. They stopped at the edge of a small wood, dismounted and tethered their horses to a couple of trees. They made their way towards the cottage. It looked deserted and more tumble down than it had been before. They made their way stealthily towards the back part of the cottage and as John was just going to tell Will that they had made a mistake, a gunshot rang out and whistled past by John's right ear.

They both threw themselves down onto the ground and hoped that they were out of the man's sight for long enough for them to take better cover. They couldn't believe that they were being shot at, they didn't have a gun between them.

Obviously, they didn't know how the Squire's mind worked. They also didn't appreciate the hell that he was going through when he realised that James had killed his son, William. His mind was in turmoil, that is why he had beaten James so badly, thinking what could have happened, the thought of that lovely son of his, struggling in the river to survive, how he did he would never know, neither would anyone else know why Merlin came back to help the child survive. It would come out one day but not at this present moment in time.

Sir Ernest was now getting into a state. He realised that it had been a mistake to come to the woodman's cottage but it was too late now. He had run out of food days ago and hadn't had a drink of brandy for hours. Things were getting rough and now he had seen two horsemen coming down the valley.

By now he was past caring and had come to realise that his life was nearly over. He had misgivings about James, his nephew. He shouldn't have whipped him like that. He had lost control when he heard what he had done to young William. He was amazed at himself. He had never had feelings for anyone like what he had for that boy and now that he was gone he didn't want to live. The sooner he died, the better, but on the other hand he wasn't going down without a fight. It would make it easier for him to leave this world.

He crouched beneath the kitchen window and could see the two men. By now he knew who they were but couldn't work out what they were doing here. They couldn't possibly know anything about the situation, unless William's body had been found. By now David and his men had come into sight, the Squire was really baffled and couldn't make any sense of it.

As the horsemen came closer, the Squire took a pot-shot at anything, not meaning to hit anyone but just to show that he meant business.

On hearing the shot, David and his men rode harder towards the cottage and the river. He realised that things were going to come to a head. He had no idea who was doing the shooting but had a good idea who it could be.

They rode towards some trees, dismounted, tethered their horses and kept out of sight for a while.

John could now see David and motioned him to come over to the right of the cottage, as there was a blind spot there.

David was like a cat moving towards John. He had a terrible look on his face, John couldn't ever remember seeing him like this before, it scared him for a minute.

John didn't know about James, the Squire's nephew. Nobody really knew what had happened, but all the bad things pointed to the Squire.

Unlike John, David had brought his gun and was ready to use it if need be. He had nothing but contempt for the Squire. Not only for the way he had treated his sister. The years of turmoil that he had put her through, that was bad enough, but this thing with William was the last straw. David knew it was either going to be the Squire or him. As much as he loved Nan and the children, if it meant him losing his life, it had to be done. This man could not be allowed to live and do these terrible things to anybody else.

He was now at John's side. They were both trying to calm each other. John wasn't having much success with David. John had the work of the world to keep him from storming the woodman's cottage. He surely would have been gunned down if John had let him go. That would not have solved anything.

By now, the Squire was getting very nervous, he jumped at the slightest sound. He had an idea that he could get out of the cottage, but after some serious thought, he changed his mind. He either had to go out to the men without any sort of fight and go straight to gaol, bluff his way out, or fight to the death.

He now realised that David Jones was one of the men waiting for him to make a move. He knew David hated him. If only he had behaved himself, he wouldn't be in this predicament. Why hadn't he let Barbara adopt little William after Annie had abandoned him? William would still be alive and so would Barbara, but he had been such a fool. Everything in his life that had meant anything to him had been taken from him. Now if things were going to plan, his life was going to be taken from him.

What was he going to do? He could go out and speak to David but he didn't think that was going to be any good. On the other hand, he could kill himself, he knew that he couldn't do that either.

It was make up your mind time.

David was now beside himself; he just wanted to get this over with.

The Squire was very lucky that John had some control over David, or he would have been dead a long time ago.

In the Arms of Merlin

The Constable was next to arrive, with a couple of men from town. One of the young lads had been sent in to tell him about the situation. John thought it would be better if the Law was at hand in case anything went wrong, which he certainly thought was definitely on the cards.

When the Constable arrived at the scene, David and John drew back and crouched behind the pig sty at the back of the cottage. They had a few words with the Constable and filled him in with details that had taken place at the Plas.

David had now calmed down a little. John also felt a bit better with the presence of the Law, who had decided that he was going to approach the cottage door and speak to the man.

David and John didn't think that way wasn't going to work, but the Constable was now in charge and they couldn't go against him, or they would be as bad as the Squire.

He got up from his crouched position, straightened his coat and helmet, gave a gentle cough and made his way to the front door of the cottage. He gave the door a good rap with his knuckles, waited a few seconds and said in a very deep voice, "this is Constable James Davies of the Carmarthen Constabulary. I would be very grateful sir, if you would remove yourself from this cottage, for us to have a word about everything that has happened at your home and the abduction of a small boy. There is no use you staying, we have just as much time as you have, so why not come out for us to have a chat?"

A shower of abuse came from the man in the cottage. That only made James Davies more determined to stand up to this man.

"You can carry on like that as long as you like, sir," the constable said, "but it will do you no good."

The Squire shouted, "do you know who you are talking to?"

The Constable certainly knew who he was talking to, that was why he was so nervous about the whole situation.

He knew that he was in his right as an Officer of the Law, but one didn't know how things could turn out with these rich land owners. He could turn the tables on this poor man, if he knew someone on the bench (and probably he did) but somehow or other James Davies thought things were going to be different this time.

While those thoughts were going through his mind, the Squire called out from behind the door.

It was quite a surprise for James, he thought he would have had more of a fight from this man, obviously he was wrong.

The door opened and the Squire came into sight. David gasped as he caught sight of the Squire's haggard face.

John felt a little pang of sympathy for him and was just going to tell David how ill he thought the Squire looked. Before he uttered a sound, David's voice was just a hiss as he saw the Squire. He was about to leap forward onto the Squire. John realised what he was going to do and caught hold of him in time.

"David," John said, "that is not going to solve anything is it?"

David had to give in to the sensibility of John.

Constable Davies took the Squire by the arm and said quietly, "are you going to come without any fuss sir?"

The Squire nodded and they made their way back to the trap that the Constable had arrived in.

As David mounted his horse, he looked over at the Squire and mumbled something to himself. John couldn't catch what he said, but he could see the hatred on his face.

It took them about an hour to get back to town, the men disbanded and the Squire was taken into custody.

David was going in with them but the Constable put his arm up and told David that it would be better if they all went home and so they did.

CHAPTER 30 – ANSWERING MY PRAYER

It was very late by the time the two men had got to the Plas, everything was topsy tuvey, no work of any sort had been done, since the men had left.

As soon as their Master came into sight, everyone started to walk towards him. They stood around awkwardly, waiting for David to tell them something, but he just dismounted, gave the reins to the nearest to him, then he walked briskly away from his workers.

John realised that it was up to him now to tell the men they deserved to know they had helped in every way since the start of the trouble. John gave his reins to one of the stable lads, then walked over to a small wall, sat on it and started to tell them all about the saga.

There were mumbles of approval and of disapproval, but they were all happy that the Squire was in custody.

John also apologised for David not saying anything to them or even thanking them, "you must realise how he is feeling."

The men all spoke, no-one condemned David for his brusque manner.

John was so tired, he was nearly dropping with fatigue. The last hours just flowed all over him. He told the men that he was going to bed for a few hours and could they just get on with the work at hand until one of them surfaced from bed.

By the time David had got onto the first step of the large sweeping staircase, Nan was running down to meet him. He cradled her in his arms, while they both sobbed.

Nan said, "oh my dearest, I thought that I would never see you again. I really thought that terrible man would get to you, but my prayers were answered. Thank you Lord."

In the Arms of Merlin

David had put his arms around Nan and they were walking up the stairs to their room. David said, "I am not even going to have a wash, I am just going straight into bed. I will have a bath when I get up."

Nan didn't worry at all that David was absolutely filthy, he had taken his boots off in the kitchen. Nan helped him to strip off, for him to go to sleep. By the time she drew the covers over him, he was fast asleep. She bent down and kissed him full on the lips but there was no response whatsoever. The man was mentally and physically exhausted. She turned away from the bed and thanked God once more as she pulled the door gently behind her.

By lunchtime, William was playing out on the lawn with little Margaret. He had got over his experience very well. Nan didn't quiz him at all but as the morning was going on, he was offering bits of information to her. That was how they learned everything about the whole fiasco.

It must have been around tea-time when the Constable arrived. He went to the kitchen, had a cup of tea and a big slice of cook's cake, before James the Butler went upstairs to tell them that he was her to ask Master William some questions.

Nan didn't know what to do about letting the Constable loose on William, without David being present.

She explained to James about her predicament and asked him to relay the message to the Constable.

As James was leaving the room, Nan asked him to apologise to him about the delay in him seeing William.

James said he would convey the message to the Constable, but thought to himself, *I shall not apologise to him.*

He knew that his Master wasn't quite like the other aristocrats living in the house, yet he thought the world of Nan. She treated all the staff as if they were family. That went down a long way with them all.

James explained to the Constable about the delay because his Master hadn't woken up yet, "if you want to stay, cook will see to your every whim, or if you have to go back to town you can come back later.

"As much as I would love to stay here, eating cook's food, I have got to go back to town to meet the Magistrate."

"I tell you what," James said, "as soon as the Master gets up, I will send one of the stable lads to tell you."

"That will be fine," the Constable said, "it will save a lot of time. Thank you very much."

"You are welcome," James said, as he closed the kitchen door behind him.

It was three hours later that David woke up. Nan had arranged for the bath water to be brought up as soon as David was ready for it.

Everybody was scurrying around the bedroom after David had had his bath. The maids stripped the bed and put clean white linen on, David had really dirtied it.

He was now seated at the dining table eating, when Nan told him about the Constable.

He looked up from his plate and asked, "why didn't you call me?"

"You needed to rest, the Constable is coming back when you are ready."

David pushed the plate away from his body, went to stand up and said, "I am ready now."

Nan put her hands on his shoulders, pressing him down back onto the seat, she said "wait, by the time you finish eating, he will be here."

James had told her what he intended to do.

David listened to her, drew his plate towards him and started to eat his food again.

Nan thought that he was calm, but she didn't know how David felt.

His insides were seething, he didn't know how he was going to contain himself until the Constable arrived, but that was what he had to do. He didn't want to upset Nan any more than she had been, but one thing the Squire had in his favour, he was in gaol. That was the only thing that was keeping David sane.

Breakfast was over. David had to admit that he felt a bit more civilised after eating something. He didn't think he ate anything the day before. He felt nice and clean and warm and on his way back to normality.

When the constable arrived, James ushered him into the study.

David was seeing to some papers regarding his business when he saw the Constable. He was quite surprised to feel so calm, he rose his hand and motioned him to a chair near to his desk. The Constable nodded and proceeded towards the very large armchair, put his helmet on his knees as he sat down.

He then proceeded to tell David all about the Squire's nephew. That it was the young man that had endangered William's life, not the Squire.

David was shocked. He was sure that it was all down to the man who had more or less killed his beloved sister, but had to listen to the Constable.

He didn't realise that Ernest Langley was capable of any sort of feeling in his body until now. The boy was his flesh and blood.

On thinking this, it upset David so much to think that William was the Squire's son and not his. He felt as if he wanted to growl with rage, but managed to control himself with great difficulty.

It must have been an hour later that the Constable was being ushered out from the Plas. As he was going through the kitchen, Cook gave him a parcel covered in muslin, very discretely. He doffed his forehead and out to the courtyard he went, with a very big grin on his face. He knew that he was all right for food tonight.

A few days later, news came to the Plas that Ernest had been moved to the Infirmary in the gaol. It seemed that he was quite ill.

As David heard the news, he thought to himself; *I hope he dies so that everything will be over*. He was worrying about Nan, everything would have to come out in the open once again.

There was no use worrying about it, it was going to happen one way or another.

David didn't mention anything to Nan, but he knew that she was thinking about the next few months too.

As the days went by, William seemed to be getting over his experience. He would call out sometimes at night. Nan would rush into him, he would mumble something about the old man, then he would go back to sleep.

He still hadn't gone back to school. Every day he would go down to the stables and chat to Will, the coachman. He would be with him for hours until one of the maids would come and fetch him back to the house.

It was on one of these afternoons that he started to talk to Will about his time in the woodman's cottage. He told him all about Jimmy and what he did to him. There were tears rolling down his cheeks, as he was relating the story when Jimmy told him where to go into the river. He had trusted him and did as he was told, by going into the river. The little boy had such a shock, when the cold water went over his head. He went up to the surface twice and called to Jimmy for help.

William would never forget the look on Jimmy's face as he shouted for his help. The little boy didn't realise that Jimmy's intentions were not honourable. He also told Will all about the old man who came from nowhere and saved his life. William could never figure out where he came from or where he went.

When Will went to the house after he got home from work, he would relate the story that William told him. It grew a little more every time he went to have a drink. By the time it got back to the Plas, the story was changing bit by bit.

One of the kitchen maids told the Mistress's personal maids and Nan was told about it in the evening, while the maid was doing her hair.

Nan was quite taken aback with the story that she told her mistress. The story had completely changed and had changed for the worse. Nan couldn't wait for David to come home; the day was never ending.

By the time he arrived, she was beside herself. David couldn't understand what was the matter with her until he realised what she was talking about. She also told him that the story had come from the house and that it had been highly exaggerated from the story that young William had told Will.

David was very cross. He listened quietly to what Nan told him. He then sat for a while, before deciding to look for William and confront him. He wanted to know what he had told Will. He thought about it for a while then decided to have it all out in the open with William, then no more lies would be told.

David went downstairs to look for William and was told that he was in the stables. He went down straight to fetch the boy. By the time he got to the stables, he was looking a bit wild and when William saw the look on his face, he wondered what was the matter.

He caught hold of the boy's arm and marched him back to the house. Neither of them spoke a word. All the staff were on the look-out, but scampered away when they saw the duo coming. David took him upstairs to his study, called Nan, as he was passing the drawing room.

David put William to sit in an armchair. He closed the door and promptly started asking questions. William was quite taken aback with the questions that David was asking. The little boy thought that everything was all over. He wasn't even thinking so much about that terrible time he'd had, but here it was again.

David plied him with questions for about half an hour and waited patiently for the answers. After David had heard all he wanted to hear and was satisfied that William was telling the truth, he told the boy; "there you are son, you can go back to the stables, but you must come to the Police Station with me and tell everything you have told me to the Constable. You will be all right son, won't you?"

"Oh yes dada, as long as you will be with me."

It gave David a good feeling to hear William say that. His confidence has nearly all come back, thought David.

Eventually the constable arrived and informed David that there was no need for them to go into town to the police station to make a statement.

David was quite relieved really, because he thought that William had had enough traumas already in his young life without going to the police station.

All the business was seen to in David's study. Constable Davies was seen off the premises and things were back to normal once again.

By lunchtime, David was back in the office. John had also arrived and they talked about the situation. Everything seemed to be going into place, except the old man.

The stores that were going around the village were getting out of hand, but John told David, "leave well alone, the truth will out one day."

CHAPTER 31 – A NEW ARRIVAL

It was a week later that Nanny came to Nan and David's bedroom, they had just woken up wondering what she wanted. They were quite shocked to hear that little Margaret had been fractious all through the night.

Nan usually slept lightly in case one of the children was ill or something, but after all the things that had happened during the last few weeks, she must have been exhausted.

She jumped out of bed and made her way to the little girl's bedroom. She had quite a shock when she saw the child and promptly asked Nanny why she hadn't called her sooner.

Nanny justified herself by saying that she was not so bad in the night but had got worse as the day dawned.

Nan believed her because she was a good nurse and she loved the children.

The first thing David did, was to send one of the stable boys to get Will. By the time David got back from the boy's room, he could see that the child was burning up. He also queried why she hadn't called them sooner, but Nan explained to him what Nanny had told her. They both knew that she was a very efficient girl and knew all about the children, especially their two.

Nan took the child out of her bed and tried to lull her in her arms, but she wouldn't have anything to do with Nan, she was screaming for Nanny.

Nan was getting upset now. David tried to explain to her that the child was delirious.

Nanny had brought a large sink bath upstairs with the help of two maids. They put it in front of the fire, which Nanny had kept in all night. She took the little girl from Nan and started to take her nightgown and her chemise off. She struggled hard but Nanny was gentle and firm.

Nan was shocked to see her putting Margaret in the bath. "Why are you doing this?" Nan asked her.

"Whenever children have a fever, I have always done this and it works."

Nan wasn't very happy about the situation, but didn't ask any more questions.

As soon as the child was in the bath she stopped screaming. She just lie there whimpering and shivering.

Nan was going out of her mind, thinking Nanny was doing more harm to the child.

David made her keep away, he had every confidence in the girl.

Will came bursting through the door.

"Oh thank God." Nan screamed out.

David went over to Nan and took her in hand, she was getting hysterical. David couldn't believe his eyes. He had never seen Nan losing it before.

Will, by this time, had taken over and congratulated Nanny for putting Margaret in the bath. "That was the best thing you could have done," he said.

Nan cooled down a little when she heard Will's comment, turned to Nanny and apologised to the girl.

"It's all right," she told Nan; "you must have been wondering what I was doing. This is a new method now, but not many people use it. The old fashioned way is to pile loads of quilts on them but they get hotter and more often than not they go into convulsions and sometimes they die."

God forbid, David thought. They had had enough shocks and bumps in the last few months, but here they were in the middle of it again.

Will examined the child, held back for a minute and eventually told them that it could be one of two things.

Nan waited with baited breath. She could feel herself going down to the floor but couldn't stop herself. In the distance she could hear Will saying, "it could be typhoid, on the other hand, it could be a bad attack of measles."

Nan was now in a heap on the floor.

David ran over to her, picked her up in his arms but couldn't make out why his darling was so weak. She was the strongest woman that he had ever known. He would ask Will to have a look at her after he finished with little Margaret.

Will was quite happy with the child at the moment. He didn't think that it was typhoid but he would have to keep an eye on her for the next few hours.

"Are you all right now Nan?" he asked.

She was as white as a sheet.

"You realise, that even if it is not typhoid she will have to be nursed in a darkened room and once the fever leaves her she will then have to be kept nice and warm."

"I will leave her in your capable hands Nanny, you know what to do. I shall be back in two hours. We should know by then which way the wind is blowing. By the way you did well, keep up the good work and don't tell any of the staff until I have really found out which it is. Keep sponging her down and give her plenty to drink."

He left the room; David followed him and asked him to have a look at Nan.

He hesitated and told David, "I have left a young girl in labour to come to see Margaret, she is a young unmarried mother living in a hovel. I don't think there is anything too wrong with Nan. If you don't mind, I will see her when I come back. Is that all right David?"

He nodded his head with accession, David trusted Will as a man and as a doctor. He mounted his horse and rode off.

As Will arrived at the shack under the bridge, an old lady was coming from the door. She looked so old and dirty, Will didn't think that people were as bad as this in the town but he supposed there must be many, many more like this woman. Most of them were poor but they mostly struggled to keep their homes and their children clean.

He walked into the hovel, the girl was on the bed with a few filthy rags over her body. At first sight, Will could see that she had departed from this cruel world that she had been living in. By the side of her was a little bundle that moved and screeched. Will bent down and drew the rags to one side. There lay a beautiful baby. It was perfect with a head of blonde fluffy down. He picked the child up; by then he could see that it was a boy. Will's eyes filled with tears. He had never been affected like this before. He wondered if he hadn't gone to the Plas first would the girl have died?

He decided that the call to the Plas was an emergency too. He had tried to do his best.

He was now looking around the room for something to cover the girl's face, which was in a terrible state. He wondered what had happened to her, she must have taken a terrible beating. Who could have done such a thing. I suppose no-one would ever know what had happened. The only thing will could do was to report it to the Constable and he could try and find out.

It seemed a long time before will could get his head around the problem. He went out through the front door, looked around – there wasn't a soul in sight, until an old lady came out from her shack. She came straight up to Will and was shouting to him that she couldn't look after the baby because she was too old and didn't have any money.

Will calmed her down and told her not to worry about the baby. (He didn't have a clue what he was going to do with the baby). He assured the woman that she wouldn't have to look after it, "but," he said. The woman held her breath and looked up at him. "Will you look after him until I come back tomorrow. I have got to go immediately to visit a patient. Take the baby to your room, I will come back later with some milk and clothes for him. I will take him off your hands tomorrow. Will that be alright with you?"

Deep down Will knew that she was a good woman, that is why he risked leaving the boy there until the morning. God knows what he was going to do with him. He would think of something.

Will made his way back to the Plas and was hoping against hope that little Margaret didn't have typhoid. Measles was bad enough but most children came through that if they were looked after properly, as he knew this one would be.

By the time he arrived at the Plas, the raging fever had subsided and the child was covered from head to toe with a fine rash. *Thank God*, he thought to himself, there might have been an epidemic.

The last epidemic we had in town spread like wildfire. Will knew that the measles wouldn't be much better, but it didn't kill as many people as typhoid.

After he had seen to little Margaret, Will turned his attention to Nan. He had noticed that she looked a bit peaky, even thought that she might be having another child, which was very unlikely.

David and will returned from the nursery and waited on the landing for Nan to come out. She came eventually. David guided her to their room. She started to object but David just kept ushering her towards the door and in she had to go.

Will asked her to lie on the bed. While David looked out of the very large bay window, Nan had a thorough going over with Will. "I don't think it is anything serious, it is just the past few months catching up with you. You have both had a very hard time. I think that today's episode with little Margaret was the straw. Now that you know that you have nothing to worry about, only the measles, I have a proposition for you."

Both David and Nan were puzzled with what Will had said. He motioned to David to come on the chaise-longue, while Nan went into her dressing room to get dressed. When they were all settled, he started. "What would you think if I asked you to take a new born baby?"

Nan and David both looked at each other.

Nan was the first to speak, "how do you mean?" She asked.

"I don't suppose you remember when I came here this morning in answer to your call? No, I don't suppose you do. Well I had been for a few hours with young unmarried mother who was in labour. When I got your message, I left her because she didn't seem to be going anywhere while I was there. I told her that I wouldn't be long, which I wasn't, so to cut a long story short, when I got back the baby had arrived but the girl was dead.

I found an old lady living next door, who obviously delivered the baby. She thought a lot of the young girl, who had been deserted and beaten up by one of the soldiers billeted in the town. It is nothing new to me, it happens all the time. These soldiers have a good time with these silly girls, then they drop them when they get with child, but this one didn't make it.

Shivers went up and down Nan's spine, her whole life passed in front of Nan's eyes. She looked at David and burst into tears.

"Oh look," Will said, "I didn't mean to upset you, but I thought that you were the perfect family for this handsome boy. He has even got the same colour hair as your children. What's more, I thought that it would take your mind off the past. I don't want you to make up your mind now, but think about it will you? I shall be indebted to you both." He then got up and started to make his way over to the door.

"Are you going so soon?" David asked.

"Yes," he said, "I haven't had time to tell the Constable yet. I know her name, she has no family and that is all. She will also have to be buried poor thing. It will be a pauper's grave I suppose. The father of the child won't want to know. I am off now."

Both Nan and David said, "we will see you in the morning, we can talk then."

Will was a happy man as he left the Plas. He felt responsible. The girl had died but deep inside he knew that things would have gone wrong even if he had stayed. It only took a few hours to sort everything out. Will sent home a very sad man but there was nothing he could do to change things.

CHAPTER 32 – LIZZIE

A few days later Lizzie was buried in an ordinary grave in St Peter's Church. The whole family went, even Lady Elizabeth. Poor Lizzie was lucky in some ways.

Little Margaret was getting better by the hour; she was kept in her nursery with just Nanny seeing to her and two maids, who took it in turns to help.

Will brought the new baby two days after the funeral. They had another Nanny for him because of the measles, thinking that after Margaret got better, they would just have one Nanny like before, but David thought about it and decided to keep the two.

Nan fell in love with the little boy as soon as she saw him, so did everyone else. He was the spitting image of William, they could truly have been brothers. Little did they know that they were half-brothers, through fate landing the new-born baby in their arms. It was history repeating itself. The same thing had happened to Lizzie that had happened to Annie, but Lizzie was very frightened, she was quite a striking looking girl when Sir Ernest Langley first saw her.

She had left home at a very young age, just wanting adventure. Her parents had been devastated when she left, she had a good home, plenty to eat, decent clothes and good parents to look after her but one of her friends had persuaded her to go to London and off they went.

Life in London was not as she thought it would be. She had had a very hard time until she had this job in the Alehouse. It also acted as a whore house too.

She had survived for three years, her friend had long gone home, but Lizzie had stuck it out. She had word that her parents had both passed away. She didn't bother to go home when her mother died and there was no need to go back when her father died.

In the Arms of Merlin

Lizzie carried on with her life.

After Sir Ernest had asked her the second time, she felt a little worried. She wasn't sure of this man, she had been with many men in the past and had got to know the difference between good and bad. She had a feeling about this one, but she could not put her finger on it. There was no good or bad with this man, there was something evil about him, which she found out all too soon.

In the beginning, Lizzie was very flattered with the attention that he lavished on her. She also showed off to the other girls that were working with her. She now was the cock of the walk and she knew it.

Things began to change when he took her to meet some of his friends. Then the trouble started; from then on her life was hell. She had money and he dressed her. She either had to shut up, or put up and that is what she did.

After a few weeks, Lizzie was getting tired of all his friends, some of them were quite nice, but all of them had their way with her.

One evening, Ernest called for her and took her to his usual private club. The first time she went there, she couldn't believe what was going on, but she put up with things so as to live a little better. By now, she had given up her job at the Ale-house, she had better fish to fry, or so she thought. While they were eating, Ernest was quite sweet to her. She was a little surprised, he had a dark mood on him for a while, so she thought to herself, I am going to make the most of this tonight.

As the evening wore on, she realised what he was trying to tell her. She breathed a sigh of relief, there were going to be no more friends. Lizzie couldn't believe her ears; she was delighted and snuggled up to him and squeezed his hand. He drew his hand away sharply and showed her that that didn't please him at all. She soon got round him.

In the Arms of Merlin

Before the evening was over, he had explained to her what he wanted. In bed that night Lizzie was quite pleased with what Sir Ernest wanted of her. She thought it was marvellous that he wanted her to have his child. He would take the child and he would keep her for the rest of her days. What an offer. Lizzie was really excited with the proposition. She didn't think that anything could go wrong. She was in seventh heaven and just lie in bed thinking of the days to come.

As the weeks were going by, Lizzie still hadn't started a baby and Sir Ernest was getting crosser and crosser. Poor Lizzie couldn't make out what was going wrong. She didn't have any friends to ask or talk about things to. She was quite ignorant about the facts of life.

One night, late in the month, Sir Ernest arrived at her rooms. He was the worse for wear with drink. As soon as he saw her, he started, he wanted to know if she was with child. Poor Lizzie had to tell him that she wasn't yet.

"Yes," he said; "I have waited for months for you to tell me that you are having my child."

Lizzie started crying, that seemed to make Sir Ernest go berserk. He lunged at Lizzie, dragged her to the floor and gave her such a hiding that she didn't know where she was after he had finished with her.

She didn't hear him ranting and raving at her. Before he left her room, he gave her a good kicking. Days went by before Lizzie was able to go out, she hadn't eaten because she couldn't open her mouth. She was black and blue, he had really done a good job on her.

As the days went by, she didn't hear a word from him. Deep down, she knew that her hey days were over. What on earth was she going to do now? She didn't have any work and couldn't ask for her job back, she had more or less told them to keep their job. There would be no money from anywhere.

In the Arms of Merlin

She stayed in her rooms until she was put out on the street. She called around to see one of the girls that used to work with her in the Ale-house but she didn't want to know. "You have made your bed gel" she said, "now you must lie on it." Poor Lizzie, what was she going to do? She picked up the small bundle of clothes that she was able to bring with her, the landlady kept most of her nice clothes to pay for her back rent.

Lizzie walked for hours. She was nearly collapsing when she came across a small park. She walked in through the gates hoping there might be a bench there.

There were loads of benches but tramps, whores and different sorts of people took them all. It was quite warm for that time of year. Lizzie's only hope was to get under a tree and that is what she did. She spent the whole evening crying softly into the crook of her arm. She must have gone to sleep eventually and woke with a start. Someone was fumbling with her bundle of clothes. She was horrified. She sat up and started shouting at the woman who was trying to steal from her. Usually Lizzie was a very quiet girl, but she realised that from now on she would have to fight to live in the world that she was entering and fight she did.

She fought for that small bundle tooth and nail, kept it and had the other woman running for her life.

Lizzie got up from the grass. She was so uncomfortable, her clothes were soaking, it must have been the dew. She could do nothing about it. She picked up her bundle and started to walk out of the park.

Another day went by just wandering around looking for somewhere to sleep.

It was a week later, Lizzie was still wandering around. She had found a bench for two nights, but the rest of the time she lay under a tree.

Lizzie now was looking like all the other people who were unfortunate enough to be homeless. She was at her wits

In the Arms of Merlin

end, she felt so ill, she really hadn't got over the beating that she had with Sir Ernest. There was something else, but she couldn't put her finger on it. The only thing she knew was that she felt really ill.

Another week went by. Lizzie was in a dreadful state. She felt as if she just wanted to lie down and die. She made her way to the usual park and found a place to lie under a tree. She tried to sleep but couldn't settle down. First of all, she was hot, then she was cold.

She realised that she had a fever and drew her shawl tighter about her, but it didn't do much good. She must have fallen into a deep sleep and that was the last she knew about anything until she woke up.

The sun was streaming down on her. Her body was feeling nice and warm. She thought for a minute that she had died and gone to heaven.

Her eyes had focused on a crucifix on a wall. Where on earth was she? She had stirred quite a bit, there must have been someone watching her.

A hand came down on hers and a gentle voice said, "come on now dear, it's all right, you are in safe hands. I am glad that you have woken up, you have been sleeping for days."

Lizzie couldn't believe her ears. She turned and the prettiest face she had ever seen faced hers. Her mouth dropped and she was lost for words. There by her side was a nun. By the way she spoke, she came from the same part of the country as she did.

Lizzie was sitting on the side of the bed now with questions pouring out of her mouth.

In time it was all revealed. It seems that two nuns had taken a short cut through the park to visit an old lady. They had come across Lizzie lying under a tree, delirious, shouting and crying out. They went to help her, saw the state she was in and Sister Mary, who was with her now, saw to her, while

In the Arms of Merlin

Sister Hannah went back to the Convent to get a cart or something to carry the girl.

Lizzie was really sitting up and taking notice now. She felt a lot better and was quite hungry. It was Sister Hannah who realised that Lizzie was hungry, so without any fuss she went through to the kitchen and brought back some gruel for the girl. In no time Lizzie had eaten it all, together with the three pieces of bread that were by her bowl.

Lizzie could have eaten more but didn't like to ask. She could just lean back on the pillow, quite contented and warm, wondering what was going to happen next.

Sister Mary was born in Wales, her father was in the army, met her mother, got married, had a family, got posted down to Wales where Mary was born. After a year or so, he got posted out to India and was killed in action, therefore, Mary's mother took her family back to London where she was originally from. Being a devout Catholic, Mary's mother was very happy for Mary to join a Convent and become a nun.

Sister Mary felt sorry for Lizzie but couldn't find any way to help her, but she would think of something.

In the meantime, Sister Hannah had told the Mother Superior that Lizzie was awake, so she scurried out from her room to have a chat with Lizzie.

At that moment, Lizzie didn't really want to tell her story to anybody, let alone a Mother Superior, so she did the next best thing, she cried. The women stopped asking her questions and left. Sister Mary felt more sorry for her than even before and decided to find some way to solve Lizzie's problems.

More than a month had gone by. Lizzie was working in the convent for her keep. She didn't mind the work but it was so boring. She didn't see a man the whole time she had been there and Lizzie had got used to her lifestyle.

In the Arms of Merlin

She was scrubbing the kitchen floor one morning very early, she felt a bit sickly when she got up, but now she felt awful. She was going to tell someone that she didn't feel so good when everything went black. The next thing she knew, she was in her little room, flat out on the bed with an elderly nun feeling parts of her body.

Lizzie tried to protest but Mother superior held her down. Lizzie was really frightened, but mother superior spoke to her quite gently and calmed her down. Lizzie found out later that the other nun was a midwife, she used to go round to houses to women in childbirth.

After the nun had finished with Lizzie, Mother Superior raised Lizzie to a sitting position, brought her feet over the side of the bed and took her hands in hers and looked deeply into her eyes and said, "have you got something to tell us child?"

Lizzie was puzzled with the question and shook her head. The elderly nun looked at the Reverend Mother. They both realised that the young girl was ignorant of the fact that she was with child.

After Mother Superior had explained to Lizzie what was wrong with her, Lizzie was very quiet, she didn't show any feeling at all. The two women thought that she might have been in shock, but little did they know that Lizzie was rejoicing, she would go to see Sir Ernest and tell him her good news.

She didn't want to show too much to the women, so she pretended to cry. They looked at each other and left the young girl alone for her to have time to think and let the problem sink in.

It took Lizzie hours to get to Sir Ernest's house, she was exhausted but she was excited to hear what he would say when she told him.

She tidied her skirt, put her hat straight and gave her shoes a gentle rub with her glove. Her mind was thinking about the change in her life after the father of her child heard the news that he was longing to hear.

Lizzie rang the heavy bell. She waited with bated breath, the door opened and there stood the housekeeper in all her glory. Lizzie knew that she didn't like her, so here was the first obstacle.

The first cold stare lasted a few seconds. Lizzie thought an hour had gone by, she was scared of the woman. She drew a deep breath and said, "I would like to see Sir Ernest."

The woman's eyes didn't flinch, she said, "I am sorry but the Master is not in residence and will not be for a few months, he has gone overseas." She closed the door.

Lizzie knew that the woman was lying, it was written all over her face. She rang the bell again.

"I shall call the Constable, so it is up to you."

Lizzie was in tears. She turned away from the door, stumbled down the steps and made her way to a park that was opposite the house. She found an empty bench, sat down and sobbed her heart out.

She sat on the bench for about half an hour, oblivious of anything that was going on around her. She felt a hand on her shoulder. She looked up and there was the housekeeper with a shawl over her shoulders. I suppose she could see the shocked look on Lizzie's face.

She said "don't think badly of me child but I have got to do my job. I know you don't believe me. I could see that you were upset, so I have taken this chance to slip out to tell you that I have orders what to tell you if you arrived on the doorstep."

Lizzie looked up and said "why?"

"The Master has got another woman, she is with child and there is talk that he is going to marry her. Don't know when. I just keep my ears open when I go downstairs. They get to hear everything. I just pick up scraps of news. The best thing you can do my girl, is to go back to where you came from. Go home. I wish that I had done so years ago. I wouldn't be the hard, miserable old woman that I have become. Take my advice and go. Goodbye and good luck."

Lizzie was drained; she just sat and stared into space. What was she going to do now? It was starting to get dark. Lizzie thought that she had better make tracks for the convent. She was so hungry and tired; she wondered what time she would get back. It would be very late. She started to wonder if she could find somewhere to stay the night, it might be dangerous walking back in the dark.

The next Ale-house she saw, she would see what was going on there. It was starting to rain and she was getting quite wet. In front of her she could see the place that would take her right down to hell and back. Poor Lizzie, she walked in through the door, the place was a rough old doss-house that had started selling ale.

She knew it was a mistake the minute she walked in through the door, but there was no turning back. She pushed and shoved, trying to get near to the room where the young girl was carrying the jugs of ale from, but it was hopeless.

The place was full of soldiers and young girls, all screaming and shouting, it was bedlam there.

She was desperate.

She felt a strong pair of hands take hold of her waist and passed her through the crowd without any problem. She sighed a sigh of relief.

She had her back against a wall, she couldn't go any further, the soldier was keeping bodies away from her with his own. She could feel his hard body against her own and it thrilled her and she showed him too. From then on things went as nature had intended it to.

Lizzie met Alfred during the next few weeks and they were very happy. He had set her up in a room where other soldiers' women were, so it was one happy family. The room was very damp and dark, but it was somewhere to sleep and it was safe.

Alfred was very attentive when they first got together; also he was quite a good looking man. Lizzie thought that she could put up with his bad temper and spend the rest of her life with him, but it wasn't to be.

It had been a very fine day and Lizzie had been for a walk. When she got back to her room, Alfred was sitting there. She hadn't seen him for days. He put his arms around her and kissed her. He really liked Lizzie but didn't think that he would marry her but on the other hand he didn't want to lose her. He put her to sit down on the sofa, asked her how she was.

She showed him that she was pleased to see him.

The next minute, he was telling her that his regiment was moving out from London and going down to Wales.

Lizzie felt quite flat. *Oh!* She thought, *here I go again, no home, no money.*

He could see that she was upset and he told her not to worry because she could come with him.

She was so happy, she was laughing and crying at the same time.

He was quite impressed with her reaction, told her to pack her things and to go down to the Ale-house and find the girls.

She didn't understand why she had to meet the girls, but by the time she got to the Ale-house, she knew why. It seemed that every soldier who wanted to take his woman with him had clubbed together and paid the owner of the Ale-house to take the girls to Wales.

It would be a very long journey but Lizzie was quite happy about it. She had never been to Wales, neither had anybody else. Eventually they got to Carmarthen. It was a small town, Lizzie thought as they drove through the narrow

In the Arms of Merlin

streets. She also thought there wouldn't be much fun down here either, but she wasn't going to complain.

They were dropped outside another Ale-house, a much smaller one than the one in London. The noise was just as much, if not more. The girls were all tired on their arrival and were starting to get picky, but Lizzie didn't interfere, she kept herself to herself and waited for Alfred.

Lizzie found an old tree stump on a grass verge opposite the Ale-house. She leaned forward, put her head between her hands and quietly went to sleep.

It had been a terrible journey down. There were about six girls, all sitting at first, then they lay on the floor of the wagon. Lizzie had put her small bundle under her bottom for a while, then she put it under her head. She got to sleep all right, but the noise of the big wheels was grinding in the background the whole time. Lizzie was very uncomfortable, but she was thankful that she was able to follow Alfred.

All the other girls were out of sight when Lizzie woke up. They must have gone into the Ale-house, but Lizzie wasn't going to go in.

It was getting dark by the time Alfred arrived. Lizzie was beginning to panic. She was so pleased to see him, she didn't complain at all. He was shocked to see her sitting outside the Ale-house, he thought that she would have gone in with the others. He had realised that she was quite a quiet girl, a bit different to the others. He said, "Come on, luv, I'll take you up to the room."

Lizzie could have cried with relief as he took her arm and guided her through the crowd of people.

The room was very small and sparsely furnished but Lizzie didn't grumble, it would be better than a park bench.

Alfred was very tired too; he had an early start in the morning. He had seen that she was all right, then left her to go back to barracks.

In the Arms of Merlin

Lizzie slept the clock round; she got up, dressed, then made her way downstairs. She was hoping to find a bit of work to help Alfred to pay for her keep.

Alfred didn't ask her for money mind, but Lizzie was thinking ahead, she would need money for a few things for the baby.

Sal, the Landlord's wife took to Lizzie straight away, she also realised that she wasn't like the other women. She didn't really need anyone else, but she took to Lizzie as soon as she spoke to her.

Two days went by before Lizzie saw Alfred. In the meantime she had worked in the kitchen, washing up and even doing a bit of washing. She didn't mind at all; the day was long. The other girls were downstairs with any soldier that would give them a drink, or anything.

Alfred arrived late. She had finished her jobs and was quite tired. She lay the bed with Alfred and they talked until midnight. Alfred was surprised that she was doing a job there and was quite please. *There is more to this girl than I realised*, he thought.

Lizzie had worked hard all day; she didn't mind though. She got on well with most of the girls who were working with her, she certainly liked her boss, Sal. For once, since she had run off for London, the felt safe and happy.

A month must have gone by. Lizzie was definitely getting heavy but nobody seemed to notice, only Sal. One morning Lizzie came down to the kitchen to have a bite to eat and start her work.

Sal took one look at her and said, "what is the matter with you Madam?"

Lizzie blushed and looked down to the floor, answering, "nothing Mum."

Sal had seen that sight before, she told Lizzie, "I'll pop up to your room later for a chat, I think you need to talk to someone."

Lizzie got flustered and said, "No, please don't come tonight, Alfred will be with me."

"All right," Sal said, "we will have a chat in the morning."

Lizzie nodded her head, carried on having her breakfast, didn't open her mouth, only to eat and every mouthful tasted like sawdust.

Morning went into afternoon. It was now late afternoon and Lizzie had to go out to the front because someone had thrown up outside the front door. In the corner of her eye, Lizzie saw three soldiers walking towards her. One of them, whom she didn't like, was passing remarks about her, really personal ones. The biggest of them was always like that with her, she hated going near him whenever he called at the Alehouse.

I'll ignore him, she thought to herself and turned her back to him. That was the worst thing that she could have done. He caught hold of her around her waist and swung her round and round until she felt dizzy. Eventually he put her down and she fell to the floor. She didn't know where she was by now. The soldier was roaring with laughter and said, "this is where I've wanted you all along my girl." He pounced on top of her, started kissing her and was trying to put his hands up her clothes.

She realised what was going on and started to scream. He seemed to get worse. The other soldiers were laughing and egging him on more. There was so much noise going on inside that nobody took any notice.

Things were really getting out of control. The top of her bodice was ripped and there was blood coming from her lip and from his.

Lizzie thought that her end had come, when suddenly the weight was lifted from her body. There was shouting and screaming, she couldn't make out what had happened.

In the Arms of Merlin

She sat up and scrambled out of the way, only in time, a body well down where she had been lying. It was a soldier. He lunged forward and waiting for him was Alfred. They kept on hitting each other.

Everything was above board until Alfred had the soldier down too many times. He started to squawk like a chicken. The two other soldiers were now beating Alfred unmercifully.

The men had come outside now and were just looking on as the three were all hitting Alfred. The first soldier, the one that Lizzie didn't like, raised his arm and brought it down full force onto Alfred's right eye.

Alfred reeled backwards and was clutching at fresh air, he just went backwards until he fell. There was a dull thud and he lay there without moving.

Everyone was outside now. Lizzie got up with great difficulty, made her way over to Alfred. He was a terrible colour, Lizzie wondered where she had seen it before.

By the time she got to him, Sal had hold of her and held her back. She was crying and struggling to get free to get to Alfred. Joe, Sal's husband, came over to the two of them and told them both that the lad was dead.

Lizzie couldn't believe her ears, she just screamed and screamed. She felt arms around her body and felt herself being lifted up. The next thing she knew, she was in bed, with brandy being poured through her lips. She sat up coughing and spluttering and threw up over everybody.

It took Lizzie two days to come to herself. She was still in a bad way, but was sitting up and taking notice. Sal had been to see her this day, told her that she didn't have to worry about somewhere to live, she could stay where she was and still do a few odd jobs. Sal also told her that she was having a child.

"Please don't tell anyone else," she begged.

"Don't worry about it, " Sal said, "everyone knows already."

That's that then, Lizzie thought.

Four months had gone by. Sal asked Lizzie if she would do a favour for her. "Would you go and order a large sack of flour down on the Quay? The boy will bring it up on the cart."

"Certainly," said Lizzie. She put her shawl on and off she went, feeling brighter than she had felt for a long time. She made her way to the Quay, went into the store, gave the order, had a few laughs with the boys and started making her way back home.

Suddenly she felt herself being drawn backwards. A large hand came over her mouth. She didn't know what was happening, there must have been more than one person, she could feel and hear them. She was terrified, but couldn't do anything to save herself.

She thought *if I am going to die, I am going to go quietly.* She relaxed completely.

She knew no more.

Once again, she awoke in a strange room with a strange face looking down at her. There wasn't one place in her body that wasn't in agony. She tried to pick her head up but only raised it a few inches. She could hardly see. Her eyes must have been swollen. She tried to get her brain going, to remember what had happened. Who could have done such a thing to her? She tried to grip the hand that was pushing her hair from her face, but things seemed to change. She slipped back into unconsciousness.

Lil Davies was a down and out, who lived in an old shack under the bridge. She was going back to her home when she heard screaming. It scared her. She knew that someone was in trouble but she couldn't do anything about it.

The bridge area was very rough, therefore she was afraid to see what was going on. She stood in the alley until she heard the screaming stop. Two soldiers were running from a bundle on the ground. She waited for a few minutes, then she could see that the way was clear. She bent over the bundle and was still in shock hours later. Some poor girl had been beaten to a pulp.

There wasn't a soul to be seen to give her some help. Lil had to drag the girl along the wet and dirty road. There was an empty shack next to hers. She managed to get her onto an old bed after a great struggle. She covered her with a quilt and some other rags from the floor, as best she could.

Lil sat on an old chair that was in the corner, to get her breath back. A few minutes later, she went over to take a good look at her.

Lil now realised that the girl was having a child and it would be in the very near future. Lil knew that she hadn't done much good to the girl by manhandling her, but she couldn't do any better for her.

She then tried to get some quilts under her, because the bed looked so uncomfortable. As she turned her over, she could see that she was in a pool of blood.

Lil panicked and ran outside to see if she could get some help. There was one Doctor who she knew would help. She ran the whole length of the Quay, until she saw a young man. She garbled her story to him and he ran like the wind to fetch the Doctor.

Lil waited a good few hours for the Doctor to come. By this time, the girl was in true labour. Lil could see the head. She just kept an eye on it, because she didn't know what to do. She just sat and waited.

Things started to happen quickly now, the head, the shoulders and the whole body came out in a gush of blood and fluid. Lil was flabbergasted. She never thought that the girl could bring the baby herself, because she was out for the count.

In the Arms of Merlin

Lil was getting flustered now, she didn't know what to do next, when she suddenly remembered her mother talking about cutting the cord and tying it. She did this by taking an old lace from her boot, cut it in half and tied both ends off. She was very pleased with herself until she realised that the girl had stopped breathing.

Lil was so upset; she just sat on the chair crying, when she heard the loudest cry she had ever heard. She stopped crying, looked up and thanked God, for her was a miracle if ever there was one.

She wasn't a religious woman, but she kneeled down and gave thanks to the Lord for that live little bundle. God only knew what was going to happen to it.

CHAPTER 33 – CONCLUSION

Nan was now back to her old self. She took to the baby as if it was her own. She did most things for him, more than she had done for her other two. It must have been good for her to take her mind off all the terrible things that had happened over the last few years. Will thought that she was well out of the woods and congratulated her one day when he called.

Nan couldn't remember what life was like before David, which was his name. It was three months later that the boy was christened in St Peter's Church, as David William Edward. William after Will, the doctor. They couldn't call him William, as they already had one in the family.

Everyone loved David, he was such a sweet little boy.

William and Margaret adored him, they weren't a bit jealous of him.

Weeks grew into months and months grew into years.

William was a strapping young man, going off to University to further his education, with the intention of going into Law. Little Margaret was also the beauty of the county and thought of as a very good catch. She was invited to all the places that mattered. It didn't seem to change her, she had both feet firmly on the ground and had no airs and graces about her.

Nan and David had done a good job bringing their family up. They knew it and were quite pleased with themselves.

David was growing up too. They knew what he wanted out of life.

They both knew that the Plas was going to be run by a very efficient man, who adored every acre of the land that his parents owned.

Nan and David knew that one day, young David would be running the Plas. Whatever he did, he did it to perfection.

He had even tried his hand at pulling a calf and did it as good as any experienced farmer.

David was delighted; it was a joy to seem him sitting a horse. A horseman through and through.

He was also kind to the animals, unlike his true father. He was a good horseman, but could get very angry if anything went wrong, then he would beat the animal unmercifully.

As the years went by, William got to be a well-known Barrister and lived most of the time in London. He eventually married and had his own family, while Margaret met a doctor, settled down just outside Carmarthen and went on to have six children.

Nan would ride out there most days and spent time with Margaret and her big brood.

David wasn't a county man; he loved to ride over the land and didn't gad about like most young men of his age.

Nan used to tease him about girlfriends, but he didn't want to know.

My goodness, she thought; *this boy is going to be a bachelor and spend all his time with us.*

Nan was mistaken though. It was coming up to Christmas and as always, they had a big Ball about three weeks before. Everything was going full swing, when Lady Elizabeth told Nan that Sir George's nephew, wife and daughter were coming over from America to stay for a while. They would be here for the Ball.

Nan was so excited and so was Lady Elizabeth. She had never met George's nephew, but George knew that he was a good fellow.

Lady Elizabeth was now an old lady. She was quite shonk and as bright as a button. She was all prepared for the family; they were going to stay in her apartment.

They had stayed in London for a few days with relatives of his uncle George and with William and his family, then had come down to Wales, glad to get away from London, from the bustle, to the peace of the countryside.

Jack, whose father had gone out West, had a huge ranch in Texas. They were very wealthy, but very lowly. They arrived at long last.

Lady Elizabeth and Nan were on the steps of the Plas as the coach arrived. They were all tired and dusty after their long coach journey.

Jack was a very good looking man, his wife was a beautiful blonde with eyes as blue as cornflowers and a deep Texan accent. Nan could hardly understand her. There was nothing loud about her, but you certainly knew that she was there.

The daughter was a different kettle of fish; she was tall and looked as strong as an ox. Beautifully dressed, but one knew that she was out of place dressed like a lady.

In the next few days they all learned the length and breadth of Emma.

As the days went by, Nan took to the trio. They were really nice people, down to earth, with no nonsense.

Emma was as dark as Ellen was fair, she had a head of long curls. She only had to brush it and it was done. She had golden brown eyes, just like a tiger and skin that was beautifully tanned and teeth like pearls.

As soon as breakfast was over, she excused herself and went down to the stables to pick her horse up. David had allowed them to choose a horse each, as soon as they arrived.

Jack and Emma were delighted, but Ellen didn't have anything to do with animals at all. She kept on to Emma every time she saw her astride a horse. Her words were always the same: "You will never find a husband dressed like that and astride a horse."

Emma didn't care much what her Mamma said, she wasn't disrespectful to her mother, but she just loved riding, especially her precious Beauty, out on the range back home.

In the Arms of Merlin

He was a wild horse, which the hands had caught one night when they were out branding. Every night the horses were tethered together. This wild stallion would come down from the mountains, he was trying his best to get the herd of horses free, for them to come away with him, but it didn't work out like that.

The boys realised what he was trying to do, so they kept an eye on things.

One night, he came too close and got too cocky. Before he knew what was happening, they had about six lassoes around his neck. He did give them a good fight. The hands had never come across such an animal.

It took them months to break him in and when he was tamed, he wouldn't allow a man to get on his back. Jack gave up on him, but Emma had her own ideas.

As soon as her father got out on the range, she would go up to him and talk. In the beginning, he would go wild, but as the time went by, he started to calm down and let Emma get closer.

Time by now was running out, Jack wanted to let him go back out on the range, but Emma persevered, things got better every day.

Her father talked to her about letting him go and each time she talked him out of it.

All the family had gone to San Antonio to meet someone. Emma had the day and the ranch to herself; most of the hands were out on the range, which left six of the older men with Emma.

She was delighted, especially that Rufus was left. He knew more about horses than even her father did, and that was saying something.

She knew what her father was saying about the horse but she didn't want to hear it.

The day in question was a very hard and long one for Emma and Ruf, as the boys called him. She was on the ground more than she was on the horse. Ruf was getting worried about her, he knew that he would have a row from the boss if he found out what was going on, but she wouldn't give in.

They had been at it all day, they were both exhausted and so was the stallion.

Even Emma was starting to doubt her capability as she mounted the horse for the umpteenth time. She said to herself, *this is the last time*. As she sat on him she finished the sentence out loud and said, "You can go to hell you unruly beast." The next minute, she was racing out from the ranch. She went for miles until he stopped, exhausted.

Emma knew that she had won, This horse was hers now and hers alone.

Ruf caught her up and was really worried about Emma, but when he saw the combination of horse and girl, he knew that she had won. From that day, Emma has treated her horse with respect; there is a bond between horse and woman. Beauty will not allow anyone else to ride him at all.

Days turned into weeks and the time came for the family to return to Texas. Nan hadn't noticed how Emma and David had been getting close to each other but David Snr. had.

They were talking in bed one night when Nan suddenly realised what could happen if they decided to get together. Shivers ran down her spine, how would she live without her darling David, he had never left them, not even for a few days.

"Now stop this at once," David said. "Perhaps when they get back home, things will go back to how they used to be and he will meet a girl from this area."

"David," Nan said, "how can you be so blind?"

"We will see," said David. "Don't go upsetting yourself with something that may never happen."

But happen it did.

Jack and his family had been gone for three months and young David was really pining for Emma.

David Snr and Nan were discussing the situation one night; David suggested something that Nan couldn't believe her ears.

After a lot of thinking about all they had discussed, David said, "I think I will tell him to take a holiday out in Texas and see what happens."

Nan cried for days, but young David was in seventh heaven.

The time care for David to leave. Nan couldn't go down to the carriage to see him off; she just kissed him as he ate his breakfast. She went back to her bedroom and she wasn't seen all day.

As the days went by, she got used to the idea of David not being there. She had started going back and forth to Margaret's to see her and her family. Margaret tried her best to help her mother and by the time the letter arrived, Nan was in a better frame of mind.

David read it first and was smiling when he passed it over to Nan, her hands were shaking so were her insides. She took a deep breath and started reading the letter and was laughing and crying at the same time. She couldn't believe that God had been so good to her, by giving her son back to her.

David and Emma were betrothed to be married and were coming home to get married and were staying at the Plas, "that is if father is willing?" David put in the letter.

Nan, David and everybody were rejoicing. Nan and David lay in each other's arms that night. They hadn't been as contented since David had gone to America. Deep down, neither of them thought that they would see him again, though in their hearts, they knew that David would come back.

In the Arms of Merlin

It was three months later; all was ready for the wedding of the year. The whole county was being invited.

Most of Emma's family had been taken in by John, even Will had a few.

Nan was surprised that so many of them had come all the way from Texas, but there you are, money was no object and she was their only child.

It was going to be very hard for them, leaving Emma behind, but Emma was a very strong willed girl, which she had inherited from her mother.

The only thing that bothered Emma was leaving Beauty back home. Her father had told her that if there was a way, he would get him to her.

It was a beautiful day. The bride was dressed simply in white silk with fresh flowers in her hair and a small posy of similar flowers.

She had all Margaret's little girls dressed in white and gold. It was a pleasure to see them. Nan and David were truly proud of their family.

The night of the wedding saw a grand Ball at the Plas.

By the end of the evening, Nan was fit to drop. She sat for a while on the veranda, remembering the Ball on the night of her wedding.

If there ever was girl going from rags to riches, she was one.

Nan had never forgotten her past life. She thanked God every time she prayed. Things could have been very different. As the children grew to an age where they understood, she told them all about her life and how it could have been. She thought that it had made a different to the three children, it kept their feet firmly on the ground.

It would have been easy enough for the children to join the regiment of spoilt, rich children.

Nan often wondered how many young girls had come out of life as she had.

In the Arms of Merlin

God had certainly been looking after her and hers, with some help from Merlin.

Why?

Nobody knew, but it would come out one day. That is another story! ……

6043643R00253

Printed in Great Britain
by Amazon.co.uk, Ltd.,
Marston Gate.